Emerging Insights on the Relationship Between Cryptocurrencies and Decentralized Economic Models

Dhanapal Kesavan
SRM Institute of Science and Technology, India

N. Mari Anand
Department of Business Studies, University of Technology and Applied Sciences, Salalah, Oman

IGI Global
PUBLISHER of TIMELY KNOWLEDGE

A volume in the Advances in Finance, Accounting, and Economics (AFAE) Book Series

Published in the United States of America by
IGI Global
Business Science Reference (an imprint of IGI Global)
701 E. Chocolate Avenue
Hershey PA, USA 17033
Tel: 717-533-8845
Fax: 717-533-8661
E-mail: cust@igi-global.com
Web site: http://www.igi-global.com

Library of Congress Cataloging-in-Publication Data

Names: Dhanapal, Kesavan, 1988- editor. | N, Mari Anand, 1989- editor.
Title: Emerging insights on the relationship between cryptocurrencies and decentralized economic models / edited by Kesavan Dhanapal, Mari Anand N.
Description: Hershey, PA : Engineering Science Reference, [2022] | Includes bibliographical references and index. | Summary: "Cryptocurrency is the real market attractive topic in todays scenario. Significant number of people are seriously searching for many questions relating to cryptocurrencies and their business model. Crypto is the new research platform for many institutions around the world. Several government and policy makers are awaiting research articles, papers and books relating to cryptos in order to have more insight. This book intends to cover major topics that are highly resourceful for knowledge seekers. This book will be highly useful and will contain vital information related to cryptos"-- Provided by publisher.
Identifiers: LCCN 2022041670 (print) | LCCN 2022041671 (ebook) | ISBN 9781668456910 (hardcover) | ISBN 9781668456927 (paperback) | ISBN 9781668456934 (ebook)
Subjects: LCSH: Cryptocurrencies.
Classification: LCC HG1710.3 .E44 2022 (print) | LCC HG1710.3 (ebook) | DDC 332.4--dc23/eng/20220916
LC record available at https://lccn.loc.gov/2022041670
LC ebook record available at https://lccn.loc.gov/2022041671

This book is published in the IGI Global book series Advances in Finance, Accounting, and Economics (AFAE) (ISSN: 2327-5677; eISSN: 2327-5685)

British Cataloguing in Publication Data
A Cataloguing in Publication record for this book is available from the British Library.

For electronic access to this publication, please contact: eresources@igi-global.com.

Advances in Finance, Accounting, and Economics (AFAE) Book Series

ISSN:2327-5677
EISSN:2327-5685

Editor-in-Chief: Ahmed Driouchi, Al Akhawayn University, Morocco

MISSION

In our changing economic and business environment, it is important to consider the financial changes occurring internationally as well as within individual organizations and business environments. Understanding these changes as well as the factors that influence them is crucial in preparing for our financial future and ensuring economic sustainability and growth.

The **Advances in Finance, Accounting, and Economics (AFAE)** book series aims to publish comprehensive and informative titles in all areas of economics and economic theory, finance, and accounting to assist in advancing the available knowledge and providing for further research development in these dynamic fields.

COVERAGE

- Applied economics
- Internet Banking
- Applied Finance
- Development Economics
- Investments and Derivatives
- E-Finance
- Economic Policy
- Fiscal Policy
- Behavioral Economics
- International Economics

IGI Global is currently accepting manuscripts for publication within this series. To submit a proposal for a volume in this series, please contact our Acquisition Editors at Acquisitions@igi-global.com or visit: http://www.igi-global.com/publish/.

The Advances in Finance, Accounting, and Economics (AFAE) Book Series (ISSN 2327-5677) is published by IGI Global, 701 E. Chocolate Avenue, Hershey, PA 17033-1240, USA, www.igi-global.com. This series is composed of titles available for purchase individually; each title is edited to be contextually exclusive from any other title within the series. For pricing and ordering information please visit http://www.igi-global.com/book-series/advances-finance-accounting-economics/73685. Postmaster: Send all address changes to above address.

Titles in this Series

For a list of additional titles in this series, please visit:
http://www.igi-global.com/book-series/advances-finance-accounting-economics/73685

Handbook of Research on Changing World Economic Order in the Post-Pandemic Period
Sushanta Kumar Mahapatra (IBS Hyderabad, The ICFAI Foundation for Higher Education, India) and Vishal Sarin (Lovely Professional University, India)
Business Science Reference • © 2023 • 470pp • H/C (ISBN: 9781799868965) • US $325.00

Concepts, Cases, and Regulations in Financial Fraud and Corruption
Abdul Rafay (University of Management and Technology, Pakistan)
Business Science Reference • © 2023 • 419pp • H/C (ISBN: 9781668450079) • US $250.00

Exploring the Dark Side of FinTech and Implications of Monetary Policy
Sheraz Ahmed (LUT University, Finland) John Agyekum Addae (LUT University, Finland & Ghana Communication Technology University, Ghana) and Kwame Simpe Ofori (International University of Grand-Bassam, Côte d'Ivoire & University of Electronic Science and Technology of China, China)
Business Science Reference • © 2023 • 281pp • H/C (ISBN: 9781668463819) • US $250.00

Tax Audit and Taxation in the Paradigm of Sustainable Development
Bistra Svetlozarova Nikolova (University of Economics, Varna, Bulgaria)
Business Science Reference • © 2023 • 300pp • H/C (ISBN: 9781799890676) • US $215.00

Future Outlooks on Corporate Finance and Opportunities for Robust Economic Planning
Siraj Kariyilaparambu Kunjumuhammed (Modern College of Business and Science, Oman) and Nithya Ramachandran (University of Technology and Applied Science, Oman)
Business Science Reference • © 2023 • 278pp • H/C (ISBN: 9781668453421) • US $240.00

Exploring Business Ecosystems and Innovation Capacity Building in Global Economics
Mihir Joshi (Banasthali Vidyapith University, India) Mohsen Brahmi (University of Sfax, Tunisia) Luigi Aldieri (University of Salerno, Italy) and Concetto Paolo Vinci (University of Salerno, Italy)
Business Science Reference • © 2023 • 325pp • H/C (ISBN: 9781668467664) • US $250.00

For an entire list of titles in this series, please visit:
http://www.igi-global.com/book-series/advances-finance-accounting-economics/73685

IGI Global
PUBLISHER of TIMELY KNOWLEDGE

701 East Chocolate Avenue, Hershey, PA 17033, USA
Tel: 717-533-8845 x100 • Fax: 717-533-8661
E-Mail: cust@igi-global.com • www.igi-global.com

Table of Contents

Detailed Table of Contents

empirical evidence on the fit of conditional volatility. The research is based upon daily U.S. dollar price indexes of Bitcoin (BTC/USD). The data were collected for a time period from October 2021 to April 2022. The every-day price data was further drilled down to arrive at OHLC (open-high-low-close) price for every quarter of the day. The dataset for the analyses were compiled from the website https://cryptowat.ch/ which is an open source and offers free downloadable dataset using Power BI. The first part of the article will focus on the introduction of topic matter concerned. The second part covers around a few literature reviews in the light of volatility in cryptos. The third part will focus on the methodology adopted followed by the results and discussion in the fourth part. Finally, the fifth and last part will provide concluding remarks.

Investing in the unregulated cryptocurrencies has showed a rising tendency since 2020, despite uncertainty surrounding its future in India. There is no ban on the use of cryptocurrencies in India, nor is there any regulation governing their actual use. This uncertainty is disturbing Indian startups developing blockchain-based products. But this hasn't altered investors' positions in investing in cryptocurrencies; they continue to be positive. For longer-term investments, investors have historically employed fundamental analysis. By analyzing the underlying company's operations and the state of its industry or the overall economy, fundamental analysis seeks to find stocks with high growth potential at fair prices. The issue with conducting a fundamental analysis of cryptocurrencies is that they cannot be evaluated using the same criteria as conventional businesses. Therefore, the authors must focus on several frameworks. Finding good metrics is the first step in that approach. This chapter examines the emergence of cryptocurrency in India and its implications on investments.

Any technological innovation is as reliable as the technology itself. The block chain technology, which is the basis of cryptocurrency, runs on a decentralised distributed ledger system which technically promises immunity from any government interference. The popularity of this notion and its variations have forced governments to think about a central bank digital currency. This chapter has been written with the objective of identifying whether lesser reliability of cryptocurrencies can be overcome by central bank digital currencies and issues involved with anonymity. While cryptocurrency ensures no counterfeiting, the feature of anonymity still carries the risk of being used for illegal activities. However, it is now perceived as the future of money. Cryptocurrencies do not create any financial liability but have been adopted as a store of value and medium of exchange. They are also used for micro-payments and decentralised applications. All these issues require a critical assessment of the reliability of cryptocurrencies as against the digital currency backed by central banks.

Cryptocurrency is a widely used word. As e-commerce becomes increasingly important, more Techno-Indians are buying online. Bitcoin was created in 2009 as an internet currency. Financial institutions bridged the buyer-seller divide. They processed trustworthy e-payments. Even if the gap was filled, buyer and seller trade operations remained dependent. This research examines cryptocurrency's influence on Indians. This reliance helped create Cryptocurrency. This will help India advance in e-commerce. Cryptocurrency will help Indians, but not necessarily the country.

This chapter scrutinizes the dynamic linkages between major cryptocurrencies and fiat currencies of developed and emerging countries. To do this, the authors estimate the Scalar-BEKK GARCH models from September 2017 to January 2022. To shed light on the effects of specific events, the authors also estimate the models for the sub-periods: the great crypto crash, the Covid-19 pandemic, and the vaccination. Empirical results suggest that the time-varying relationships between the crypto- and fiat currencies highly depend on the country- and crypto-specific dynamics. By the decentralized nature of cryptocurrencies, it is not an easy venture to define the stylized facts on those dynamic relationships. The most striking result shows a sharp and massive decline in the conditional covariances between the cryptos and the fiat currencies of developed countries except the Japanese Yen at the onset of the Covid-19 pandemic.

explored the feasibility of using DAOs as a new model for economic governance in the blockchain era. The authors examined the key features and functions of DAOs, assessed the potential benefits and challenges of using these organizations as a model for economic governance, and considered the legal and regulatory implications of DAOs. The authors also examined case studies of existing DAOs and analyzed their successes and failures in order to identify best practices for implementing and operating DAOs effectively. The findings suggest that DAOs have the potential to disrupt traditional models of economic governance by providing a new way for organizations to operate and make decisions in a transparent and decentralized manner. However, there are also challenges and limitations to using DAOs as a model for economic governance.

Chapter 10
Cryptocurrencies: Changing the Face of Online Gaming.................................155
Srimathi T., SRM Institute of Science and Technology, India
Bharathi R., St. Joseph's College of Engineering, India

In this digital age, the rise of new technologies has caused a significant change in how we go about our daily business. The invention and adoption of cryptocurrencies have been one of the most significant recent developments. Given the surge in smartphone usage, cryptocurrency has had a big impact on a number of industries, including the mobile gaming sector. The use of cryptocurrencies has dramatically increased in recent days, with a wide range of uses including investments and transactions in the online gaming sector. With a billion-dollar market cap, the gaming sector is booming and not expected to stop. Every year, new systems and video games are released, giving players fresh things to look forward to. How players pay for their gaming is one area where the i-gaming industry has failed in making changes. The majority of the time, gamers have been forced to use conventional means like credit card payments or Google wallet. But what if a better option existed? What if cryptocurrency could be used by gamers to purchase their games?

Chapter 11
Cryptocurrencies: Issues and Challenges in Financial Reporting 167
Fathima Farzana J., St. Joseph's University, India

With the advent of cryptocurrency during 2009, a new regime of exchange consideration, as well as an investment avenue without physical existence and centralized regulatory authority, started attracting the investors. These extremely volatile neo currencies created regulatory issues among apex monitoring authorities and also raised various challenges in the front of financial reporting. The main purpose of financial reporting is to present the true and fair view of the financial statement of a company. Any violation in this regard creates serious issue of corporate governance. On acceptance of cryptocurrencies as a legal tender, disclosure of such

Preface

As we stand at the forefront of a new digital age, we are witnessing an unprecedented evolution of economic systems. Cryptocurrencies have emerged as a new form of digital currency that has the potential to disrupt traditional economic models. The impact of cryptocurrencies on the global financial system has been a topic of debate for several years. The idea of decentralized economic models has emerged as a potential solution to address the limitations of traditional centralized economic models. With the rise of blockchain technology, we have seen the development of decentralized economic models that offer transparency, security, and flexibility.

This book, *Emerging Insights on the Relationship Between Cryptocurrencies and Decentralized Economic Models*, aims to provide an overview of the subject matter, highlighting key insights and perspectives from leading experts in the field. The book explores the relationship between cryptocurrencies and decentralized economic models and examines the opportunities and challenges presented by this emerging field. The book includes a collection of scholarly articles that address a range of topics, including the impact of cryptocurrencies on traditional financial systems, the potential of blockchain technology to enable decentralized economic models, the regulatory landscape of cryptocurrencies, and the future of cryptocurrencies as a viable economic system.

We hope that this book will serve as a valuable resource for students, scholars, researchers, and professionals who are interested in the subject matter, and we look forward to the insights and ideas that will emerge from this rapidly evolving field. The topic of the relationship between cryptocurrencies and decentralized economic models is highly relevant in today's world, as we are witnessing a rapid shift towards a more decentralized, digitized economy. Cryptocurrencies, such as Bitcoin, Ethereum, and Litecoin, have disrupted the traditional financial system by enabling decentralized, peer-to-peer transactions without the need for intermediaries, such as banks. In addition, the emergence of decentralized economic models, such as blockchain-based smart contracts and decentralized autonomous organizations (DAOs), has the potential to transform industries beyond just finance. These models can enable more transparent, secure, and efficient processes for a variety of applications, including supply chain management, voting systems, and intellectual property rights. However, as with any disruptive technology, there are also challenges and potential risks associated with the adoption of cryptocurrencies and decentralized economic models. These include issues related to regulation, security, scalability, and sustainability.

Therefore, it is essential to have a deeper understanding of the relationship between cryptocurrencies and decentralized economic models, their potential benefits and risks, and their impact on various industries. The insights and perspectives shared in this book can help inform and shape the ongoing evolution of this important area of innovation in our rapidly changing world.

RELEVANCE OF THE TOPIC IN THE CONTEMPORARY WORLD

In recent years, the rise of cryptocurrencies and blockchain technology has brought about significant changes to the global economy. Cryptocurrencies such as Bitcoin, Ethereum, and others have gained popularity as alternatives to traditional currencies, with their decentralized nature and lack of reliance on central authorities making them appealing to many individuals and businesses alike. The decentralized economic models that underlie these cryptocurrencies have also sparked interest in a wide range of industries, with many seeing them as a way to disrupt traditional business models and empower individuals and small businesses. As such, the study of the relationship between cryptocurrencies and decentralized economic models has become increasingly important in understanding the potential implications of these new technologies.

Moreover, the COVID-19 pandemic has further highlighted the importance of decentralized economic models and digital currencies, as more and more people have turned to online transactions and remote work. As governments around the world continue to grapple with the economic impacts of the pandemic, there is a growing interest in exploring new ways to create a more resilient and inclusive global economy. In this context, the book *Emerging Insights on the Relationship Between Cryptocurrencies and Decentralized Economic Models* is a timely and valuable resource for scholars, researchers, and practitioners in a variety of fields. By exploring the latest research and insights on these important topics, this book provides a comprehensive overview of the current state of the field and offers insights into the potential future of cryptocurrencies and decentralized economic models.

The Target Audience

Emerging Insights on the Relationship Between Cryptocurrencies and Decentralized Economic Models is broad and diverse, including academics, researchers, policymakers, business leaders, investors, and anyone interested in understanding the impact of cryptocurrencies and decentralized economic models on the global economy.

For academics and researchers, this book provides a comprehensive analysis of the latest research on the relationship between cryptocurrencies and decentralized economic models. It offers insights into the role of these emerging technologies in disrupting traditional financial systems and creating new economic models. The book also provides a platform for researchers to share their work and collaborate with others in the field.

For policymakers and business leaders, this book offers an in-depth analysis of the opportunities and challenges presented by cryptocurrencies and decentralized economic models. It provides a framework for understanding how these technologies can be leveraged to promote economic growth and financial inclusion while minimizing risks such as money laundering, terrorism financing, and market instability.

For investors, this book provides insights into the potential of cryptocurrencies and decentralized economic models to create new investment opportunities and disrupt traditional markets. It offers guidance on how to navigate the risks and opportunities presented by this emerging asset class. "Emerging Insights on the Relationship Between Cryptocurrencies and Decentralized Economic Models" is a valuable resource for anyone looking to stay up-to-date on the latest trends and developments in the cryptocurrency and decentralized economic model space. It offers a comprehensive analysis of the subject matter, along with real-world examples, case studies, and best practices that will help readers understand how these technologies can be leveraged to create a more equitable and sustainable global economy.

Description of Chapters

"Public Perception on Awareness and Adaptation of Cryptocurrency in Brunei Darussalam": This chapter presents a case study of public perception and awareness of cryptocurrency in Brunei Darussalam, highlighting the challenges and opportunities for widespread adoption in the region.

"Price Volatility in Cryptocurrencies – A Modelling Approach": This chapter presents a modelling approach for analyzing and predicting price volatility in cryptocurrencies, which is critical for investors and traders in this highly volatile market.

"The Emergence of Cryptocurrency in India and Its Implications on Investments": This chapter discusses the emergence of cryptocurrencies in India and its implications on investments. It explores the challenges and opportunities associated with investing in cryptocurrencies in India, and provides an analysis of the regulatory landscape and the future of cryptocurrency investments in the country.

"Reliability of Cryptocurrencies and the Central Bank Digital Currency Architecture": This chapter analyzes the reliability of cryptocurrencies and discusses the potential for central bank digital currencies to provide a more stable and reliable alternative to traditional cryptocurrencies.

"Cryptocurrencies on New Rise": This chapter provides an overview of the recent rise of cryptocurrencies and how they have become an important part of the global financial system. It explores the different types of cryptocurrencies and their applications, as well as the factors driving their popularity and growth.

"Modeling Time-Varying Co-movements between Major Cryptocurrencies and Foreign Exchange Markets": This chapter examines the dynamic relationships between major cryptocurrencies and foreign exchange markets, providing insights into the market interdependencies and risk exposures.

"Cryptocurrency may Prove Financial Crime – A Conceptual Analysis": This chapter provides a conceptual analysis of how cryptocurrencies can be used for financial crime. It explores the different types of financial crimes that can be committed using cryptocurrencies, and discusses the measures that can be taken to prevent and detect such crimes. It also explores the challenges associated with regulating cryptocurrencies to prevent financial crime.

"Digital Currencies and Its Relationship Towards Economic Instability": This chapter examines the relationship between digital currencies and economic instability, highlighting the potential risks and benefits of this emerging technology.

"Exploring the Feasibility of a Decentralized Autonomous Organization (DAO) as a New Model for Economic Governance in the Blockchain Era": This chapter discusses the feasibility of using a Decentralized Autonomous Organization (DAO) as a new model for economic governance in the blockchain era. It explores the advantages and limitations of DAOs and discusses how they can revolutionize economic governance in the future.

"Cryptocurrencies - Changing the face of Online Gaming": This chapter explores the impact of cryptocurrencies on the online gaming industry. With the rise of blockchain technology and the use of decentralized platforms, the chapter discusses the benefits of using cryptocurrencies in online gaming. It provides an analysis of how the gaming industry can benefit from the use of cryptocurrencies as well as the challenges that need to be addressed.

"Cryptocurrencies – Issues and Challenges in Financial Reporting": This chapter focuses on the financial reporting issues and challenges associated with cryptocurrencies, providing guidance on how to properly account for and disclose these assets.

"A Revolutionary Impact on Cryptocurrency": This chapter explores the impact of cryptocurrencies on the financial industry and the economy at large, providing insights into the new business models and market opportunities that have emerged as a result of this disruptive technology.

IMPLICATION

Emerging Insights on the Relationship Between Cryptocurrencies and Decentralized Economic Models offers a comprehensive and multifaceted analysis of the impact of cryptocurrencies on various aspects of the economy and society. The book covers a wide range of topics, including financial reporting, economic governance, online gaming, price volatility, and the reliability of cryptocurrencies, providing valuable insights into the opportunities and challenges associated with this emerging technology. By bringing together contributions from a diverse group of experts, the book provides a unique perspective on the subject matter and contributes to the ongoing discourse on the relationship between cryptocurrencies and decentralized economic models. This book will be valuable to academics, researchers, policymakers, and practitioners interested in understanding the impact of cryptocurrencies on the global economy and society, and will serve as an important resource for years to come.

Dhanapal Kesavan
SRM Institute of Science and Technology, India

N. Mari Anand
Department of Business Studies, University of Technology and Applied Sciences, Salalah, Oman

Acknowledgment

It is great privilege to express our gratitude and respect to all those who have guided and inspired us in preparing this book.

First and foremost, we thank GOD, the Almighty for enlightening and showering His Blessings on us for the successful completion of this work.

With profound gratitude, respect and pride, we express our sincere thanks to the Management of SRM Institute of Science & Technology, Chennai, India and University of Technology & Applied Science, Salalah, Oman for providing all the facilities.

We are indeed thankful to all our authors, from around the globe and from India for contributing their in bringing out this book.

Finally, we would also like to thank IGI Global for giving us the opportunity to prepare this project. We are happy to contribute to the field of cryptocurrency and its relation with decentralized economic models through the creation of this book.

Last but not the least, we are privileged to record a deep sense of gratitude tour family members for their valuable support, appreciation, encouragement and inspiration through this process.

Chapter 1
Public Perception of Awareness and Adaptation of Cryptocurrency in Brunei Darussalam

Nur Aqilah Adilah Hj Abd Rahman
https://orcid.org/0000-0003-2215-8661
Universiti Teknologi Brunei, Brunei

Heru Susanto
Universiti Teknologi Brunei, Brunei

ABSTRACT

Cryptocurrency has been around since 2008 when Satoshi Nakamoto issued a white paper. Satoshi also claimed to be the creator and developer of Bitcoin, the first type of cryptocurrency. This research looks at Bruneians' understanding of Cryptocurrencies, their perceptions, and their awareness and acceptance of cryptocurrency in Brunei Darussalam. This research used questionnaires as a method of gathering data. Who would have thought that cryptocurrency was known to almost all levels of age, it did not only focus on higher education respondents, and that the fact it was male-dominated? Cryptocurrency in Brunei is not widespread yet. The awareness of cryptocurrency in Brunei is deficient because information is inadequate. Bitcoin is yet to be the most well-known cryptocurrency. Cryptocurrency is seen as an asset instead of currency by the general public. Information primarily obtained is mainly from social media, family, friends, word of mouth, and press releases from AMBD.

DOI: 10.4018/978-1-6684-5691-0.ch001

INTRODUCTION

This paper aims to investigate further the adaptation and awareness of cryptocurrency in Brunei on whether it has a positive, negative, or null impact when used in transaction processes or payments. Positive in a way that it may help settle loans and hire purchases or negative in a way that it was not regulated by the government, making it not seen as currency as fiat currency is. Cryptocurrency is not banned in Brunei but is also not accepted as a means of payment. AMBD has announced to the public through a press release dated 22nd December 2017 that people should exercise high caution with cryptocurrency. AMBD also stated that cryptocurrencies are not legal tender, and AMBD did not regulate cryptocurrency.

Bruneians can obtain cryptocurrency through buying and selling, and mining bitcoin. This paper will also discuss information on how Bruneians get cryptocurrency. Currently, Brunei is facing the pandemic Covid19. Everything needs to be done online, especially in terms of payment; therefore, to see whether cryptocurrency is coming in handy in light of this pandemic. Cryptocurrency uses blockchain technology which is currently a modern technology that provides perfect security because of its cryptographic function. Cryptographic function means decryption is needed to obtain information.

With few adaptations in Brunei, this paper also aims to see the users of cryptocurrency and the demographic of cryptocurrency in Brunei. As one who has experience seeing people investing in cryptocurrency, authors have developed an interest in exploring cryptocurrency adaptation in Brunei Darussalam. In the author's opinion, accurate and adequate information about cryptocurrency and guidelines for using one can positive impact (profit) on whoever has invested in it and even a negative result (loss).

PROBLEM STATEMENT

Cryptocurrency is quite a new concept of currency, there are few types of cryptocurrencies, and various questions and challenges arise in this research. Cryptocurrency is quite well known outside of the country, and it is now known to several populations in Brunei Darussalam. Cryptocurrency is virtual or online money, and for it to work, it needs to be done online. The reason for this study is to investigate whether, in light of the pandemic covid-19, is to know whether Brunei is applying the online approach to every process concerning payments and whether an adaptation of cryptocurrency is widespread or not.

The problem is to investigate whether the public is aware of cryptocurrency and know the consequences of using it and the advantage and disadvantage of using it. By establishing a hub or licensed company in Brunei's "crypto hub", the public may have been aware of the existence of cryptocurrency and have enough or adequate information about crypto, which would be a waste to investigate something that already exists has the answer to it. However, it seems that the crypto hub is not yet well known to the general public in hope that through this study, the public will start to be aware of the existence of cryptocurrency.

METHODOLOGY

Research Design

This paper will use the quantitative method to address the critical research goals and combine primary and secondary sources. The first part consisted of a series of structured public questionnaires with knowledge of cryptocurrency and pieces of literature on research papers related to cryptocurrency.

Study Area

Population refers to a complete set of individuals with a common characteristic that researchers are interested in. Researchers choose the study area via random sampling. Researchers collected data from the middle of May until the middle of June 2020.

Data Sources

The researcher collected primary data sources via questionnaires in English and Malay, distributed to 100 to 150 people. Preliminary data were more reliable and had a more confident level of decision-making as they directly interacted with the occurrence of an event. Researchers collected secondary data from the literature, journals, different articles, books, newspapers, newsletters, press releases, websites, blogs, and other sources related to adaptation and awareness of cryptocurrency.

Population and Sample Size

The study population were Bruneians who know cryptocurrency and its adaptation in Brunei Darussalam. About 125 respondents participated in answering the questionnaire.

Data Collection Method Through Questionnaires

Questions asked will be basic demographic questions; gender, age, education level, employment, and whether respondents are aware of cryptocurrency. How did the respondents know about cryptocurrency (bitcoin)? Have they ever used bitcoin as means of payment? Have they ever withdrawn money using a bitcoin ATM? What is their point of view on cryptocurrencies? Does cryptocurrency help in light of the pandemic Covid-19? Questionnaires will be developed based on a multiple-choice question, Likert-type scale question, checkbox question, and short answer question. Questionnaires were prepared and distributed to various people via email, Facebook, and Whatsapp.

Method of Data Analysis and Interpretation

The data analysis section will answer the questions raised in the problem statement. The analysis provided from questionnaires on public perception of adaptation and awareness of cryptocurrency in Brunei Darussalam was analyzed, discussed, compared, contrasted, and synthesized. Responses from questionnaires were analyzed using SPSS for chi-square, t-test, and ANOVA.

RESEARCH OBJECTIVES

The primary objective is to determine how widespread bitcoin use is in Brunei Darussalam and how overall cryptocurrency awareness is. The secondary objective is to determine the preferred cryptocurrency, perceptions about cryptocurrency adaptation and awareness, and what they believe are cryptocurrencies' benefits, drawbacks, and essential factors.

RESEARCH QUESTIONS

1. What is the gender-wise familiarity of cryptocurrency in Brunei Darussalam?
2. What is the age-wise understanding of cryptocurrency in Brunei Darussalam?
3. What is the occupation-wise understanding of cryptocurrency in Brunei Darussalam?
4. What is education-wise familiarity with cryptocurrency in Brunei Darussalam?
5. What are the essential advantages and disadvantages of cryptocurrencies?
6. What are the factors affecting cryptocurrency investment?
7. What is the most preferred cryptocurrency in Brunei Darussalam?

8. Does cryptocurrency fulfil the properties of fiat currency? As means of payment?

HYPOTHESIS

H1: There is a significant relationship between gender and cryptocurrency awareness

H2: There is a significant relationship between occupation and cryptocurrency awareness
H3: There is a significant relationship between age and cryptocurrencies adaptation
H4: There is a significant difference between education level and cryptocurrencies adaptation
H5: There is a significant difference between gender and factor in investing in cryptocurrency

HYPOTHESIS FRAMEWORK

An illustration of the hypothesis framework can be seen in Figure 1.

LITERATURE REVIEW

Cryptocurrencies currently are widely used virtual currencies around the globe. People use them as daily payment methods, savings, or investment tools. Some countries banned the use of cryptocurrencies, but some support the use of cryptocurrencies. Countries that banned the use of cryptocurrency are Algeria, Egypt, Nepal, UAE, etc. Some countries also issued a warning against trading cryptocurrencies due to the extremely high risk. Countries that prohibit or do not entirely ban the use of cryptocurrency are Bangladesh, Colombia, Iran, Kuwait, Macau, Oman, etc. However, Bahraini citizens are allowed to use cryptocurrency outside of Bahrain. (Said 2019)

(Karels, 2018) discussed the impact of cryptocurrency on the economy through the environment. Bruneians uses bitcoin; bitcoin is generated through a process called mining. At the same time, own mining bitcoin will use 24-hour electricity. Massive data centers are being built to mine bitcoin, consuming a vast amount of energy. Studies were done on recognizing the amount of energy a bitcoin has consumed. Charts are used to show the percentage of energy consumption of bitcoin mining. With the increase in energy consumption, a new market for utility companies within the economy have an opportunity to be created. Mining consumes a lot of energy

Figure 1. Hypothesis framework for public perception on adaptation and awareness of cryptocurrency in Brunei Darussalam

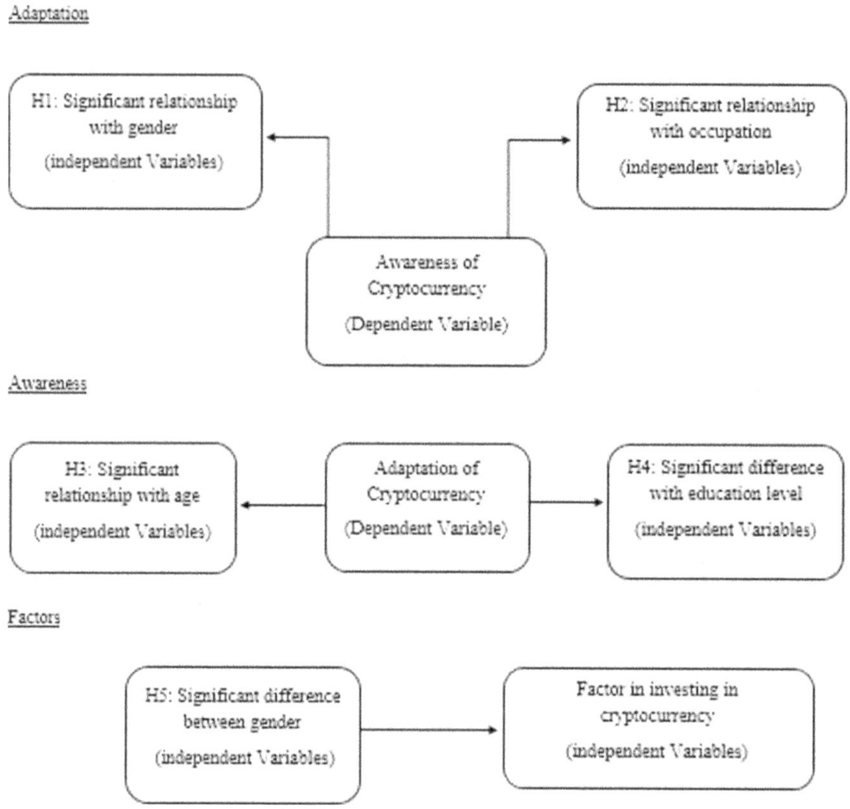

and can produce a vast amount of heat. Similar to other electronics, its server needs to be cooled off too. Karels added that companies across the globe are investing in additional sustainable solutions to decrease the negative impact that energy-intensive bitcoin mining brings. Due to the overload usage of power, Venezuelan authorities have shut down mining operations, with 11,000 computers allegedly running on power illegally. This overload of power usage caused severe repercussions for Venezuela, including an electricity shortage (Karels, 2018).

(Bondarenko, Kichuk, and Antonov, 2019) discussed whether cryptocurrency could be used as an investment tool in developing the national economy. Online questionnaires were distributed to 450 respondents aged 17 to 70 years to research the demand for cryptocurrency in Ukraine. In Ukraine, 45.4% of respondents consider cryptocurrency as means of payment. The report concluded that Ukraine and the world's attitudes towards cryptocurrency are ambiguous. However, in Ukraine, cryptocurrency has not been recognized with money. Even though few online stores in Ukraine accept cryptocurrency, it is also not banned in Ukraine.

Legal and economic review written on cryptocurrency effect on financial journal stability by (Srokosz and Kopciaski, 2015) stated that in the economic dimension with references to the concept behind the emergence of virtual currency, researchers can find different strands of the economic theory. Austrian School of Economics claimed that currency interventions triggered the occurrence of business cycles. Excessive credit expansion caused by fractional reserve banking contributes to increased money supply hence low-interest rates. Using Bitcoin as a common currency, as a specific example, is not the solution to escaping various kinds of danger involved in cash circulation. When exchange rates are unstable, legal risks related to using new currency are not essentially easily avoided.

(Kunjadić, 2018) wrote that because of blockchain technology, cryptocurrency requires technology that allows database credibility where historical data cannot be changed from inside or outside, which can completely reform the financial sector—for example, transferring money for Southeast Europe, which costs around 3 to 12 per cent interest rates but with cryptocurrency lower interest rates, attracts cryptocurrency users, which can lead to temporary savings. (Kunjadić, 2018) assumed that powerful countries that significantly increased their state debts and money in pre-crisis and crisis times are behind the development of cryptocurrencies. The occurrence and purchase of cryptocurrencies accomplish the sterilization of surplus but limited conventional money. In time, debts in traditional currencies can be converted into obligations in cryptocurrencies. Since cryptocurrencies are not regulated like conventional currencies are, nothing prevents the various nation-states from proclaiming illegal money and criminal activities if a significant portion of their debt is found. Crytpcorruncey would resolve part of the state debts would be fixed overnight.

In his bachelor thesis, (Stancel, 2015) concluded that the most fantastic feature of cryptocurrencies is allowing users to make their cash smarter and automate the economy's cash and cash flows. It will enable users to designate certain coins, such as specific services such as creating allowance even in dollars or euros. The designed budgets can only be used to pay for healthcare at certified parties. In addition, doing so would not require a specific bureaucratic body to oversee this method. Cryptocurrency can program money. Another point is that the company can keep its expenditure under control, for example, salaries, materials, maintenance, etc. Such an earlier specification may have prevented the money from being spent otherwise. In addition, automating such processes could lead to a tremendous reduction in bureaucracy, saving resources in terms of human energy. It would dramatically reduce the burden on accountants and controllers. It is fair to say that it will keep the organisations a significant amount of time.

(Nica, Piotrowska, and Schenk-Hoppp, 2017) wrote a report on cryptocurrencies' economic benefits by reviewing several academic literatures on their potential benefits and risks. Due to the pseud anonymity they provide and the lack of strict independent regulations, cryptocurrencies have been used in multiple illicit activities, especially those in cyberspace/the internet (black market), such as fraud offences, for instance, money laundering and tax evasion. (Nica, Piotrowska, and Schenk-Hoppp, 2017) analyse how cryptocurrencies have been utilised in financing illegal activities by terrorist groups and contributed to the development of dark markets, the online marketplaces used for selling forbidden items such as drugs.

(Naboulsi, 2018) wrote articles on the impact of digital currencies on economic development in Kenya by discussing whether the digital currency can reduce international fund transfers and remittance fees. Taking website material, press articles, and case studies as examples, (Naboulsi, 2018) used them as a purposive sampling process. The data analysis started with a single source after a cross-comparison of the findings collected from various proof sources. Results showed that using cryptocurrencies in Kenya can reduce remittance fees but did not reduce international fund transfers in Kenya. A widely used cryptocurrency, BitPesa, proved attractive to the Kenya market.

(Geetha and Girisha, 2018) conducted a conceptual study on the impact of bitcoins on the Indian economy through secondary data, including periodicals, journals, reports, websites, business lines, economic times of India, and research articles. Geetha and Girsiha claimed that bitcoin is a potential way to improve essential financial services and people's quality of life in developing nations, a promising anti-poverty technique. Until now, India's government is only watching and studying how it works before adopting it.

(Said 2019), in his conference paper on the impact of digital currency, noted that digital currency (bitcoin) is used in international money laundering because bitcoin can't be monitored, predicted, and even traced. Cryptocurrency has created a new environment where no one person has complete control, unlike the present financial system. He also noted that dark web transaction has now been made easier because a person can complete an unlawful transaction with Bitcoin without disclosing any identifying information that could increase cybercrime. Digital currency has advantages, too, though. Ahmed noted that cryptocurrency could reduce the cost of cash (cost of printing and producing fiat money), ease of flow of funds without blocking leaks with efficient administration, and increase the use of e-commerce and mobile financial services. Lastly, it provides the highest security to enhance trust in the digital ecosystem.

ADAPTATION AND AWARENESS OF CRYPTOCURRENCY IN BRUNEI DARUSSALAM

Authors obtained information from several blogs, articles, and websites, for instance, Reddit, and blogs written by locals on where to get and how to earn cryptocurrency in Brunei Darussalam. It is pretty challenging to get as much information regarding cryptocurrency due to the limitation of news and how the adaptation is not as comprehensive as expected. The public seems only to be using bitcoin as a preferred cryptocurrency. Although some are aware of cryptocurrency, their information is still minimal.

Where to get Bitcoin?

Buying Bitcoin is simply finding a place where cash can trade with Bitcoin. These places are known as exchanges, authors can find several exchange places, but these places also did not serve Bruneian customers. Some deals require users to scan their ID or passport and proof of address and upload it to them, which can prevent money laundering and other shady business or the black market.

Websites

Brunei crypto is a local website that acts as the first cryptocurrency hub for Brunei Darussalam. Its vision is to enable the widespread application of cryptocurrency products and services in Brunei Darussalam and, at the same time to promote an economic and financial ecosystem that can benefit the local population. Brunei crypto is a company based locally registered under 16/17 and subject to local regulations as determined by His Majesty's government. This company is not charging any fees, minimal or no commissions, because all transactions are via local banks, online payments that are virtually free. Banks available for the transactions are BIBD (Bank Islam Brunei Darussalam), TAIB (Tabung Amanah Islam Brunei), Baiduri Bank, and Standard Chartered. Transactions use cash deposit online transfers. Brunei crypto is protected against malicious attacks with valid SSL certification. If the customer faced any problem, the company would contact the customer personally to resolve any issues by the company's terms and conditions. Brunei Crypto accepts payments made through Visa/Mastercard debit and credit cards from the listed bank above. CDM (cash deposit machines) are also available as means of payment.

Exchange of Bitcoins

Four cryptocurrency exchanges are Coinbase, Bitstamp, Gemini, and Cex.io. Still, the most trusted exchange commonly used by Bruneians, according to a Bruneian blogger Saveyfox.com who is personally a bitcoin owner, is Bitstamp. Bitstamp is a leading and most extended cryptocurrency exchange that allows users to deposit cash and exchange it for Bitcoin. As it suggests, users would need to transfer money from their bank account into their Bitstamp account before getting Bitcoin and vice versa in terms of reselling its Bitcoin.

Bitcoin Mining

In Brunei, one company currently sells a machine that mines its cryptocurrency, especially Bitcoin mining and OKVY mining. OKVY mining offers various kinds of devices used to mine Bitcoins. The company also provides information such as how much income will be generated monthly by a machine (more expensive machines, more revenue it can develop) and the total amount of energy that the device will require because mining will require a 24hr electricity. Recently, one machine only cost less than 1k; this may be due to no bitcoin left to mine, only a few left. Initially, there was 21 million bitcoin ever produced; mining it can make 900 bitcoins per day. Only 1,961,319 bitcoins remain mined; nevertheless, according to bitcoinblockhalf.com, 90.66 per cent of bitcoin has been excavated until the next block half (miners are given a set amount of bitcoin whenever a block is is produced as part of bitcoin's coin issuance).

Bitcoin ATM

Because Bitcoin is not acknowledged as legal tender in Brunei, no local bank works with a cryptocurrency exchange. (AMBD, 2017). Therefore, no ATM, especially for Bitcoin, is available yet. But there is one source from YouTube, a video showing a Bruneian would go to Malaysia, Glomac Plaza, where he can withdraw his bitcoin money using the ATM.

From Other People

The fastest way to get Bitcoin is by buying it from other people. However, users have to socialize face-to-face, and the price can be pretty high for a seller to profit. Although it may be possible to find individuals, who wish to sell bitcoins in return for a credit card or payment from PayPal, such payment methods do not allow at most places to finance. Someone buys bitcoins with PayPal and then reverses their half of the transaction, usually referred to as a chargeback. Of course, because of the price, 1 Bitcoin nowadays is equivalent to 41,294.23 Brunei dollars as of May 2022.

How to Store Bitcoin?

Physical money has a physical wallet, so digital money must also have a digital wallet. Before purchasing Bitcoins, the user must first install a wallet, a software program that stores private and public keys and interacts with a blockchain that allows users to send, receive and trace their Bitcoins. There are three types of wallets (online web-based) desktop wallets, mobile wallets, and hardware (physical) wallets offered by Brunei Crypto.

Two primary things about digital wallets are receiving addresses and paper keys or seeds. The receiving address is the location where cryptocurrency is transferred. It consists of alphanumeric characters, including capital letters, such as "1GpRptYjiNNghyu49JIHklIhKHmP3SV." It can also take the form of a QR code, which the payer can scan while making payments. Payers need to always double-check the address before issuing a send command. A paper key comes in handy when a user loses their wallet. Setting the wallet prompts the user to write down a series of words from 12 to 24 randomly generated words; these are the seeds used to recover bitcoins. If somehow the user loses their wallet, this sheet of paper needs to be kept safe.

Desktop Wallets

Desktop wallets are downloaded and installed on a single computer and can only be accessed from that computer. Desktop wallets offer one of the highest levels of security, but if the computer is hacked or receives a virus, all funds may lose. According to Brunei crypto, examples of desktop digital wallets currently offered for Bruneians are Bitcoin Core, Blockchain, Electrum, and Bither.

Mobile (Online) Wallets

Mobile / online wallets operate on a mobile app and are helpful as they can be used anywhere retail stores are involved. Digital wallets are usually much smaller and more accessible due to the limited space on a cell phone. Online wallet stores online and third-party controlled private keys make them more vulnerable to hacks and theft while making them more accessible. Examples of desktop wallets offered under Brunei crypto for Bruneians are GreenAddress, Breadwallet, Jaxx, and Mycelium (Android only).

Hardware (Physical) Wallets

Hardware Wallets Vary From software wallets in that they store the private keys of a user on a hardware computer such as a USB device, or in the simplest sense, the wallet looks like a pen drive. Although hardware wallets do online transactions, they are stored offline, increasing security. Hardware wallets can be compatible with multiple web interfaces and can support different currencies, depending on which one is chosen to use. Users may plug in their system to any machine or device allowed on the internet, insert a password, send currency and confirm. Hardware wallets allow easy transactions while keeping money offline and away from danger. Examples of hardware wallets are **Nano Ledger S** and **Trezor**.

DESCRIPTIVE STATISTIC (QUESTIONNAIRE SURVEY)

Gender Wise Familiarity on Adaptation With Awareness of Cryptocurrency

Authors distributed two questionnaires online and by hand to the public in English and Malay versions. The aim of having two different languages of the questionnaire was to target people who have difficulty understanding the English language and thus can answer the questionnaire created in the Malay language; hence more excellent responses were provided. Initially, the target responses were 100 – 150 and ended up with a total of 125 surveys distributed to the public at random; out of 125 questionnaires, 66 were female respondents, and 59 were male participants.

According to website financial times Kuchler stated that cryptocurrency's anonymity features make finding accurate data about who holds or owns cryptocurrency difficult. The identity with the cryptocurrency was sealed and kept anonymous. However, 75 per cent of crypto owners or holders are men through Uphold's research, a virtual wallet service that does background checks on its users. Bitcoin statistics found that 97 per cent were male. (Financial Times, 2018).

Anna Dreber, an economics professor at the Stockholm School of Economics, cited one study showing a 64 per cent probability that men would take risks compared to women, which may be why the male-dominated cryptocurrency is. Risks such as when the price of cryptocurrency is highly volatile and sometimes digital exchange that can be hacked, which women are not prone to take. However, Anna Dreber still thinks that alone is not enough to account for the difference between males and females in cryptocurrency investment. Bitcoin and cryptocurrencies first became popular in the geekiest parts of the technology and finance industries, where both industries are proven to be male-dominated. Despite the larger number of female respondents who participated in the survey, male respondents were more aware of the existence of adaptation of cryptocurrency compared to female respondents. 45 out of 59 male respondents were aware of cryptocurrency. Only 38 out of 66 female respondents are mindful of the adaptation to cryptocurrency. However, some stated that they are not conscious of cryptocurrency but aware of the types of cryptocurrency, I.e. Bitcoin, Ethereum, Litecoin, Ripple and etc.

Age Wise Familiarity on Adaptation and Awareness of Cryptocurrency

Source to bitcointalk, the highest number of respondents are at the age of 22 – 30 and the second are age 31 – 40, and following is the age group of 16 – 21—Researchgate. net paper written by Bohr and Bashir. Bohr and Bashir, professors of sociology, conducted research on "what age demographic are aware of cryptocurrency" and received about 1200 responses. From their study, they concluded that the average age was about 33 years old. They also concluded that surveying a random sample of the cryptocurrency community is nearly impossible because cryptocurrency offers a lot of privacy to its user also. The currency is not regulated by any centralized agency, and the adoption of cryptocurrency is still not widespread. (Bohr and Bashir 2014)

Research done on Brunei Darussalam has shown that the 18 – 28 age group and the 29 – 38 age group seem to lead the chart on awareness. Both of these age groups know what cryptocurrency is and have heard of bitcoin, Litecoin, etc., especially people of age 29 – 38. This group seem to have shown more interest compared to the other age group. The shocking result for researchers was the fact that the percentage of people aged 25 – 44 old heard less about the crypto industry.

Education Level Wise Familiarity on Adaptation and Awareness of Cryptocurrency

Respondents whose highest education level is Diploma are about 40 respondents in total, 35 respondents whose highest education level is High School, five respondents are PhD, 20 respondents are undergraduates, 17 respondents are postgraduates, and eight respondents chose other; HNtec and HND. Out of 40 diploma graduates, about 27 respondents are aware of cryptocurrency. Out of 35 high school leavers (all respondents who chose high school are mainly public sector workers), 26 are aware of cryptocurrency, and out of 5 PhD, four are aware of cryptocurrency; out of 17 postgraduates respondents, 13 are aware of cryptocurrency, 14 out of 20 undergraduates are aware of cryptocurrency while respondents who chose other, 5 out of 8 aware of the existence of cryptocurrency.

This result concluded that despite the level of education, cryptocurrency is known to different educational levels, not specifically just respondents who have a higher level of education. Outside the country, Coinbase is trying to increase crypto awareness by regularly engaging with students and universities across the country as part of recruiting efforts; by partnering with Qriously, Coinbase is trying to ask students' thoughts and opinions on cryptocurrency (Coinbase, 2018). From their findings, 42 per cent of the world's top 50 universities currently offer at least one course on crypto or Blockchain.

Employment Wise Familiarity on Adaptation and Awareness of Cryptocurrency

Question 4 of the questionnaire on public perception of adaptation of cryptocurrency in Brunei Darussalam is about employment. Questions require multiple-choice answers of housewife, private sector, public sector, self-employed, unemployed, student, etc. There were a total of 125 respondents; ten respondents were housewives, 40 respondents were working in the private sector, 38 respondents were working in the public sector, 20 respondents were students, seven respondents were self-employed, seven respondents were unemployed, and the other 3 were respondents who chose other. Out of 10 housewives, nine housewives are aware of the existence of cryptocurrency, about 90%. Out of 40 private-sector workers, 31 people were aware of cryptocurrency, about 77.5% and 38 workers who work in the public sector, about 24 people are aware of cryptocurrency, and 63% of whole respondents were from the public sector. Out of 7 self-employed respondents, five are aware of cryptocurrency, around 71%. While for 20 students who participated in the questionnaire, only seven were aware of cryptocurrency, 35% and 43% from unemployed respondents, where 3 out of 7 respondents were aware of cryptocurrency and respondents who chose other, 2 out of 3 were mindful of cryptocurrency.

From the results above, housewives in the private and public sectors seem to be dominating the familiarity with cryptocurrency in Brunei Darussalam. In contrast, students expected to understand Information technology did not seem to be aware of cryptocurrency. Using image sources from coindesk.com below, 43% who know about bitcoin and use crypto have full-time employment. Comparing it to results obtained from questionnaires, public sector and private sector workers are aware of the existence of cryptocurrency.

Awareness of Cryptocurrency and Adaptation in Brunei Darussalam

Out of 125 respondents, 83 respondents responded yes to knowing cryptocurrency, and 42 respondents responded no to learning cryptocurrency. There are about 459 500 in 2019, according to the department of planning and statistics, and with 83 respondents aware of the cryptocurrency, about 0.018% of the whole population is aware of cryptocurrency. Therefore, the results showed that the awareness of cryptocurrency in Brunei Darussalam is very low. Few respondents did not know what cryptocurrency is but were aware of the types of cryptocurrencies; for instance, they did not know what cryptocurrency, when asked about cryptocurrency, is but when asked whether they have heard about bitcoin, Litecoin, or Ethereum (types of cryptocurrencies) they have heard of such types.

Question 10 is a Likert-scale question to analyze how the public is aware of cryptocurrency adaptation in Brunei. The first question is how much the respondent knows about its adaptation in Brunei. The results concluded that the public only has little information on its adaptation in Brunei Darussalam. The second question is whether the public knows where to get cryptocurrency in Brunei, and similar to the above result, the public has only a little information on where to get it. The third and fourth question is quite similar, whether the public knows that cryptocurrency is banned or is it illegal in Brunei, and the people again only have little information on whether they are unlawful or prohibited, basically meaning they did not know whether crypto is legal or illegal to use but still invested in it. The fifth question asked about where to withdraw cryptocurrency in Brunei, and the public responded that they had inadequate information. These supported the above result that awareness of cryptocurrency in Brunei Darussalam is still deficient.

Most Preferred Cryptocurrency in Brunei Darussalam?

From results obtained through distributed questionnaires through social media and hardcopy, Bitcoin is the most known cryptocurrency in Brunei Darussalam, and Bitcoin cash follows after Bitcoin. Litecoin and Ripple fell after Bitcoin Cash. Hence, the most preferred cryptocurrency or known cryptocurrency is Bitcoin._

Elizabeth wrote an article that listed a list of the popular cryptocurrency. Top of the list of the most popular cryptocurrency as Bitcoin (BTC), following second is Ethereum (ETH), Ripple (XRP) following in third place, Litecoin (LTH) place at fourth place, and Bitcoin cash (BCH) placed in fifth, and from above result, BTC and BCH is the most known cryptocurrency by the public.

Cryptocurrency as Means of Payment

Of 125 respondents who answered the questionnaire, 83 respondents were aware of cryptocurrency, while the other 42 responded no. Out of 83 respondents, 97% never withdrew cryptocurrency money, and only 3% of respondents withdrew cryptocurrency money which is expected due to almost all respondents only having a little information on the adaptation of cryptocurrency in Brunei Darussalam. Very few have adequate information on where to withdraw and where to get cryptocurrency.

Question no 16 in the questionnaire asked whether they have used cryptocurrency as means of payment. 3% out of 100% used cryptocurrency as means of payment; the 1st respondent wrote that he had used it for online shopping, the 2nd respondent wrote that he had used it for online gaming purposes, and the 3rd respondent is a female who has used it also for online shopping. The aim of asking this question is to see whether cryptocurrency has helped its users in Brunei to pay for debts or to make any payments using cryptocurrency, and as a result, none have shown that cryptocurrency actually helps in making any necessary payment, for instance, hire purchase due to the adaptation of cryptocurrency was not yet widespread.

Cryptocurrency as an Investment and Factor Affecting From Investing

Fifty-seven respondents claimed that they did not invest in cryptocurrency even though they know its adaptation. This may be due to its features. As explained in an article by the federal trade commission on "what to know about cryptocurrency", before buying cryptocurrency, consumers need to know that it does not have the same protection as when the user is using fiat money. Scammers are prone to ask people to pay with cryptocurrency as they know that such payments are typically not reversible (FTC, 2018) and may be due to the disadvantages that cryptocurrency has, which will be discussed further in this dissertation.

Question 28 in the questionnaire asked about what are the factors that affect the public from investing. And 19% actually said lack of knowledge in cryptocurrency because according to results from adaptation of cryptocurrency, public basically only know little information about cryptocurrency hence lacking in the knowledge of cryptocurrency.

The second factor is regulatory/legal concern because cryptocurrency uses blockchain technology and Blockchain is a decentralized technology system. A decentralized system requires parties to make their independent decision as discussed by Khare, 2006 in the PACE project website, and even though any portion of the network goes offline, the payment mechanism stays intact (Ccoingossip,2018). Cryptocurrencies are not protected by the government, meaning currencies are digitally deposited and do not have the same security as the money in a bank. If user store their cryptocurrency in a company's digital wallet and the company is being hacked, the government may not be willing to step in to help bring back the user's money (FTC, 2018).

The third factor that affects investing in cryptocurrency is the lack of finances because the price of one bitcoin to date May 2022 is BND40, 337.77 according to Coindesk, and it can change constantly. The value of a crypto-currency can change by the hour. An investment worth billions of BND dollars today may only be worth hundreds tomorrow. If the deal goes down, no guarantee is given that it will go up again. (FTC, 2018).

Important Advantages and Disadvantages of Cryptocurrency

Audrey Conklin wrote an article on the advantages of cryptocurrency and the widespread benefits: no intermediary or no third-party involvement. When cryptocurrency doesn't use an intermediary, transactions are usually easier and faster and will require less or no additional transaction fees. Just below no third-party involvement, the second advantage is more secure because cryptocurrency uses decentralized technology called Blockchain. Decentralized means no one is controlling it, no authority, not even the government is handling the technology, meaning that users have freedom over their cryptocurrency. Other than using Blockchain, cryptocurrency also uses cryptographic functions. Cryptographic provides a very complex process, meaning for a user to send or receive bitcoin; with cryptographic, they need to have a unique code to encrypt the information on their cryptocurrency, thus minimizing fraud or counterfeiting.

From results obtained from questionnaires, the top 3 advantages of cryptocurrency are lower cost, more automation and new revenue sources. The public seems to think that a lower price is essential for cryptocurrency. More automated was chosen the most, maybe due to the technological advancement relating to covid-19 in 2020; everything has to be done online and automated.

According to an article in Altcoin Magazine by volt technology (2019), the top 5 disadvantages of cryptocurrency are volatility, no reverse payment, excessive security threat, and regulation and storage security. According to Warren, when cryptocurrency is characterized by the ecosystem as a bubble, meaning market volatility, price volatility associated with a lack of inherent value proves to be a severe problem. The public thinks that cryptocurrency is not accepted everywhere as the essential disadvantage of cryptocurrency.

The second disadvantage would be no reverse payment; if a user mistakenly pays someone by using cryptocurrency, then there is no way to get a refund of the amount paid. All that the user can do is to ask the person for a refund and if the user's request is turned down, then forget about the money (Ccoingossip, 2018)

The third disadvantage is the black market, as personal identity isn't shown anywhere, meaning anonymity as the features of cryptocurrency, users are prone to penetrate the black market. Users can use it to conduct unlawful activities (Koirala, 2019). According to www.top brokers. Trade, the infamous "dark web" marketplace Silk Road used Bitcoin to facilitate illegal drug purchases and other illicit activities before the government shut it down in 2014.

Bitcoin in Pandemic

Out of 125 respondents, 72 voted yes on cryptocurrency helping generate additional income, especially in light of covid-19 in 2020. One respondent who commented on the questionnaire wrote that "even with only little profits, for instance, BND200 invested at the first week, at the end of the week, you might get 220, 204 and 230. Depending on the market of bitcoin. But it will always give profit and never a loss."

Although the impact of the covid19 pandemic may differ from country to country, poverty and inequalities will most likely increase on a global scale (UNDP, 2020). Gregory Klimov wrote articles on "Covid19 changing the way the world sees money", in which Covid19 made an impact on various industries to a level that until now has hardly been estimated. Digital currencies, which had posed concerns and problems before, now saw strong demand from ordinary and even institutional investors. What couldn't be accepted or changed naturally for a long time has shifted rapidly during the crisis, and digital payments and cryptocurrencies have begun to be adopted globally. Klimov also mentioned that the virus has caused a drastic increase in fintech (financial technology) applications worldwide as more people now work or conduct commercial operations remotely or work from home.

Use of Cryptocurrency

Results obtained from questionnaires further understand the public view of cryptocurrency transaction value and whether it is more useful in general for payment transactions within the country or a foreign country. 34% of respondents don't know whether it is more valuable internally or externally. 25% think that cryptocurrency is more useful in a foreign country, and 24% believe that cryptocurrency is helpful both in and outside of the country. 9% assume that cryptocurrency is dangerous, while only 8% think it is valuable internally.

Information About Cryptocurrency

The general public mostly gained information from social media, family and friends, followed by word of mouth. As an investor personally, information about cryptocurrency is mainly from family and friends and, of course, Whatsapp group. The group admin will update weekly profit gain or loss from the investment made on cryptocurrency. If one of the participants wishes to withdraw money from their investment, the group admin will transfer money online through the respective banks of participants weekly.

The last ten questions in the questionnaire did ask whether the public would want to know about cryptocurrency in-depth, and about 85 respondents responded yes, and 39 respondents responded no. The survey results show that they have limited knowledge of cryptocurrency, including where to buy it, how to adapt it, whether it is legal or illegal, and where to withdraw bitcoin money.

INFERENTIAL STATISTICS

Relationship Gender and Awareness of Crypto

H1: There is significant relationship between gender and awareness of cryptocurrency in Brunei Darussalam

H0: There is no significant relationship between gender and awareness of cryptocurrency in Brunei Darussalam.

According to the website "statistics by Jim," The Chi-square test of independence works by comparing the observed distribution and that to be expected to have the relationship between variables. In the context of Chi-square, the word "expected" is equivalent to where the null hypothesis is expected to be true. If the observed distribution is sufficiently different from the expected, the null hypothesis can be rejected and predicted that the variables are related. (Frost, 2020)

Hypothesis 1 used the goodness of fit of Chi-square, whether there is a significant relationship between gender and cryptocurrency awareness in Brunei Darussalam. The value of the test statistic is 3.446, and the reference for this statistic is the expected cell count assumption (i.e., expected cell counts are all larger than 5): no cells had an expected count less than 5, indicating that this assumption is satisfied. (Ken State Uni) The corresponding p-value of the test statistics is 0.63, meaning that the p-value is greater than the alpha value of 0.05. By having a greater value than the conventionally accepted significance level of 0.05, the null hypothesis (H0) cannot be rejected but instead suggests insufficient evidence to indicate an association between gender and awareness of cryptocurrency. Therefore, based on the results, there is no significant relationship between gender awareness of cryptocurrency in Brunei Darussalam with a chi-square of 3.446 and a p-value of 0.634 and hence concluded that variables are independent of each other.

Significant relationship between occupation and awareness of crypto.

H2: There is significant relationship between occupation and awareness of cryptocurrency in Brunei Darussalam

H0: There is no significant relationship between occupation and awareness of cryptocurrency in Brunei Darussalam.

Table 1. Table on chi-square test on gender and awareness

Chi-Square Tests

	Value	Df	Asymp. Sig. (2-sdd)	Exact Sig. (2-sdd)	Exact Sig. (1-sdd)	Point Probability
Pearson Chi-Square	23.036[a]	6	.001	.000		
Likelihood Ratio	23.740	6	.001	.001		
Fisher's Exact Test	22.632			.000		
Linear-by-Linear Association	4.079[b]	1	.043	.046	.026	.006
N of Valid Cases	122					

a. 5 cells (35.7%) have expected count less than 5. The minimum expected count is .34.
b. The standardized statistic is 2.020.
c. sdd: sided

Chi-square test and Fisher's Exact test were used to test hypothesis 2, where there is a significant relationship between employment and cryptocurrency awareness. The test statistic's result is 23.036; the footnote for this statistic said that five cells had an expected count of less than 5, indicating that the assumption was not met; hence the hypothesis was concluded using Fisher's exact test.

P-value is .000, meaning that the p-value is lesser than that alpha value of 0.05. By having a lesser value than the conventionally accepted significance level of 0.05, the null hypothesis is rejected and accepted the alternative hypothesis of a significant relationship between occupation and adaptation of cryptocurrency in Brunei Darussalam. For a Chi-square test, a p-value that is less than or equal to the significance level or alpha indicates sufficient evidence to conclude that the observed distribution is not the same as the expected distribution. Authors can conclude that a relationship exists between the categorical variables. (Ken State University)

Significant Relationship Between Age and Adaptation of Crypto

H3: There is significant relationship between age and adaptation of cryptocurrency
H0: There is no significant relationship between age and adaptation of cryptocurrency

Table 2.

ANOVA

		Sum of Sq.	df	Mean Sq.	F	Sig.
Adaptation in Brunei	Between Groups	1.185	3	.395	.735	.534
	Within Groups	45.714	85	.538		
	Total	46.899	88			
Where to get crypto in Brunei	Between Groups	1.905	3	.635	1.343	.266
	Within Groups	40.185	85	.473		
	Total	42.090	88			
Is it illegal in Brunei	Between Groups	2.613	3	.871	.838	.477
	Within Groups	88.376	85	1.040		
	Total	90.989	88			
Is it banned in Brunei	Between Groups	.702	3	.234	.227	.877
	Within Groups	87.680	85	1.032		
	Total	88.382	88			
Where to withdraw in Brunei	Between Groups	.742	3	.247	.306	.821
	Within Groups	68.763	85	.809		
	Total	69.506	88			

ANOVA test above shows the output from a test conducted to generate a relationship between age and adaptation to cryptocurrency. The degree of freedom is 3, and the value of the test statistic on awareness of adaptation of crypto in Brunei is .735, corresponding to the p-value of the test statistic is p = .534. Since the p-value is higher than the significance value (level of confidence is 95%) 0.05, we cannot reject the null hypothesis. The degree of freedom is 3, and the value of the test statistic on where to get crypto in Brunei is 1.343, corresponding to the p-value of the test statistic is p = .266. Since the p-value is higher than the significance value (level of confidence is 95%) 0.05, we cannot reject the null hypothesis.

With degrees of freedom 3, The value of the test statistic on is crypto legal in Brunei is .838, corresponding to the p-value of the test statistic is p = .477. Since the p-value is higher than the significance value (level of confidence is 95%) 0.05, we cannot reject the null hypothesis. The value of the test statistic on crypto banned in Brunei is .227, degree of freedom three corresponding to the p-value of the test statistic is p = .877. Since the p-value is higher than the significance value (level of confidence is 95%) 0.05, we cannot reject the null hypothesis. The value of the test statistic on awareness of where to withdraw crypto in Brunei is .306. Also, the degree of freedom at 3, corresponding to the p-value of the test statistic, is p = .821. Since the p-value is higher than the significance value (level of confidence is 95%) 0.05, we cannot reject the null hypothesis; hence there are no association or relationship between variables.

Significant Difference Between Education and Adaptation of Crypto

H4: There is significant difference between education level and adaptation of cryptocurrency

H0: There is no significant difference between education level and adaptation of cryptocurrency

Table 3.

Kruskal Wallis

	Adaptation in Brunei	Where to get crypto in Brunei	Is it illegal in Brunei	Is it banned in Brunei	Where to withdraw in Brunei
Chi-Square	1.049	4.418	4.512	3.637	10.209
df	5	5	5	5	5
Asymp. Sig.	.959	.491	.478	.603	.070

a. Kruskal Wallis Test
b. Grouping Variable: Education

The Kruskal Wallis test was used for hypothesis 4, which is the significant difference between education level and cryptocurrency adaptation in Brunei Darussalam. Kruskal Wallis H test, also called-Way ANOVA on ranks, is an alternative to one-way Anova, a nonparametric rank-based test that can determine if there are statistically significant differences between two or more groups of an independent variable on a continuous or ordinal dependant variable. This test allows comparison of more than two independent groups (Laird Statistics). To test is to measure whether a higher level of education results in the higher information or awareness of cryptocurrency. The dependent variable would be the adaptation of crypto in Brunei, and the independent level would be levels of education.

According to the Minitab support website, to determine whether any of the differences between the medians are statistically significant, compare the p-value to assess the null hypothesis. The null hypothesis states that the population medians are all equal. Usually, a significance level (denoted as α or alpha) of 0.05 works well. A significance level of 0.05 indicates a 5% risk of concluding that a difference exists when there is no actual difference. If the p-value is less than or equal to the significance level, you reject the null hypothesis and conclude that not all the group medians are equal.

Test statistics above show the output from a test conducted to determine the significant difference between education and awareness of cryptocurrency adaptation. The value of the test statistic on awareness of adaptation of crypto in Brunei is 1.049, corresponding to the p-value of the test statistic is $p = .959$; since the p-value is higher than the significance value (level of confidence is 95%) 0.05, we cannot reject the null hypothesis. The value of the test statistic on where to get crypto in Brunei is 4.418, corresponding to the p-value of the test statistic is $p = .491$; since the p-value is higher than the significance value (level of confidence is 95%) 0.05, we cannot reject null hypothesis.

The value of the test statistic on is crypto illegal in Brunei is 4.512, corresponding to the p-value of the test statistic is $p = .478$; since the p-value is higher than the significance value (level of confidence is 95%) 0.05, we cannot reject the null hypothesis. The value of the test statistic on crypto banned in Brunei is 3.637, corresponding to the p-value of the test statistic is $p = .603$; since the p-value is higher than the significance value (level of confidence is 95%) 0.05, we cannot reject the null hypothesis. The value of the test statistic on awareness of where to withdraw crypto in Brunei is 10.209, corresponding to the p-value of the test statistic is $p = .070$; since the p-value is higher than the significance value (level of confidence is 95%), 0.05, can reject the null hypothesis. Hence, the result concluded that an alternative hypothesis needed to be accepted that there is a significant difference between education and adaptation of cryptocurrency.

The Significant Difference Between Genders and Factors in Investing in Crypto

H5: There is a significant difference between respondents' gender and factor in investing in cryptocurrency

H0: There is no significant difference between respondents' gender and factor in investing in cryptocurrency

T-tests were used to interpret the significant difference between gender and factors affecting investment. Interpretation of T-Test result for significant difference between genders and adaptation of cryptocurrency, the p-value is less than the level of significance or alpha value which is 0.05. Therefore, the authors can reject the null hypothesis of no significant difference between gender and factors in investing in cryptocurrency. If the null hypothesis is rejected, the alternative hypothesis is correct, and the data are significant. If the hypothesis fails to be rejected, there is no significant difference between variables (Sciencing, 2017).

LIMITATIONS

1. (Bulut 2019) discusses methods applied in cryptocurrency research through a case studies, interviews, web surveys, regression modelling, statistical analysis, and data analysis with a literature review, framework, etc. Ani is providing researchers with what method can be applied for cryptocurrency research. Ani stated that accessible literature on cryptocurrencies could not cover all literature regarding cryptocurrency. Due to limited sources of information. It is still very insufficient and uncovered issues related to cryptocurrency from legal and regulatory points of view.
2. Coronavirus Covid19 is affecting Brunei Darussalam; authors cannot conduct interviews as the company did not wish to do the face-to-face interview concerning covid-19 issues that did not allow close contact with one person or another. However, the country is not on lockdown, but restrictions on movement and the public is advised to stay at home.
3. The data is collected from 125 respondents only where generalization to the population of Brunei is inevitable. An interpretation of this study is based on the assumption that the respondent has given the correct information. Despite the intensive effort, variables confined to the study may have been influenced by the interest and the known limitations.

CONCLUSION

In conclusion, from findings and discussion, an adaptation of cryptocurrency is not yet widespread in Brunei Darussalam. The author concluded that cryptocurrency awareness and adaptation are still not widespread. The public only has little information on how, where, and which cryptocurrency to get despite their existence. It is safe to say that cryptocurrency is male-dominated; despite the higher number of female respondents, male respondents are more aware of the existence of cryptocurrency.

Age demographic where people of age group 29 – 38 are more prone to investing and know of the existence of cryptocurrency due to knowledge in technology compared to the age group of 18 – 28 who would seem to have more knowledge in Information technology.

Respondents with an education level of high school seem to be aware of cryptocurrency compared to respondents with a diploma, undergraduates or postgraduates, or even PhD. Results from the analysis conclude that a higher level knew cryptocurrency from all education levels. The public sees cryptocurrency as an asset instead of currency. Still, it did help them in generating additional income, especially with Coronavirus currently hitting Brunei Darussalam, and the public suggested that more information be shared by the authorities, or maybe through social media to help Bruneians understand what cryptocurrency is in-depth.

To conclude, the general public still does not trust online payment technology because of the disadvantages and risks that they may face if they were adapting one. Moreover, cryptocurrency is still very new to the people of Brunei. Even though it has been on the market since 2009, in 2020, over 11 years, the widespread in Brunei is still very low.

REFERENCES

Ali, H. Abdullah, R. Zaini, Z. 2019. Fintech and Its Potential Impact on Islamic Banking and Finance, Industry: A Case Study of Brunei Darussalam and Malaysia.

Baur, D., Lee, A., & Hong, K. (2020). *(PDF) Bitcoin: Medium Of Exchange Or Speculative Assets?* ResearchGate. https://www.researchgate.net/publication/321988034_Bitcoin_Medium_of_Exchange_or_Speculative_Assets

Bitcoinblockhalf.com. (2020). *Bitcoin Block Reward Halving Countdown*. Bitcoin BlockHalf. https://www.bitcoinblockhalf.com/

Blockgeeks. (2020). *What Is Cryptocurrency: [Everything You Need To Know!]*. Block Geeks. https://blockgeeks.com/guides/what-is-cryptocurrency/

Bondrako, O., Kichuk, O., & Antonov, A. (2019). The possibilities of using investment tools based on cryptocurrency in the development of the national economy.

Bulut, A. (2018). Cryptocurrencies in the new economy. Journal of International Trade. *Logistics and Law*, *4*(2), 45–52.

Cambridge English Dictionary.. (2020). *Awareness*. Google.com https://www.google.com/amp/s/dictionary.cambridge.org/amp/english/awareness

Ccoingossip.com. 2018. *Advantages And Disadvantages Of Cryptocurrency*. C-Coin Gossip. https://ccoingossip.com/advantages-and-disadvantages-of-cryptocurrency/

Chillieh, V. (2020). *What Is Public Perception?* Powers That Beat. https://powersthatbeat.wordpress.com/2012/08/24/what-is-public-perception/

Coinbase. (2018). *The Rise Of Crypto In Higher Education*. Coinbase. https://blog.coinbase.com/the-rise-of-crypto-in-higher-education-81b648c2466f

Conklin, A. 2020. *What Are The Benefits Of Cryptocurrency?* Fox Business. https://www.foxbusiness.com/money/what-are-the-benefits-of-cryptocurrency

Consumer Information. 2018. *What To Know About Cryptocurrency*. Consumer Information. https://www.consumer.ftc.gov/articles/what-know-about-cryptocurrency

Geetha, R.S., & Girisha, M. C. (2018). A conceptual study on the impact of Bitcoins on the Indian economy. *International journal of Business and Management Invention (IJBMI)*.

Hao, K. (2018). The First Rule Of Being A Woman In Crypto. [online] *Quartz*. https://qz.com/1262167/the-first-rule-of-being-a-woman-in-crypto-is-you-do-not-talk-about-being-a-woman-in-crypto/

Honest Pros and Cons. (2019). Advantages And Disadvantages Of Cryptocurrency - Honest Pros And Cons. *Honest Pros and Cons*. https://honestproscons.com/advantages-and-disadvantages-of-cryptocurrency/

Hulliet, M. (2019). 1 In 5 European Crypto Holders Are Women, New Report Reveals. *Cointelegraph*. https://cointelegraph.com/news/1-in-5-european-crypto-holders-are-women-new-report-reveals

Ingham, L. (2019). Cryptocurrency May Replace Cash Within A Decade, Says Deutsche Bank. *Verdict*. https://www.verdict.co.uk/cryptocurrency-replace-cash/

Jovic, Z. Kunjadic, G. (2018) *Economic, Security and Information aspects of the application of cryptocurrency and their impact on the South East European countries*. Research Gate.

Karoles, R. (2018). *Cryptocurrencies and the economy: a review of literature*. University Honor Capstone.

Ken State University. (2020). Spss Tutorials: Chi-Square Test of Independence. *Libguides*. https://libguides.library.kent.edu/SPSS/ChiSquare

Khare, R. (2006). *What Is Decentralization?* Isr.uci.edu. https://isr.uci.edu/projects/pace/decentralization.html

Klumov, G. (2020). From Cash to Crypto: Covid-19 is changing the way the world sees money. *Coin Telegraph.* https://cointelegraph.com/news/from-cash-to-crypto-covid-19-is-changing-the-way-the-world-sees-money

Koirala, B. (2021) 16 advantages and disadvantages of cryptocurrency. *Honest Pros and Cons.* https://honestproscons.com/advantages-and-disadvantages-of-cryptocurrency/.

Kuchler, H. (2020). *Bitcoin: Why Is It So Male-Dominated?* Ft.com. https://www.ft.com/content/259734ca-0b95-11e8-839d-41ca06376bf2

Macroanalyst.blogspot.com. (2020). *Economic Assets Vs Speculative Assets.* Blogspot. https://macroanalyst.blogspot.com/2011/04/economic-assets-vs-speculative-assets.html

Merriam-Webster. (2020). *Adaptation.* Merriam-Webster. https://www.merriam-webster.com/dictionary/adaptation

Naboulsi, N., & Neubrt, M. (2018). *Impact of digital currencies on economic development in Kenya.* ACBSP Region 8 Annual Conference, Paris, France.

Nica, O., Piotrowska, K., & Reiner, K. 2017. Economic benefits and risks. *Fintech Working paper no 2.* University of Manchester.

Radar, C. (2019). *Largest Bitcoin Ownership Survey Reveals 6.2% Of Americans Own Bitcoin, While 7.3% Are Planning To Buy Some.* Prnewswire.com. https://www.prnewswire.com/news-releases/largest-bitcoin-ownership-survey-reveals-6-2-of-americans-own-bitcoin-while-7-3-are-planning-to-buy-some-300928651.html

Said, A. (2019). The economic impact of Digital Fiat Currency (DFC): Opportunities and Challenges. *Econstar.*

Seetharaman, A. Saravanan, A.S. Patwa, N. Mehta, J. (2017). Impact of Bitcoin as world currency. *SciEdu.*

Stancel, D. (2015). *Economic Consequences of Cryptocurrencies and Associated Decentralized Systems.* Research Gate.

Statistics How To. (2020). *Chi-Square Statistic: How To Calculate It / Distribution – Statistics How To.* Statistics. https://www.statisticshowto.com/probability-and-statistics/chi-square/

Technology, V. (2020). Top 5 Disadvantages Of Cryptocurrency. *Medium*. https://medium.com/the-capital/top-5-disadvantages-of-cryptocurrency-925d6679195d

United Nation Development Program. (2020). *Covid-19 Socio-economic impact*. UN. https://www.undp.org/content/undp/en/home/coronavirus/socio-economic-impact-of-covid-19.html

Chapter 2
Price Volatility in Cryptocurrencies: A Modelling Approach

Sivaprakkash S.
https://orcid.org/0000-0003-4642-0660
Department of Commerce, Central University of Tamil Nadu, Thiruvarur, India

Vevek S.
Department of Commerce, Alagappa University, India

ABSTRACT

Cryptocurrency is a digital currency which works as a medium of exchange through a computer network. This study aims at modelling the volatility of selected cryptocurrencies by adopting different models of the GARCH family and providing empirical evidence on the fit of conditional volatility. The research is based upon daily U.S. dollar price indexes of Bitcoin (BTC/USD). The data were collected for a time period from October 2021 to April 2022. The every-day price data was further drilled down to arrive at OHLC (open-high-low-close) price for every quarter of the day. The dataset for the analyses were compiled from the website https://cryptowat.ch/ which is an open source and offers free downloadable dataset using Power BI. The first part of the article will focus on the introduction of topic matter concerned. The second part covers around a few literature reviews in the light of volatility in cryptos. The third part will focus on the methodology adopted followed by the results and discussion in the fourth part. Finally, the fifth and last part will provide concluding remarks.

DOI: 10.4018/978-1-6684-5691-0.ch002

INTRODUCTION

Volatility plays a humongous role in an actively traded market. Volatility is a measurement of how much an asset's price has changed across time. In single day trade consisting of 24 hours, volatility is defined as "the dispersions the price of an asset has shown from its starting price". In general, the more volatile an asset is, the riskier it is to invest in it, and the more potential it has to deliver either larger gains or greater losses over shorter timeframes than less volatile assets. Crypto is generally viewed as volatile, being such a newer asset class with the potential for big upward and downward moves over short time spans. Any investment instruments are considered to be volatile if the everyday price movement of the particular instruments is very threating, which is evident in the case of cryptocurrency market. In a nutshell, volatility is the movement in the markets. It is a double-edge sword in the sense that if there are no movements, the investor will not lose any money, but will not gain any either.

Volatility is mediated factor risks and returns relationship of an investment instruments. Volatility is amongst the most significant elements when assessing investment risk. Traditionally, investors consider on a high degree of risk if they believe the possible gain exceeds the chance of losing some of their money. Understanding one's risk appetite is often the first step for investors and traders before investing in any type of investment. Varied people have different levels of risk tolerance, which influences their investment choices. A fresher into an employment, young investor focuses on growth-oriented investment will naturally take bigger risks than a retired investor who is just interested in maintaining his capital. Risk is proportional to returns, and it is at this point that the significance of volatility may be explained. To reduce risk, ordinary investors have traditionally been urged to diversify their investments across assets. Investing in a basket of equities rather than few individual stocks is a popular method (commonly known as diversification of investment). The diversified portfolio will be a combination of equities & derivatives (highly volatile assets) and government securities and bonds (less volatile assets) to further limit the risk of losing money.

The naive investors have an eagle's view over the crucifixion of cryptocurrency for its outrageous volatility which petrifies the novice before they get a taste of the cryptocurrency market's delicacies. Panicknees arises among people when the market turns into red (bear market) followed by huge dip in the prices of the investment instruments. When market turns green (bull market) the spillover effect makes it difficult for the people to become calm and here is where negative bias comes into play.

Figure 1. Volatility
Source: https://masterthecrypto.com/wp-content/uploads/2019/01/wsi-imageoptim-volatility1.png

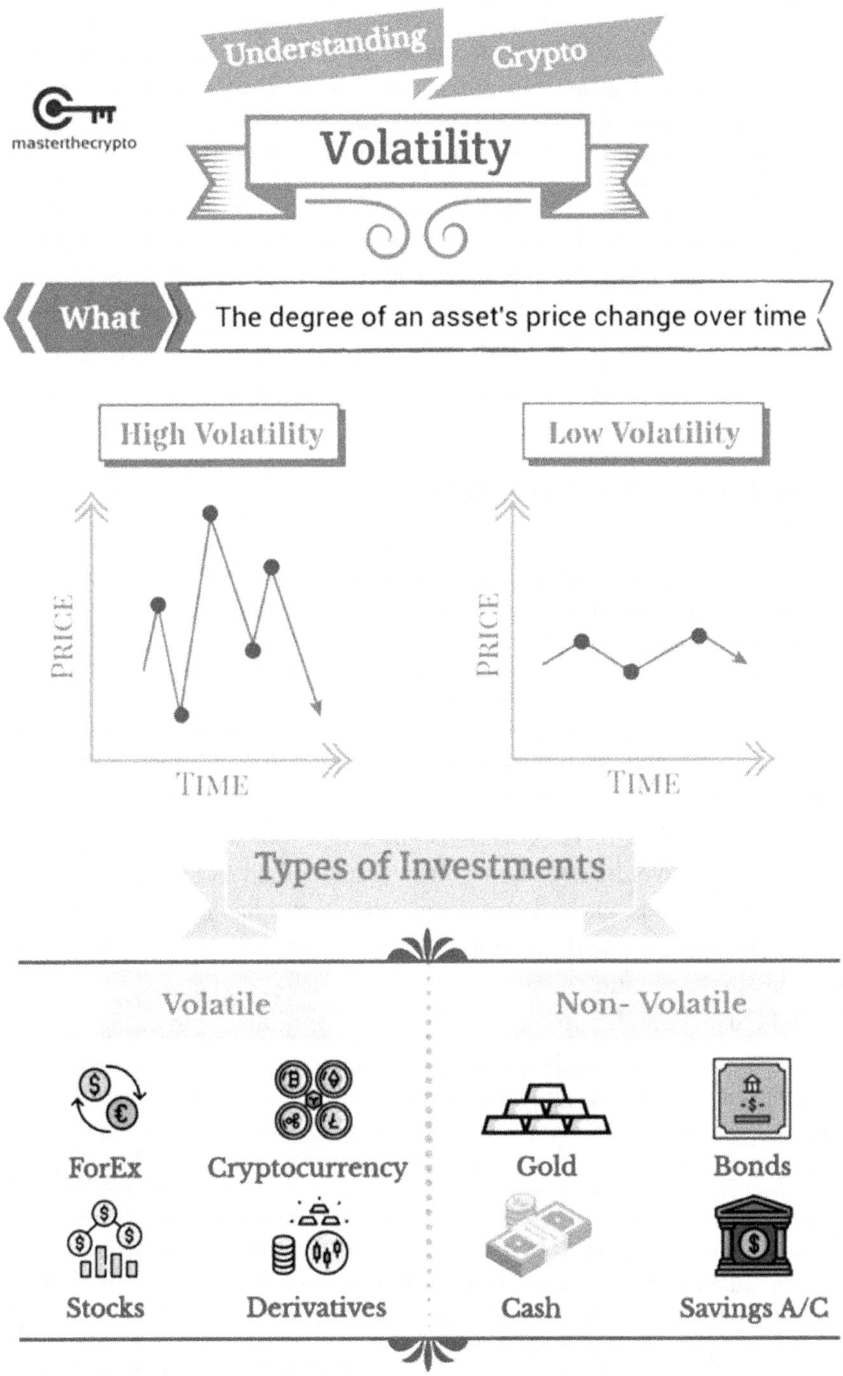

The Bitcoin (BTC) is peer-to-peer payment system with no intermediaries and its average monthly returns are highly volatile compared to gold or USD (Dwyer, 2015). The investment fraternity has a hesitation on not to christen Bitcoin as 'Digital Gold' until its volatility is reduced. Government Securities and Gold are stable investments with teensy movements. On contrary, stock and derivates are high volatile investments indeed crores and crores of money are invested in them. This pulls the mice out of the whole that volatility is not the fear factor which has hesitated the people from entering the crypto market, it's the fear of sudden heavy loss. The volatility has played a huge double game in the cryptocurrency investment in the sense that investors have lost much and also gained millions to billions overnight. Still the Indian Government and Society is hesitating to adopt cryptos as mainstream currency but cryptos possess the hidden consequential potentiality in becoming the behemoth investment vehicle in guiding the investors to gain profits.

VOLATILITY IN CRYPTOCURRENCY

The volatility in cryptocurrency were inherited from its inception and the recent time periods, it has been an unprecedented topsy-turvy ride for millions of investors pan world. Crypto has experienced a series of high gains and subsequent losses as an asset class that is just more than a decade old and is considered to be more volatile as a category than stocks. However, more institutional engagement and higher trading volumes on Bitcoin (most valuable cryptocurrency by market cap) appear to be reducing its volatility over time. When playing with these assets as a newbie, it's preferable to risk quantities you can afford to lose. Cryptocurrencies with lower trading volumes or newer crypto assets tend to have higher volatility. The investments made in the cryptos are topsy-turvy has many have made huge earning in the upswings and on the other hand many have also lost large and small investments in the bursting bubbles and sudden market downturns.

The BTC uses complex protocol and is fully decentralised payment system. It has developed quickly and this growth is accompanied by severe volatility (Katsiampa 2017, Acharya et al, 2018). The price of the Bitcoins in parlance with that of shares, commodity trading is highly influenced by demand and supply. The investors adopt bitcoins expeditiously as an investment instrument, the acceptance rate has become an ardent cause for speculation on price movement which in turn decides the bitcoin's value. Investor concerns are sparked by media sources, influencers, outspoken industry magnates and bitcoin supporters causing price volatility. When compared to already existing investment instrument's life-cycle, the crypto's are still in its infancy coupled with industry's newness, results in lot of volatility. Investors probe into experimenting their money to generate riches quickly and also try to understand how cryptocurrency prices fluctuate.

Whether cryptocurrencies have the potentiality to be used as an investment opportunity for portfolio diversification or hedging depend upon the volatility and risk revolving around it. Though cryptocurrencies are speculative in nature (Fry & Cheah, 2016), they also have the potentiality for portfolio diversification or hedging (Akhtaruzzaman, Sensoy & Corbet, 2019; Baur, Lee & Hong, 2015; Bouri, Gupta, Tiwari & Roubaud, 2017; Corbet, Meegan, Larkin, Lucey & Yarovaya, 2018; Dyhrberg, 2016; Platanakis & Urquhart, 2020). But contrary to these research articles, Klein, Thu & Walther (2018) claimed that Bitcoin is "no safe haven and offers no hedging capabilities for developed markets". There also existed a spill-over effect between Bitcoin and other commodities and Bitcoin market is not isolated separately (Bouri, Das, Gupta & Roubaud, 2018). Instead of intrinsic value, the volatilities of classic assets have a negative and delayed effect on Bitcoin exchange prices (Giudici & Polinesi, 2019). Overall, the literature believes that, for the time being, cryptocurrencies exhibit considerable interdependence among themselves, but remain somewhat separated from traditional market dynamics. Price efficiency means all the information which affects the price of an asset are publicly available to all market participant. Brauneis and Mestel (2018) found that price efficiency is positively related to liquidity. Cryptocurrencies become less predictable or inefficient as liquidity increases.

Based on the Inputs Derived From Research and Markets Report (2022)

Cryptocurrencies have evolved into a contemporary instrument for decentralised finance. The prima-face reason for cryptocurrencies investments is for supporting the never-ending financial needs of individuals coupled with for their high-risk and high-reward business models. Many international authorities and policy makers have not yet decided whether to include cryptocurrencies in monetary and financial systems, despite the fact that they are characterised by their development, complexity, volatility and potential for criminal activity. The market capitalization of cryptocurrencies has been revealed to be highly volatile and they are recognised for being dynamic.

Numerous companies have begun to explore blockchain technology. The banking sector is anticipated to participate in the global blockchain. EXIM payments & settlements, trade finance and after sale settlements are banking industry's main activities comprising of roughly 50% of total expenditure. Inspite of the uncertainty looming over blockchain technology regarding policy framework, rules and regulations, its adoption rates in financial services, trade and other markets are expected to be in the uptrend. The United States of America will have the highest outlay towards the blockchain technology followed by Western Europe and China.

Factors That Cause Volatility in Cryptocurrencies

Brauneis et.al., (2021b) in their research article identified the factors which causes liquidity in cryptocurrency. They took into consideration financial markets, global cryptocurrency markets and exchange-currency pair. The liquidity in cryptocurrencies is mostly influenced by the volatility of cryptocurrency returns, volume of dollar traded and transactions count. The general financial market variables have no impact on the liquidity of crypto. In the cryptocurrency basket, Bitcoin is highly liquid and Coinbase Pro is the most liquid exchange.

The other drivers of cryptocurrency liquidity are:

- Price Discovery Stage - As the cryptos are in the stage of infancy is the fundamental cause of their volatility. All new ideas take time to settle and become accepted, and cryptocurrencies are no exception. Cryptocurrencies have piqued the interest of some investors, but the high volatility of pricing has deterred others. Inspite of all the media hype about cryptocurrencies investment over the years, the size pf crypto market is very small compared to fiat currencies and gold. This relatively small market size means that smaller forces can have a larger effect on price. As the crypto market is still in the developing phase there are huge room for new and exciting opportunities.
- Attractiveness of BTC as digital currencies (Usage) - The number of people who use crypto coins and for what purpose has an impact on their price. The price will rise if more people use them to buy goods and services rather than just holding them. (i.e.) More people start to use BTC more will be the sharing of information and belief in it and will change the mindset of potential investor (Guizani & Nafti, 2019).
- Demand & Supply (Scarcity) - This relates to the controlled mechanism of cryptocurrency. The protocol sets the maximum number of Bitcoins that can be mined at 21 million. When a result, as more people enter the business, there will inevitably be a scarcity of Bitcoin, causing its price to increase. Some coins also use the burning mechanism to increase their value by destroying a portion of the supply. Moreover, as cryptocurrency is a digital asset, the price is determined entirely by the laws of demand and supply. The miners, who donate their computing power to confirming transactions throughout the decentralised network, are rewarded with new bitcoin. Each new block that is successfully mined now pays less than it used to since the size of these rewards is diminishing over time. The supply of bitcoin is perfectly inelastic. "A rise

in demand cannot result in the increase in supply of bitcoin or increase the speed at which bitcoin is issued," (Ria Bhutoria, former director of Research for Fidelity Digital Assets). Bitcoin prices are reflected by the demand of bitcoins in long-run and not by the supply of bitcoins both in short-run and long-run indicating that mining of new bitcoins is difficult (Guizani & Nafti, 2019). This has been even supported by Ciaian, *et.al.,* (2016) who found that price fluctuations of bitcoin are determined by its demand variation. The impact of market forces over bitcoin's price volatility increases over time.

- Whales - When people who are holding large amounts of coin start selling them it leads to fall in the prices of the coins. Those huge investors are called as Whales and my mere experience and knowledge they have the capacity to influence the movement of the market.
- Lack of Controlling Agency (or) Less Government Regulations - Unlike other asset classes that are governed or managed by an entity, cryptocurrencies are not controlled by any entity as in the case of fiat currency, stocks or bonds are. No central bank or government can artificially calm volatility. Bitcoin's volatility is a trade-off for a distortion-free market. There is currently no regulatory structure in place in India for cryptocurrencies. The anonymity is what both attracts and repels investors.
- Investor and User Sentiments - When the popularity of the cryptos improve, more investors (late majority) will comprehend to invest in them and acknowledged their movement. The early bid investors (innovators) who are speculators buy and sell based on their emotions.
- Investor Profile - If an individual has few bucks and good internet connectivity then it is a cake walk for the entering into cryptocurrency market for trading and investing. As there is no need of a lawyer or trading license or minimum amount of capital the crypto market is the first-hand choice for millions of amateur traders around the world. But institutional investors are cautious about the crypto market. The average investor far less experienced and educated than with most other markets. The cryptocurrency markets are hovered by FUD (Fear, Uncertainty and Doubt) and outright manipulation. The value of cryptos is backed entirely by faith. People are inclined to sell Bitcoin if they no longer think its value will increase. This may lower the price and persuade others to sell as well, starting a loop that swiftly drives the price lower. The inverse can also occur, driving prices up and creating exaggerated price bubbles.
- Media - The media has a significant impact on the crypto's price movement because it is a small market for digital assets with a lot of speculation. Investors and speculators continuously scan headlines in search of the next big news event that will either launch or crash the market. Everyone is aware

that when something does emerge, there is a race to purchase or sell, with the quickest making the gain and the slowest losing the money. The prices of cryptocurrencies are significantly impacted by news headlines about the sector. The fact that many people in the cryptocurrency business obtain their news from questionable sources and social media doesn't help. The media frequently tries to break intriguing news about the world of cryptocurrencies. Because of this, marketing experts found the ways to make profit from the frenzy that surrounds cryptos ups and downs. An event study was conducted by Yue, *et.al.*, (2021) regarding the impact of news on the liquidity of cryptocurrencies. The results revealed that positive news increased the crypto's liquidity and negative news decreased the crypto's liquidity. The impact of positive news stays for a longer time period that that of negative news.

- Even long-term investors are interested in cryptos because they anticipate the asset class will achieve popularity. For example, Elon Musk quoted that he owned Dogecoin because many of the employees at Tesla and SpaceX own Dogecoin.
- In terms of the bitcoin mining difficulty, it has favourable and notable short-term impact. When difficulty for mining rises, the price of bitcoin rises as well. Potential investors are becoming more knowledgeable about the bitcoin system and technological advancements are lessening impact of mining costs on the price of bitcoin (Guizani & Nafti, 2019). Macroeconomic and financial development do not determine the price of the bitcoin in short term and long term.

Cryptocurrency Volatility of Liquidity vis-à-vis Returns

The volatility of liquidity measures the level of risk related to the liquidity of the particular currency which a trader has to face when dealing with that currency. Investors need aegis when dealing with currency having high volatility in liquidity. Thomas Leirvik (2022) discovered a positive correlation between volatility of liquidity and returns of Bitcoin, Ethereum, Ripple, Bitcoin Cash and Litecoin. As the long-term investors bear the risk of liquidity volatility, they demand a higher return as liquidity might suddenly disappear (Akbas et al., 2011). Investors wanted to invest in cryptos at a discount rate which has high liquidity-volatility. Bitcoin has the least positive magnitude of relation between liquidity volatility and returns amongst the other cryptos. Crypto's liquidity can be better estimated by illiquidity ratio. The spread estimators capture the time-series variation of liquidity (Brauneis et al., 2021a). There has been an enhancement in the liquidity of Bitcoin in the recent year and disparity exist between volatility of Gold and Bitcoin (Scharnowski, 2021).

Volatility of liquidity focus on investors trading at arbitrary intervals of time would be interested in the ease of trading in the future. Investors are aware of the exact degree of liquidity and investors will be at ease in trading the assets if the volatility of liquidity remains constant. When dealing with trades in the future, there is a potential that the liquidity will be entirely different if the volatility is non-constant. Although the rate of liquidity change differs from asset to asset, it does occur over time. Investors have to tackle both liquidity level risk along with variability in the liquidity level. The relationship between volatility of liquidity and returns varies across different studies, viz market liquidity and returns are extremely volatile (Chordia, et al., 2002) but in contrary increasing liquidity volatility results in lower stock returns (Pereira & Zhang, 2010). In declining markets, liquidity drastically decreases. Investors must focus on the security's performance and tradability when the market is in red and when liquidity is scarce (Acharya & Pedersen, 2005).

A risk-averse investor prefers an investment which is easy to trade in the future over one that may be more difficult to do so. The volatility of liquidity measures variations of liquidity over time. An asset with stable but low liquidity is highly preferred by risk-averse investors. Ceteris paribus, a risk-averse investor may be willing to pay a higher price for an asset whose liquidity is less volatile and hence has a lower chance of becoming less liquid at the time of trading. As a result, it is conceivable that an asset with high liquidity volatility trade at lower price than an equivalent asset with a lower level of volatility. Therefore, asset with higher liquidity-volatility should have higher predicted returns.

DATA AND METHODOLOGY

The study is based on secondary data sourced from Cryptowatch website (https://cryptowat.ch/). The Cryptowatch website is a database for live price charts, trading and alerts for cryptocurrencies like Bitcoin (BTC), Ethereum (ETH) and many more. For this study, we focused on Bitcoin cryptocurrency. The website was further drilled down to extract dollar denominated Bitcoin close-price data at 240 minutes (4 hours) time interval. The data was available in the following link (https://api.cryptowat.ch/markets/coinbase-pro/btcusd/ohlc). Our dataset entails the period from 30th October 2021 to 13th April 2022, which represents a period consisting of 1,000 data. Those data were iterated from the website with the help of Microsoft Power BI (Data Visualization Software) using the algorithm (= #datetime(1970,1,1,0,0,0) + #duration(0,0,0,[Value.1]).

As each day had six close price data, an average of these data was calculated to arrive at an estimated single close price of bitcoin. As a result of those 1,000 data was reduced to 166 data. The price volatility in bitcoin was analyzed taking into consideration the daily return of average close price of bitcoin.

$$Return\ on\ Average\ Close\ Price\ of\ BTC = \left(\frac{P_t - P_{t-1}}{P_{t-1}}\right) * 100$$

where, P_t is present value of average close price of bitcoin and P_{t-1} is previous day value of average close price of bitcoin.

To measure volatility in bitcoin price, the GARCH (1, 1) model was employed in this study. Generalised Autoregressive Conditional Heteroscedasticity is known as GARCH (1, 1) model was proposed by Engle (1982). GARCH is used to capture the volatility clustering among the squared residuals. Bollerslev (1986) used GARCH model as a trouble shooter to the problem with the high ARCH orders.

EMPIRICAL RESULTS

Figure 2 explains the return graph of the Bitcoin (BTC) from the 31st October 2021 to 15th April 2022, total observations of 166. The return of Bitcoin is highly volatile.

Table 1 shows the descriptive statistics of Bitcoin return. The means is negative (-0.232) and the standard deviation is (2.98). The kurtosis value (5.56) is greater than three (>3) and it is leptokurtic. The skewness is small and positive, which exhibits the tail distribution is more likely to be near to the mean. The maximum return (11.29333) and minimum return (-11.67470), the Bitcoin is volatile between the max and mini. Jarque-Bera result is 44.169 and the p-value is 0.000. In this case, we fail to accept. Null hypothesis is the series are normally distributed. Hence, the series of Bitcoin return is not normally distributed.

Table 1. Descriptive statistic of Bitcoin Return of Average Close Price

Mean	**-0.232**	**Std. Dev.**	**2.984589**
Median	-0.322036	Skewness	0.081339
Maximum	11.29333	Kurtosis	5.560820
Minimum	-11.67470	Observations	166
	Jarque-Bera	44.16943	
	Probability	0.000000	

Figure 2. Return of Average CP
Source: eViews

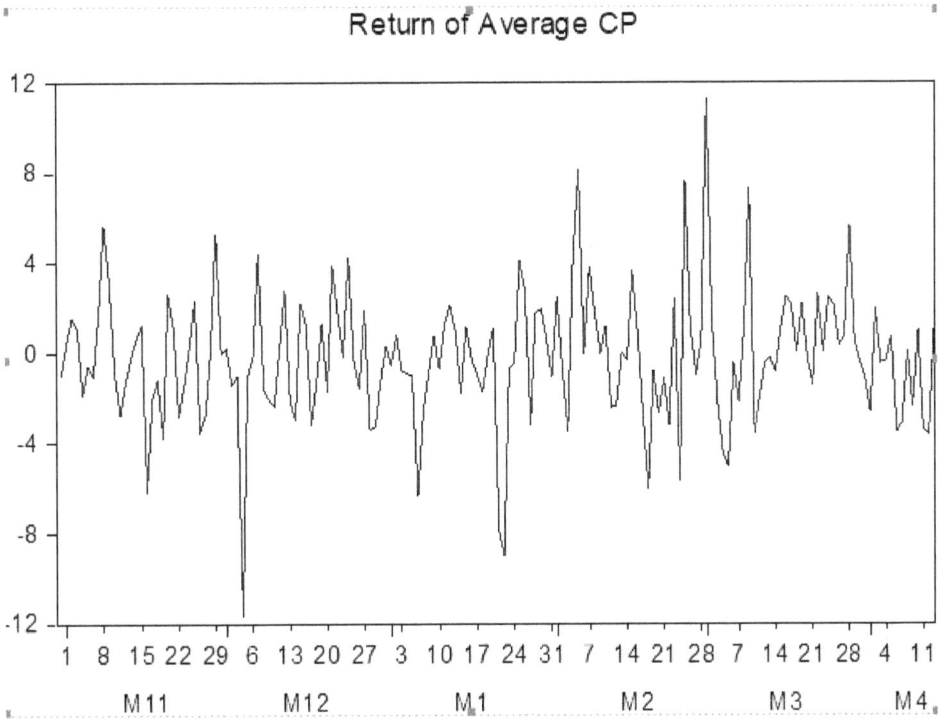

Garch Equation: GARCH = C(1) + C(2)*RESID(-1)^2 + C(3)*GARCH(-1)

Both the ARCH and GARCH parameter are highly significant with p values of 0.000. The sum of the coefficients of the ARCH and GARCH parameters (0.048470 + 0.629179) is near to one (1) which covey that the shock to the Bitcoin return series are highly persistent. The R-square (0.006074) is less than Durbin-Watson statistics (1.687737).

There is volatility in the bitcoin but the volatility is not that strong. Old information fads away when new information arrives.

Table 2. Result of GARCH (1, 1) Model

Variable	Coefficient	Std. Error	z-Statistic	Prob.
	Variance Equation			
C	3.783295	2.451760	1.543094	0.1228
RESID(-1)^2	0.048470	0.026984	1.796241	0.0725
GARCH(-1)	0.629179	0.273207	2.302935	0.0213
R-squared	0.006074	Mean dependent var		-0.231885
Adjusted R-squared	0.000175	S.D. dependent var		2.984589
S.E. of regression	2.984328	Akaike info criterion		5.056392
Sum squared resid	1433.901	Schwarz criterion		5.113810
Log likelihood	-404.0396	Hannan-Quinn criter		5.079706
Durbin-Watson stat	1.687737			

CONCLUSION

Bitcoin's volatility is the cost it pays for having a small quantity and being decentralised. Bitcoin is still in the price discovery stage because it is a new asset class. However, as an asset class, cryptocurrencies are not as widely acknowledged as more established assets like gold or stock, despite their recent rise to on a worldwide scale. Market maturity and rising acceptance go in hand. Because of this, the value of Bitcoin plummeted when Tesla said that cryptocurrency would not be accepted as a form of payment. However, Dogecoin's value increased after Tesla CEO Elon Musk typed 'Doge' in a tweet. Similar to how share prices tend to increase when a famous investor purchases stock in a certain business, such influencing events or personalities increase volatility. Given the current scenario, trading and investing in cryptocurrencies is quite speculative due to the lack of rules and awareness. The volatility in crypto's prices is caused by the speculative bets placed by the investors on the prices going up or down. Due to development of technical and commercial infrastructure, the acceptance level is expanding quickly and the value is continuously rising and this ought to result in the volatility issue being solved.

REFERENCES

Acharya, S., Thomas, A., & Pani, B. (2018). Volatility of Bitcoin and Its Implication to be a Currency. *International Journal of Engineering Technology Science and Research*, *5*(1), 1017–1024.

Acharya, V. V., & Pedersen, L. H. (2005). Asset pricing with liquidity risk. *Journal of Financial Economics*, *77*(2), 375–410. https://doi.org/10.1016/j.jfineco.2004.06.007

Akbas, F., Armstrong, W. J., & Petkova, R. (2011). *Idiosyncratic volatility of liquidity and expected stock returns*. Semantic Scholar.

Akhtaruzzaman, M., Sensoy, A., & Corbet, S. (2020). The influence of bitcoin on portfolio *diversification and design. Finance Research Letters*, *37*, 101344. https://doi.org/10.1016/j.frl.2019.101344

Baur, D. G., Hong, K., & Lee, A. D. (2015). *Bitcoin: Medium of Exchange or Speculative Assets?* SSRN. https://dx.doi.org/10.2139/ssrn.2561183

Bollerslev, T. (1986). Generalized Autoregressive Conditional Heteroscedasticity. *Journal of Econometrics*, *31*(3), 307–327. https://doi.org/10.1016/0304-4076(86)90063-1

Bouri, E., Das, M., Gupta, R., & Roubaud, D. (2018). Spillovers between Bitcoin and other assets during bear and bull markets. *Applied Economics*, *50*(55), 5935–5949. https://doi.org/10.1080/00036846.2018.1488075

Bouri, E., Gupta, R., Tiwari, A. K., & Roubaud, D. (2017). Does Bitcoin hedge global uncertainty? Evidence from wavelet-based quantile-in-quantile regressions. *Finance Research Letters*, *23*, 87–95. https://doi.org/10.1016/j.frl.2017.02.009

Brauneis, A., & Mestel, R. (2018). Price discovery of cryptocurrencies: Bitcoin and beyond. *Economics Letters*, *165*, 58–61. https://doi.org/10.1016/j.econlet.2018.02.001

Brauneis, A., Mestel, R., Riordan, R., & Theissen, E. (2021a). How to measure the liquidity of cryptocurrency markets? *Journal of Banking & Finance*, *124*, 106041. https://doi.org/10.1016/j.jbankfin.2020.106041

Brauneis, A., Mestel, R., & Theissen, E. (2021b). What drives the liquidity of cryptocurrencies? A long-term analysis. *Finance Research Letters*, *39*, 101537. https://doi.org/10.1016/j.frl.2020.101537

Chordia, T., Roll, R., & Subrahmanyam, A. (2002). Market liquidity and trading activity. *The Journal of Finance*, *56*(2), 501–530. https://doi.org/10.1111/0022-1082.00335

Ciaian, P., Rajcaniova, M., & Kancs, D. A. (2016). The economics of Bitcoin price formation. *Applied Economics*, *48*(19), 1799–1815. https://doi.org/10.1080/00036846.2015.1109038

Coinbase. (2022). *What is volatility?* Coinbase. https://www.coinbase.com/learn/crypto-basics/what-is-volatility

Corbet, S., Meegan, A., Larkin, C., Lucey, B., & Yarovaya, L. (2018). Exploring the dynamic relationships between cryptocurrencies and other financial assets. *Economics Letters*, *165*, 28–34. https://doi.org/10.1016/j.econlet.2018.01.004

Dwyer, G. P. (2015). The economics of Bitcoin and similar private digital currencies. *Journal of Financial Stability*, *17*, 81–91. https://doi.org/10.1016/j.jfs.2014.11.006

Dyhrberg, A. H. (2016). Hedging capabilities of bitcoin. Is it the virtual gold? *Finance Research Letters*, *16*, 139–144. https://doi.org/10.1016/j.frl.2015.10.025

Engle, R. F. (1982). Autoregressive Conditional Heteroscedasticity with Estimates of the Variance of the United Kingdom Inflation. *Econometrica*, *50*(4), 987–1007. https://doi.org/10.2307/1912773

Expert Commentator. (2019). *Why are cryptocurrencies so volatile?* Smart Insights. https://www.smartinsights.com/digital-marketing-strategy/volatile-cryptocurrencies/

Fry, J., & Cheah, E. T. (2016). Negative bubbles and shocks in cryptocurrency markets. *International Review of Financial Analysis*, *47*, 343–352. https://doi.org/10.1016/j.irfa.2016.02.008

Giudici, P., & Polinesi, G. (2021). Crypto price discovery through correlation networks. *Annals of Operations Research*, *299*(1), 443–457. https://doi.org/10.1007/s10479-019-03282-3

Guizani, S., & Nafti, I. K. (2019). The determinants of bitcoin price volatility: An investigation with ARDL model. *Procedia Computer Science*, *164*, 233–238. https://doi.org/10.1016/j.procs.2019.12.177

Gupta, S. (2020). *Cryptocurrency Volatility – a Friend or a Foe.* AITHORITY (AI Technological Insights). https://aithority.com/guest-authors/cryptocurrency-volatility-a-friend-or-a-foe/

Katsiampa, P. (2017). Volatility estimation for Bitcoin: A comparison of GARCH models. *Economics Letters*, *158*, 3–6. https://doi.org/10.1016/j.econlet.2017.06.023

Klein, T., Thu, H. P., & Walther, T. (2018). Bitcoin is not the New Gold–A comparison of volatility, correlation, and portfolio performance. *International Review of Financial Analysis*, *59*, 105–116. https://doi.org/10.1016/j.irfa.2018.07.010

Kumar, H. (2021). *Here Is Why Cryptocurrencies Are So Volatile*. Outlook. https://www.outlookindia.com/website/story/business-news-here-is-why-are-cryptocurrencies-so-volatile/398988

Lapin, N. (2021). Explaining Crypto's Volatility. *Forbes*. https://www.forbes.com/sites/nicolelapin/2021/12/23/explaining-cryptos-volatility/?sh=1e66d2d27b54

Leirvik, T. (2022). Cryptocurrency returns and the volatility of liquidity. *Finance Research Letters*, *44*, 102031. https://doi.org/10.1016/j.frl.2021.102031

N. D. T. V. (2021). *Volatility in the Cryptocurrency Industry: What Determines Heightened Price Fluctuation?* NDTV. https://www.ndtv.com/business/why-is-bitcoin-or-any-other-cryptocurrency-so-volatile-2546933

Nibley, B. (2021). *Bitcoin Price History: 2009-2022*. SoFi Learn. https://www.sofi.com/learn/content/bitcoin-price-history/

Online, F. E. (2022). Cryptocurrency markets project high price volatility. *Financial Express*. https://www.financialexpress.com/digital-currency/cryptocurrency-markets-project-high-price-volatility-report/2502562/

Pereira, J. P., & Zhang, H. H. (2010). Stock returns and the volatility of liquidity. *Journal of Financial and Quantitative Analysis*, *45*(4), 1077–1110. https://doi.org/10.1017/S0022109010000323

Platanakis, E., & Urquhart, A. (2020). Should investors include bitcoin in their portfolios? A portfolio theory approach. *The British Accounting Review*, *52*(4), 100837. https://doi.org/10.1016/j.bar.2019.100837

Reiff, N. (2022). *Why Is Bitcoin Volatile?* Investopedia. https://www.investopedia.com/articles/investing/052014/why-bitcoins-value-so-volatile.asp

Scharnowski, S. (2021). Understanding bitcoin liquidity. *Finance Research Letters*, *38*, 101477. https://doi.org/10.1016/j.frl.2020.101477

Sigalos, M. (2021). *Bitcoin's wild price moves stem from its design - you'll need strong nerves to trade it*. CNBC. https://www.cnbc.com/2021/05/19/why-is-bitcoin-so-volatile.html

Woebbeking, F. (2021). Cryptocurrency volatility markets. *Digital finance, 3*(3-4), 273–298. doi:10.1007/s42521-021-00037-3

Yue, W., Zhang, S., & Zhang, Q. (2021). Asymmetric news effects on cryptocurrency liquidity: An Event study perspective. *Finance Research Letters*, *41*, 101799. https://doi.org/10.1016/j.frl.2020.101799

Chapter 3
The Emergence of Cryptocurrency in India and Its Implications on Investments

Mohammed Umair
St. Joseph's University, India

ABSTRACT

Investing in the unregulated cryptocurrencies has showed a rising tendency since 2020, despite uncertainty surrounding its future in India. There is no ban on the use of cryptocurrencies in India, nor is there any regulation governing their actual use. This uncertainty is disturbing Indian startups developing blockchain-based products. But this hasn't altered investors' positions in investing in cryptocurrencies; they continue to be positive. For longer-term investments, investors have historically employed fundamental analysis. By analyzing the underlying company's operations and the state of its industry or the overall economy, fundamental analysis seeks to find stocks with high growth potential at fair prices. The issue with conducting a fundamental analysis of cryptocurrencies is that they cannot be evaluated using the same criteria as conventional businesses. Therefore, the authors must focus on several frameworks. Finding good metrics is the first step in that approach. This chapter examines the emergence of cryptocurrency in India and its implications on investments.

DOI: 10.4018/978-1-6684-5691-0.ch003

MAKING SENSE OF CRYPTOCURRENCY

A barter system of trading existed in history, although it eventually became less effective due to defects. As a result, numerous research initiatives were launched later on to create digital currency. The most common types of currency in use today are coins and paper money, which were gradually developed. In the contemporary economy, we have both physical money (such as paper money and coins) and virtual money (such as debit and credit cards, electronic wallets, and so on), all of which are governed by common or centralized authority. Speaking about cryptography, it is a similar idea to digital currency, but it operates in a decentralized fashion, meaning no servers are needed to process transactions, and there is no central authority in charge of it. Digital money known as cryptocurrency is utilized for trade and transactions. Cryptocurrency is not actual money, in contrast to paper money. Because cryptocurrencies are a decentralized form of money, they cannot be governed by a single government or set of nations.

In a formal sense, cryptocurrency is just digital money. Similar to the rupee or the US dollar, a cryptocurrency is a form of an exchange that is digital and employs cryptography to regulate the creation of new units of currency and to confirm the transfer of value. Blockchain, decentralization, and cryptography are the three terms you need to be familiar with in order to better understand cryptocurrencies. The backbone of cryptocurrency is the blockchain. It is a digital ledger that keeps track of transactions and distributes access to authorized users. Registered users receive the information and access. As a result, everything on the blockchain is transparent and irreversible. The data cannot be tampered with or hacked. No one, not even the administrator. The RBI oversees and controls the centralized money that we use. In the case of cryptocurrencies, decentralization refers to the absence of any central authority over the asset. By using this approach, cryptocurrencies become independent. In the context of cryptocurrencies, cryptography refers to secret writing, so the recipient can only read messages. It handles the transactions, safeguards operational independence, and strengthens the entire chain.

CRYPTOCURRENCY IN INDIA

Investing in the unregulated digital asset, especially Bitcoin, has showed a startling rising tendency since 2020, despite uncertainty surrounding its future in India. The scale and investment appeal of cryptocurrencies have increased, making it easier for people to acquire, sell, and trade cryptocurrencies both in India and internationally. 7.3% of Indians owned cryptocurrencies in 2021, according to the United Nations Conference on Trade and Development Report 2021. Cryptocurrencies are unaffected by influence from any central body or government. However, they have had a very awkward relationship with the Indian government.

- In the year 2018, a warning was issued that virtual currencies in India are not recognized as legal money. A committee was established by the finance ministry to craft legislation regarding cryptocurrencies in India. However, there was no virtual currency ban.
- In 2019, A bill prohibited cryptocurrency mining, keeping, selling, issuing, transferring, and use. People would have to pay a large fine or spend up to 10 years in prison if proven guilty of breaking the law.
- In the year 2020, the Supreme Court overturned the RBI's 2018 ban on cryptocurrencies. The ruling by the Apex Court is seen as a landmark decision, particularly for India's start-ups and virtual currency business.
- In the 2021, In the Rajya Sabha, the minister of finance, brought up the subject of cryptocurrencies. The minister claimed that while the RBI and SEBI will raise awareness, the government had not yet taken any meaningful action to outlaw cryptocurrency promotions in India.
- The Reserve Bank of India (RBI) suggested a ban on cryptocurrencies in July 2022, citing their "destabilizing consequences" on the nation's monetary and fiscal stability.
- In the Union Budget for 2022–2023, the Government of India stated unequivocally that any transfer of virtual currency or cryptocurrency assets will be subject to a 30% tax deduction. Virtual assets and cryptocurrencies used as gifts will be taxed in the recipient's hands.
- The Ministry of Finance in the Union Budget for 2022–2023 also announced the establishment of a CBDC known as the digital rupee. Is the digital rupee, however, a cryptocurrency? Here's some background.

DIGITAL RUPEE AND CRYPTOCURRENCY COMPARED

The Reserve Bank of India is getting ready to start using its central bank digital currency (CBDC), which it classifies as money in the digital form of legal tender. It will be exchangeable at par with current currencies, accepted for payments, and regarded as a secure store of value. It is sometimes referred to as the "digital rupee." The RBI's CBDC, also known as the "digital rupee," is a new way to utilize money that isn't much different from the banknotes that are already in circulation. The only difference is that the digital rupee is meant to be used more easily and to be transacted digitally. The accepted cryptocurrency by the RBI is the digital rupee, which has been repeatedly repudiated by the institution and described as a severe threat to the stability of the nation's financial system. The CDBC is advertised as being safer than private cryptocurrencies since it is a digital version of a sovereign currency. Here is how they will differ.

A CBDC is a form of legal money that is issued in digital form by a central bank, according to the RBI. It is interchangeable one-to-one with fiat currency and is the same as fiat currency. Its only distinction is in form. A CBDC, however, cannot be directly compared to a cryptocurrency. In contrast to cryptocurrencies, a CBDC is not a commodity or a claim on a commodity or digital asset. There is no issuer of cryptocurrencies. They are not money (definitely not currency) in the sense that the term has come to be understood historically, according to the RBI's release. No cryptocurrency will be exempt from taxes. Only the digital rupee issued by the RBI will be exempt from tax laws. The RBI hopes to solve issues with current physical currencies and international trade by adopting the digital rupee. Money transfers across borders and currency exchanges are time-consuming and expensive. The fast cross-border money transfer is expected to improve bank cash management and operations with the introduction of the digital rupee. Cash placement and tracking are difficult in India. CBDC can address anonymity, find a non-threatening solution, and lessen the need for cash.

The government will reduce operational, printing, distribution, and storage expenses, advancing its goal of a cashless society. Governments and central banks throughout the world are investigating (some of them have also implemented) the potential of digital money in light of the recent popularity of a cashless or digital financial system.

INDIAN CRYPTO MARKET'S FUTURE AND THE GOVERNMENT STANCE

The Indian government has resisted taking a firm stance on cryptocurrency. There is no crypto-specific legislation in place in India currently. However, India has continued to impose high tariffs that have contributed to the collapse of the local cryptocurrency business. The problem is getting worse due to additional macroeconomic and crypto contagion causes. India will present its budget for the fiscal year 2023–2024. The nation might introduce new tax laws pertaining to cryptocurrencies. If bitcoin is seen as an asset in India, the finance ministry can enact restrictions, but if bitcoin is regarded as a currency, the central bank of the country is in charge of enforcing them. The Reserve Bank of India (RBI) has reiterated its position that India would be best served by prohibiting the use of cryptocurrencies domestically. Both the Finance Ministry and the Reserve Bank of India (RBI) agree that the so-called wallet-to-wallet transfers of cryptocurrencies have a destabilizing effect on the country's financial stability, but the Union government is waiting for an internationally acceptable solution to track and stop them before outlawing them in India. In India right now, cryptocurrencies are unregulated.

India's cryptocurrency legislation is still under development, the government is waiting for the Financial Stability Board (FSB) to draught cross-border regulation for cryptocurrencies. The FSB supports global financial stability and deals with threats to financial systems. It comprises 68 member organisations, including central banks and finance ministries from various nations. While China has outright prohibited cryptocurrency transactions, India is yet to introduce legislation defining digital assets and deciding how to regulate them. According to the Finance Ministry, any legislation can only be effective with international cooperation to prevent so-called regulatory arbitrage, in which companies seek the most lenient jurisdiction that allows them to conduct business. The uncertainty is disturbing the clusters of Indian startups developing blockchain-based products ranging from decentralized finance applications to nonfungible tokens. It's also unclear how India's digital rupee, which is set to debut in 2023, will affect the industry.

POLICY INDECISION AND THE DANGERS OF CRYPTOCURRENCY

Policymaking in the area of digital finance appears to be more difficult than ever before. Technically, there is no ban on the use of cryptocurrencies (or crypto assets) in India, nor is there any regulation governing their actual use. During periods of market turbulence, crypto exchanges have experienced significant disruptions. There have also been several high-profile cases of customer funds being stolen as a result of hacking. So far, these incidents have had little effect on financial stability. However, as crypto assets become more mainstream, their significance in terms of potential economic implications is expected to grow. Anything that could become a national security issue is one of the primary regulatory concerns. In this regard, regulators are concerned about the misuse of crypto currencies, which use their anonymity to undermine anti-money laundering efforts. As a member of the Financial Action Task Force (FATF), India is required to follow its standards, which promote global cooperation among sovereign member nations. Investor protection is always a top priority for financial regulators. From a regulatory standpoint, crypto assets are currently viewed with suspicion about their intent-of-existence, as well as an overtly speculative asset with no underlying value. Because cryptocurrencies in circulation have high volatility in terms of value and trading volume, global regulators will need to beef up their investor protection measures until they either ban them or strictly regulate them. Because cryptocurrency is a digital mode of transaction, it has become a popular platform for hackers, terror finance, and drug transactions. This has increased people's fatigue because it provides less security and reliability. Criminals, for example, used the Wannacry virus to demand Bitcoin ransom payments. The Securities and Exchange Board of India (SEBI) has stated clearly that unlike for stocks, it has no authority over cryptocurrency "clearing and settlement" and is unable to offer counterparty guarantees.

Furthermore, neither a money, a commodity, nor a security have been used to define cryptocurrencies. Rising crypto currency markets have the potential to tip the Indian economy's circular flow of money out of balance. The process of creating cryptocurrencies differs greatly from the way the economy creates regular money. For instance, only the RBI is allowed to create cash in India, and only if the Minimum Reserve System is up and running. As a result, supply and demand are in balance. Cryptocurrency, on the other hand, is encrypted and secured rather than dependent on the rules of financial institutions, which makes it challenging to raise the money supply above a set algorithmic pace. Because there is currently no place where users can seek assistance or a means for resolving complaints regarding crypto assets, customers are exposed to transactional risk.

IS CRYPTOCURRENCIES AS AN ASSET CLASS OR NOT

An asset class is a grouping of securities with similar characteristics and responses to market fluctuations. It is common to refer to asset classes and their categories interchangeably. However, in practice, they are not related. Different risk and return on investment characteristics may be reflected in each asset class. Additionally, they behave differently depending on the market situation. Asset classes now encompass a wide range of other categories, including commodities, real estate, various financial derivatives, and cryptocurrencies. It consists of both tangible and intangible assets that investors purchase and resell in order to generate money over the short- or long-term. With a real asset class, you hold genuine property, an equity stake in a business and a portion of its potential profits in the case of stocks; Bonds are a company's guarantee to pay a predetermined sum plus interest; Real estate includes a home or a plot of land; Gold is a precious metal with industrial use and jewelry-making potential. Commodities include things like a barrel of oil, metals and agricultural commodities. A derivative is a contract whose value is based on how well an underlying entity performs. This so-called "underlying" entity, which can be a stock, an index, or a commodity. It serves as a benchmark in a popularity contest. These assets have value regardless of what the "market" claims they are worth at any one time. Nevertheless, the "market" only determines their value on any given day. (Aggarwal, 2022).

Unlike with crypto. When you purchase cryptocurrency, you have no ownership. Aside from your ability to sell your portion of nothing to another eager customer.

Your cryptocurrency's worth is solely based on what other people are willing to pay for it on any given day. It doesn't have any inherent value or independent worth. It serves as a benchmark in a popularity contest.

The majority of individuals no longer assert that cryptocurrencies are money. At least not in a direct manner, no one now asserts that it is a hedge against inflation or the stock market. Although it is innovative and employs cutting-edge technology, purchasing crypto currency does not provide you ownership of the disruptor or the blockchain.

Another viewpoint sees cryptocurrency as a great asset class, with Bitcoin and Ethereum acting as, respectively, a store of value and a reservoir of use cases. These have grown to maturity and will continue to do so. People who choose long-term gains to speculative trading are the reason that Bitcoin in particular has emerged as an asset class. The valuation of assets like bitcoin may potentially be a concern for institutional investors. There are numerous methods for estimating probable future prices for the asset as bitcoin does not provide cash flows.

CRYPTOCURRENCIES INVESTMENT TRENDS IN INDIA

Due to the introduction of new rules by the Indian government regulating cryptocurrencies, cryptocurrency investors and hodlers in India have recently faced some difficult times. That hasn't altered their position on investing in cryptocurrencies, though, and they continue to be positive and cheerful. The popularity of cryptocurrency investments began to rise as the price of Bitcoin skyrocketed. Optimists are always attracted to such extraordinary returns, and this time was no exception. More and more people began pouring into this untapped market. On the one hand, there is this untapped resource. The consequences and ramifications of this asset are not well known. More and more crypto coins are being introduced, and new blockchain networks are emerging. Where cryptocurrency will fit into our financial networks in the future is a topic of discussion. However, this unknown asset is bringing in billions. Investors are rushing to it in increasing numbers. The market is expanding, and new trading platforms are appearing. It is a hub of speculative trading activity, to put it another way.

The Indian cryptocurrency market is anticipated to reach $241 million by 2030, despite the local government's stance on digital assets and the imposition of a 30% tax on revenue derived from digital assets, according to the KuCoin research. According to the survey, around 115 million Indians between the ages of 18 and 60 own or have traded cryptocurrencies as of June 2022, making up 15% of the country's total population. Of them, 54% believe they will see long-term returns on their investments. Industry estimates point to 15 to 20 million cryptocurrency investors in India, with total holdings of about 400 billion rupees, according to Reuters. The crypto market has reached an intriguing crossroads as a result of this.

CRYPTOCURRENCY INVESTMENT EVALUATION MATRIX

For longer-term investments, investors have historically employed fundamental analysis. By analyzing the underlying company's operations and the state of its industry or the overall economy, fundamental analysis seeks to find stocks with high growth potential at fair prices. Traditional fundamental analysts typically use business indicators to determine what they believe the real worth of an asset to be. A fundamental analysis looks at a company's key ratios to assess its financial health. So, by the conclusion of the process, you should have a good sense of what the stock price of the company should be. This informs you if your purchase price was higher or lower. As a general guideline, keep in mind that you stand to earn when you purchase a stock at its fair value or below because the market price is always higher than fair value. The issue with conducting a fundamental analysis of cryptocurrencies is that they cannot be evaluated using the same criteria as conventional businesses. Therefore, we must focus on several frameworks. Finding good metrics is the first step in that approach. Fundamental analysis is now very crucial due to the cryptocurrency market's extreme short-term volatility and enormous long-term growth. Numerous cryptocurrency initiatives have failed, and new ones are always being proposed, which keeps the market lively. You can estimate a token's value before investing if you have a solid understanding of the fundamentals of cryptocurrency. The following crucial metrics are employed by the fundamental crypto analysis framework:

1. The on-chain indicators

   On-chain indicators are those that can be seen by examining the information that the blockchain provides. By running a node for the chosen network and exporting the data, we could accomplish this on our own, but that can be time-consuming and expensive. especially if we merely want to think about the investment and don't want to devote time or money in the project. Pulling the data from websites or APIs created particularly for the aim of informing investment decisions would be a simpler approach. Let's quickly review some key on-chain indicators for cryptocurrencies.

   a. Count of transactions: A network's activity can be measured well by its transaction count. We can observe how activity changes over time by plotting the number for predetermined intervals (or by using moving averages). Please take note that this metric needs to be used with caution. We cannot be certain that only one party is transferring money between their own wallets to artificially inflate the on-chain activity, as we cannot be certain of active addresses.

b. Transaction Fees: Transaction fees are common in blockchains. Similar to the gas fees paid on the Ethereum blockchain, fees also reflect the demands of transactions paying to be included to blockchains as quickly as possible. Your understanding of the fees will help you determine how secure a token is. Cryptocurrency miners will start to work at a loss and leave the blockchain if transaction costs rise and block rewards fall.

c. Active Address: On a blockchain, active addresses are those that are currently being used. You must count the numbers of both the sender and the recipient of transactions over a specified time period in order to calculate this. To determine activity and interest in a cryptocurrency, you can also observe the evolution of the number of unique addresses over time and compare the results. More popular cryptocurrencies have greater potential.

d. Rate of Hashing and Staked Amount: The two most widely used consensus algorithms for cryptocurrencies are proof of stake and proof of work. Proof-of-work, which gauges the health of the network using the hash rate, is used by both Bitcoin and Ethereum. A system that is more secure and hard to bridge has a high hash rate. However, if the hash rate falls, crypto mining operations may also slow down, particularly if miners view it as unproductive. Investor interest in the cryptocurrency asset declines as the hash rate falls. In a proof-of-stake cryptocurrency, transaction validators stake their holdings during the block validation process. The volume staked at any given time may also be a good indicator of the level of interest in a particular crypto asset.

2. Project Indicators

A qualitative method for assessing how well a cryptocurrency project is going is to use project metrics. We'll examine several facets of cryptocurrencies in this part, including its function and goal.

a. Whitepaper: Before investing in any enterprise, you must read its whitepaper. The technical whitepaper provides a detailed analysis of the project. The project's goals, strategies for achieving them, use cases, supply levels, the technology employed, and a wealth of other relevant information are all included in this document. Therefore, reading the whitepaper is simply one of the things that individuals mean when they advise doing your own research before investing.

b. The Group: The track histories of the individuals who make up the cryptocurrency network's team, if one exists, can shed light on whether the group possesses the necessary expertise to see the project through to completion. Have members ever launched profitable businesses in this field? Do they possess the knowledge necessary to meet their anticipated milestones? Have they participated in any dubious endeavors or frauds? What would the developer community look like if there was no team? Check to see how many contributors there are and how much activity there is on the project's public GitHub, if it has one. A coin whose repository hasn't been updated in two years may not be as appealing as one whose development has been consistent.

c. Competitors: We should be able to determine the use case the crypto asset is aiming towards from a solid whitepaper. It's critical to note the projects it competes with at this point, as well as the outdated infrastructure it aims to replace. Ideally, these should undergo equally rigorous fundamental scrutiny. Even while an asset could seem enticing on its own, comparing it to other crypto assets of a similar type may show that it is less strong than the others.

d. Initial distribution and the Tokenomics: Some projects use the creation of tokens as a problem-looking strategy. The project itself is viable, however its related token might not be very helpful in this situation. As a result, it's crucial to ascertain whether the token actually has any use. Additionally, whether or not the general market will recognize the utility and how much it is going to be valued at. The initial distribution of the cash is a crucial aspect to think about in this regard. Users could earn it via mining, or was it through an ICO or IEO? If the former, the whitepaper should specify how much will be available to investors and how much would be retained for the founders and team. The first distribution of the cash is a crucial aspect to think about in this regard. Users could earn it via mining, or was it through an ICO or IEO? If the former, the whitepaper should specify how much will be available to investors and how much would be retained for the founders and team. For the latter, we could look for proof that the asset's originator engaged in premining, or mining on the network before it was made public. By concentrating on the distribution, we might be able to identify any potential risks. We may conclude that this is a dangerous investment if, for example, a small number of parties control a large portion of the supply since they could ultimately.

3. Financial Indicators

Fundamental analysis can benefit from knowledge about the asset's current trading price, historical price range, liquidity, and other relevant factors. However, other intriguing measures that can fall into this category are those that relate to the protocol's economics and incentives.

a. Market capitalization: Calculating market capitalization (or network value) involves multiplying the current price by the circulating supply. In essence, it shows the estimated price to purchase each and every cryptocurrency asset now in circulation (assuming no slippage). Market capitalization on its own can be deceiving. Theoretically, it would be simple to create a worthless token with a ten-million-unit supply. The market capitalization of those tokens would be $10 million if just one of them were traded for $1. Without a compelling value proposition, it is improbable that the larger market would be interested in the token, hence this pricing is blatantly misleading. In a similar manner, it is hard to accurately estimate the quantity of a given cryptocurrency or token in circulation. Keys can be misplaced, money can be forgotten about, and coins can be destroyed. Instead, we see approximations that make an effort to weed out coins that are no longer in use. However, market capitalization is frequently used to assess networks' growth potential. Some cryptocurrency investors believe that "small-cap" currencies have a higher chance of growth than "large-cap" coins. Others think that because large-caps have stronger network effects, they have a better chance of succeeding than newly floated small-caps.

b. Liquidity: An asset's liquidity can be determined by how easily it can be traded. If a bitcoin asset can be bought or sold fast without affecting its market value, its liquidity is robust. An order book for an easily traded cryptocurrency coin or token will have a large number of buyers and sellers.

c. Volume: The trading volume of a token reveals how well it will maintain its value over time. This indicator shows the total number of individual assets that have been traded during the time frame under consideration. A trend that is going up and has a high trade volume will probably endure longer than one that is going down.

d. Mechanisms of supply: One of a currency or token's most intriguing qualities from an investment standpoint may be its supply processes. Indeed, among supporters of Bitcoin, models like the Stock-to-Flow

(S2F) ratio are becoming more and more well-liked. Decisions can be influenced by the maximum supply, the available supply, and the inflation rate. Some coins produce fewer new units over time, which appeals to investors who think there will be a greater demand for new units than there are available. On the other hand, some investors could believe that a cap that is strictly implemented would be detrimental over time. According to some worries, users may decide to hoard the coins or tokens rather than use them. Another complaint is that it unfairly favors early adopters when a consistent inflationary strategy would be preferable.

You'll have a clearer understanding of what's going on in the cryptocurrency markets with the help of fundamental analysis. You will get information from it that will enable you to distinguish between valuable tokens and those with little potential. It's not the best idea to use it as a stand-alone analysis technique, though. You will be constrained if you only use fundamental research, much like in the stock and currency markets. A solid approach that integrates basic and technical analysis must be developed. By doing this, you'll be able to spot coins with potential and properly timing your trade entry and exits. Technical analysis is concerned with the previous market performance of an asset; by analyzing price history and trade volume history, you can learn how the market perceives the asset. Is it going up or down? Are individuals adding money or withdrawing it? Is it exchanged extensively and in significant amounts? Technical analysis poses questions of this nature. The same principles apply to technical analysis in the cryptocurrency market. Traders and investors can determine the mood of the market and how that will affect the value of cryptocurrencies by examining cryptocurrency charts using technical indicators.

THE FINAL WORD

The cryptocurrency market is expanding quickly, and the current hot terms driving the excitement are Bitcoin, Dogecoin, and Ethereum. Despite the fact that the cryptocurrency sector is just decade old, new investors are attracted to it because they perceive it as a rapid way to make money.

Because there is no regulation on the cryptocurrency market, unlike the stock market, its value fluctuates daily. Here is all the information you need to know before investing in the cryptocurrency market, given the high volatility of these digital assets. Even if the success of all cryptocurrencies is not guaranteed, they might pay off for their early investors. For cryptocurrencies to succeed over the long term, widespread adoption is crucial.

Although this is an intriguing offer, it is still in its infancy. In fact, the government's near-monopoly over currency production and monetary policy appears secure for the foreseeable future. Users of cryptocurrencies must constantly be aware of this idea and its constraints. To determine why a currency will remain strong over time, they must always have a sound investment thesis.

REFERENCES

Babu, S., & Abraham, K. M. (2021). Central bank digital currencies: policy and operational perspectives for India. *CSI transactions on ICT, 9*, 85-94. doi:10.1007/s40012-021-00327-6

Rajagopal, K. (2019). Draft banning of cryptocurrency & regulation of official digital currency bill. *The Hindu*. https://prsindia.org/billtrack/draft-banning-of-cryptocurren cyregulation-of-official-digital-currency-bill

Research, H. (2022, December 12). Global Crypto Industry Overview and Trends[2022–2023 Annual Report]. *Medium*. https://medium.com/huobi-research/global-crypto-industry-ove rview-and-trends-2022-2023-annual-report-first-part-e15372f2 9c

Shubhashree A. (2018). Volatility of Bitcoin and Its Implication to be a Currency. *International Journal of Engineering Technology Science and Research*, 1017-1024. doi:10.1007/s40012-021-00327-6

Shukla, V & Misra, M., & Chaturvedi, A. (2022). *Journey of Cryptocurrency in India in View of Financial Budget 2022-23*. Research Gate.

Singh, A. K., & Raj, M. (2022).A study of Analytics and Exploration of Bitcoin Challenges and Blockchain. *2022 International Conference on Electronics and Renewable Systems (ICEARS)*, Tuticorin, India. 10.1109/ICEARS53579.2022.9751821

Chapter 4
Reliability of Cryptocurrencies and the Central Bank Digital Currency Architecture

Sayantani Banerjee
https://orcid.org/0000-0003-4223-1256
St. Joseph's University, India

ABSTRACT

Any technological innovation is as reliable as the technology itself. The block chain technology, which is the basis of cryptocurrency, runs on a decentralised distributed ledger system which technically promises immunity from any government interference. The popularity of this notion and its variations have forced governments to think about a central bank digital currency. This chapter has been written with the objective of identifying whether lesser reliability of cryptocurrencies can be overcome by central bank digital currencies and issues involved with anonymity. While cryptocurrency ensures no counterfeiting, the feature of anonymity still carries the risk of being used for illegal activities. However, it is now perceived as the future of money. Cryptocurrencies do not create any financial liability but have been adopted as a store of value and medium of exchange. They are also used for micro-payments and decentralised applications. All these issues require a critical assessment of the reliability of cryptocurrencies as against the digital currency backed by central banks.

DOI: 10.4018/978-1-6684-5691-0.ch004

INTRODUCTION

When barter system existed there was reciprocal exchange. However, there was no guaranteed fair exchange. Then came money which was considered as a generally accepted medium of exchange. Apart from that, money served as a store of value (Nag, 2021), and also provide a common unit of account to enable comparison between the value of goods and services. This money, often referred to as 'fiat money', is a currency issued by a government and not backed by any product or commodity but by the government itself. So the promise to pay plays an important role in the way money works. Therefore, the value of fiat money is largely based on the public's faith in the currency's issuer, which is normally that country's government or central bank. Fiat money is legal tender, but without any intrinsic value. In essence, it has value only because the issuing authorities say so and the value can be largely determined by how the issuer's economy performs. The fiat system allows the government or the central banks to have a lot of influence on the economy because they can control the money supply. As soon as the fiat money is more in supply there is a fall in its value which renders fiat money vulnerable to such external factors. So an individual possessing a certain amount of money at a certain point of time can never be sure of its true value. At the background of loss of faith and trust in the money issued by central banks, the concept of cryptocurrency emerged silently, which has now forced governments to evolve the way money functions at present. The chapter has been divided into 5 major segments dealing with various aspects of central bank digital currency and cryptocurrency. The first part deals with the blockchain genesis with historical reference. The second part deals with digital currency in general followed by Central Bank Digital Currency (CBDC) architecture and comparison between CBDC and cryptocurrencies. This is followed by a country-wise CBDC status and conclusion based on reliability.

THE BLOCKCHAIN GENESIS

The blockchain technology was conceptualised by Stuart Haber and W. Scott Stornetta way back in 1991. Their first work involved working on a cryptographically secured chain of blocks whereby no one could tamper with timestamps of documents. While they continued their work, in 2008 the Blockchain technology started to gain relevance under pseudonym of Satoshi Nakamoto. The first whitepaper about the technology was released in 2009 where all details were provided of how the technology was well equipped to enhance digital trust given the decentralization aspect that and hinted that nobody would ever be in control of the entirety. The new technology was discussed with lot of apprehension and many investors were not very clear about the working mechanism. Amidst the apprehension, Bitcoin came into being in 2008 as the first application of Blockchain technology. The whitepaper detailed the electronic peer-to-peer system. Nakamoto formed the genesis block, from which other blocks were mined, interconnected resulting in one of the largest chains of blocks carrying different pieces of information and transactions. In the next phase of blockchain innovation, Ethereum was conceptualised to overcome the limitations of Bitcoins. The Blockchain history and evolution did not stop with Ethereum and Bitcoin. In recent years, a number of projects have cropped up all leveraging blockchain technology capabilities. New projects have sought to address some of the deficiencies of Bitcoin and Ethereum in addition to coming up with new features leveraging blockchain capabilities. At this point a comparison between fiat currency and cryptocurrency can be drawn under the following points:

Tracking: While fiat currencies can be easily monitored and recognized by the issuer and recipient, crypto promises anonymity.

Medium of Exchange: The traditional fiat currency is a tangible cashable medium of exchange, whereas cryptocurrency is essentially digital.

Safety: While Fiat currency is safer when backed by the Government and the transfer of money can be tracked, the risk of devaluation always stays. As for cryptocurrencies, the limited supply ensures protection against devaluation.

Supply: Fiat money has a limitless supply, meaning that central banks have no limit to how much money they can print. Many cryptocurrencies have a supply limit, which ensures that only a limited number of coins will ever be accessible.

Legality: Governments regulate the supply of fiat money and issue policies that influence its value. Cryptocurrencies are digital assets that function as a medium of trade not regulated by governments.

DIGITAL CURRENCY

Digital currency is the digital format of fiat currency is carried in wallet or withdrawn from an ATM and used for payments. It is the same currency which is backed by a central authority and is used by the users with a lot of trust and reliability with an underlying assurance that what is paid for is the same value received. However, the essential element of trust and reliability has often been misused and has had its manifestation in currency devaluation (Fiedler et al., 2019). Nevertheless, digital currency has been perceived as the most worth alternative/extension of fiat money as against cryptocurrency. The difference between the two can be summarised as under:

1. Control and centralisation

The major differentiating factor between digital currency and cryptocurrency is control over the monetary value of coins. In case of digital currency, it would be the Reserve Bank in India or Fed in the US along with the government, banks and other middlemen need to have complete coordination to set the value of the currency in question. Cryptocurrency, on the other hand, follows a transparent procedure right from mining to ownership to transfer of crypto assets. Its value is also independent of central banking authorities and regional geopolitical problems.

2. Transparency and conflict management

The biggest advocates for cryptocurrency will cite the transparency afforded by the platform. The decentralised ledger that records all the blockchain details ensures that every detail regarding cryptocurrency transactions is in the public domain. With digital currency, only the banking authorities along with the sender and receiver are involved in the transaction involved. In case of conflict over any asset, cryptocurrencies are easier to manage as the records are there for everyone involved to see, whereas digital currencies could involve bureaucratic hurdles and other problems in case of any conflict. This decentralisation of data is, therefore, one of the driving forces leading to the popularity of cryptocurrencies across the world. (Sackheim and Howell, 2018).

3. Encryption

Digital currencies are essentially e-cash that not requiring any special indigenous methods to encrypt them. The process of encryption ensures the prevention of unauthorised access and may involve a code. Banks have been using digital money for quite some time now and payment gateways have also been established for online payment system. Cryptocurrencies, on the other hand, are stored on a blockchain and the coins themselves are stored in 'wallets' that offer a much higher degree of cyber security as well as anonymity (Mancini-Griffoli et al., 2018).

4. Stability and ease of access

Digital currency is stable, available in convenient ways and also relatively easy to manage because of the wider acceptance in the global market. It is the fiat version of approved currency, is traded and understood by a vast majority of the population. Hence it is more stable when compared to the new technology of cryptocurrency that has started gaining attraction but is not mainstream yet. People are skeptical about the reliability of the platform for crypto.

5. Perception

Whereas the utility aspect of a digital currency is the prime focus, the common perception about cryptocurrency is trading and volatility. People are generally wary of a new technology especially when there is no government authority backing it. The fact that the formal banking system is not a part of this technology discouraged a lot of investors. There is a lot more acceptance to any method of dealing with money which is closer to the traditional method in comparison to a new method using disruptive technology.

6. Legality

Most countries, including India, are now taking a look at the legality and acceptance of cryptocurrencies. Since these aren't backed by any governing body, most traditional frameworks don't assign any value to them. However, the swift rise in the number of depositors and various use cases of blockchain today and the upcoming metaverse, where the only method of payment remains cryptocurrencies, means that some sort of discussion around the legality of cryptocurrencies is bound to happen sooner than later. For now, countries around the world are firm in backing their own fiat currencies and the result is a central Bank digital currency.

The entire area of fintech has evolved over the past few years owing the technological revolution going on across sectors. Real-Time Gross Settlement (RTGS) is one such example of the technological revolution instituted by central banks across the world in finance and payment services. There is also Unified Payment Interface (UPI) in India, CoDi in Mexico, PIX in Brazil and the FedNow proposal in the US in the retail payment system. Narayana Kocherlakota – one of the world's leading monetary theorists, former president of the Federal Reserve Bank of Minneapolis and a former Stanford professor – argued in a famous 1998 paper that "money is memory" as it is just a substitute for a publicly available and freely accessible device that records who owes what to whom. The acceptance and success of the digital transformation in payment system goes a long way in proving that the existing system can adapt to innovation in private -public partnership.

CENTRLA BANK DIGITAL CURRENCY (CBDC)

A CBDC is a digital form of the fiat currency issued by a central bank in lieu of the paper/metal currency issued and is the direct liability of the central bank – that is, it is denominated in the national unit of account. The proposed architecture of a CBDC has been conceptualised to bridge the gap between digital currency and cryptocurrency, and in this effort central banks around the world, including those of China, Russia, Bahamas or the USA, are developing or researching the use of CBDC. As per a 2021 Bank for International Settlements (BIS) survey of central banks, 86% of central banks in the world were conducting active research to identify the potential for CBDCs, 60% of them were already experimenting with the technology and another 14% were in the process of deploying pilot projects (Sankar, 2021). China became the first large economy to carry out pilot digital currency in April 2020. When most populous countries of the world like China and India are taking a lead in launching digital currency, it has far reaching implications worldwide. Theoretically, if societies want digital money, the first choice is the choice of operational architecture. Should the payment system rely on a trusted central authority or could it be based on a decentralised governance system, where the validity of a payment depends on achieving consensus among network participants on what counts as valid payments (refer Figure 1). The second choice is around access: whether access should be around verification of identity as in bank accounts ("account-based access") or around validity of the object being traded as with physical cash, for instance with cryptography ("token-based access"). (Carstens, 2021)

Figure 1.

Choice of operational architecture

Source: R Auer and R Böhme, "The technology of retail central bank digital currency", BIS Quarterly Review, March 2020, pp 85–100.

A strong underlying system for issuance and distribution to the public is essential for a general-purpose CBDC. Depending on the model adopted, the whole ecosystem will need various players to function, which includes the central banks, public and private banks and payment service providers (PSPs) like PayPal, Paytm, Razorpay etc. Further, other financial institutions and third-party service or application providers can also be included. Whatever the model, every central bank and commercial bank will need to adopt a parallel end-to-end blockchain enabled system for CBDC issuance and circulation. There are essentially 2 categories of CBDC namely, wholesale and retail.

The wholesale CBDC works quite like the issuance of notes from central banks to retail banks. Since the wholesale CBDC can be used for interbank settlements, cross-border remittances, and capital and security markets, it is expected to make a positive impact on the existing payment transactions. In the domestic payment system under wholesale CBDC, the central bank will act as a central counterparty in a cross-border setting. So a decentralised ledger or a blockchain will be essential. In the Indian context, RBI can interface faster with and among its intermediaries and help in improving the existing real-time gross settlement (RTGS) system. (PwC, 2021).

Retail CBDC, on the other hand, could be used in daily transactions by households and businesses, and depending on their design, could topple our existing financial system (Federal Reserve System, 2022). Generally, a retail CBDC is based on the mechanism of a distributed ledger technology (DLT) which is like a private blockchain network managed by the government to trace transactions while maintaining anonymity. This technology also helps mitigate the private involvement and the prevention of fraudulent transactions and economic crimes like money laundering and other economic crimes. Bitcoin and others Cryptocurrencies also used this distributed technology but without permission from the central banks. So, the ideal setup could be a DLT with permission and a known network of validators replacing the traditional model with a single central validator. Retail CBDC can be issued **directly** to the public by the central bank. Alternatively, it can be issued **indirectly** to intermediaries (which can be public/ private banks) who then issue it to the public almost like a fiat currency. The third option is a **hybrid** issuance where the central bank issues to PSPs, which onboard clients and execute payments. The bank periodically records the retail balances. The mode of issuance will definitely impact the usage and popularity of CBDC.

CBDC and Stablecoins

With a motive to act as a middle ground for newer investors that believe in crypto and old-fashioned investors that still distrust decentralized systems, stablecoins (Koning, 2016) are essentially a collections of, stable and unstable, currencies pegged together to regulate supply and stabilize high volatile coins. JR Willett's 2012 white paper introduced it. For example, USD Coin (USDC) is a very popular stablecoin used to exchange and facilitate transactions for investment and consumption through third-party decentralised applications (Dapps). USDC is an ERC-20 token that is backed and pegged 1:1 to the American Dollar. Another example is Libra coin, introduced by Facebook (Meta), that was popularised in 2018. The concept of Libra pegged together powerful world currencies to completely stabilize prices. Backed by 50% UDS, 18% EUR, 14% JPY, 11% GBP, and 7% SGD; governed by the Libra Association.

While the primary function of stablecoins was to regulate volatile price fluctuations to make a blockchain-based currency to mimic fiat currency better, it has instead seemed to act as a substitute, in people's minds, to digital currency.

The concept of stablecoins is based on a concept of automated regulation. They are built on smart contracts that execute microtransactions anytime the currency needs to be stabilized. Most whitepapers reference the Classical economic concept of quantity theory of money being an inspiration to the genesis of stablecoins. In brief, economist Irving Fisher introduced the following equation to represent the correlation between money supply and demand:

$$MV = PT$$

- Where M is the supply of money,
- V is the velocity of circulation,
- P is the level of price
- T is the volume of market transactions

This small equation shows the responsiveness of money demand to changes in money supply. For example, if a smart contract is written with a code that executes response to M doubling (Money supply is doubled), keeping V and T constant, the contract will half P. This implies that the automated response is regulating price through circulation.

Regulation in stablecoins vs CBDC. Do governments benefit from stablecoins?

CBDC offers no extra freedom in regulation as it is essentially fiat currency on the blockchain. However, since there is dealing with a decentralized system, it is only natural that the public don't want a centralised power having control over the decision making on money supply and/or price. So, let's go through a small thought process:

- Imagine a country that has entirely accepted a functioning CBDC, and there are no alternate cryptocurrencies, stablecoins, cash, or other forms of currencies. Now, what does life look like here? Firstly, unlawful behaviour is limited as the only form of exchange is a highly regulated, tracked currency that acts as a blaring alarm for crime or anything similar. This is from a citizen's perspective. The same can be said from a lawmaker's perspective too. Every transaction of the politician is tracked, recorded, and viewed by millions of people affected by the decision-making. Now, the assumption here is that this data will be made public. However, lawmakers have no compulsion to do that. People in power will not have any of their data made public, but those living with the consequence of their decision-making will be. When governments promote such alternates, it is difficult for the public not to accept transparency as a 2-way street.

- Here, it may be observed how the same country works with stablecoins as an accepted mode of conducting transactions. It is also assumed that fiat currency exists to promote and withhold foreign exchange keeping foreign trade stable while also acting as legal tender to uphold the concept of stablecoins. Here, the public or lawmakers don't have a distinction in exchange of money. The same liberty that crypto provides exists here i.e. the government cannot depreciate or appreciate currency (keeping in mind the loss of trust in a central system due to continued currency devaluation).
- However, the question remains whether the government benefit from this. Lawmakers here have a few responsibilities to keep up with new technological advancements. For example, a complete, laid-out form for regulation that abides by pre-set laws providing sufficient data and legal clarity for thc end user. Using this laid down structure, governments can adapt by approving stablecoins as legal tender

CRYPTO vs CBDC

A cryptocurrency thrives on the disadvantages of sovereign money. So, a low return offered by alternative safe assets could contribute to the success/demand for cryptocurrencies. The strongest advocates of cryptos like bitcoin use it as a store of value asset to shield themselves from inflation and economic instability. However, a committee of the IFRS(international financial reporting standards) Foundation pointed out that the currently available cryptocurrencies, including Bitcoin, cannot be treated as financial assets as it does not give rise to a contractual right for the holder. It is not a contract that will or may be settled in the holder's equity instruments. A comparison between cryptocurrencies and CBDC are provided below based on several aspects like technology, reliability, applicability etc.

Table 1. Comparison between cryptocurrencies and CBDC

Features of distinction	Cryptocurrencies	CBDC
Type of blockchain	Permissionless (public) blockchains without the interference of any centralised authority	authorized (private) blockchains under centralised supervision.
Decentralisation	The authority in crypto networks is given to the user base, which makes choices through consensus.	A central bank determines the regulations for CBDC networks.
Anonymity	Anonymity is a benefit for cryptocurrency users.	CBDC customers' identities will be linked to an existing bank account as well as a similar quantity of personal information. (choice between account based or token based)
Valuation	Not recognised as financial assets	recognised as an acceptable medium of exchange and a store of value
Use case	may be used for both speculation and payment.	can only be used for payments and other monetary transactions.
Third-party verification	essential	not required
Risk of investment	High due to high volatility	Not applicable unless interest-bearing
Ease of use	Only limited users due to high technical knowledge, also more time taken to verify the authenticity of a crypto transaction	Can be widely used with modification in existing payment structure
Scalability	Low scalability as they need more validators, more computing resources, and more fees.	CBDCs can theoretically scale better than cryptocurrencies since they function on permissioned networks similar to databases.
Money-laundering	Identifying responsibility for AML/ CFT compliance, supervision/ enforcement is a challenge.	helps in implementing anti-money laundering (AML) and combating financial terrorism (CFT) measures by acting as a highly secure way for cross-border transactions.

Existing secluded cryptocurrencies like Bitcoin lack regulatory standards and are thus inclined to money laundering, extortion, and other criminal activities. So public (permissionless) blockchain cannot fulfil the necessities of financial systems in regulation, scalability, and efficiency and is not appropriate for blockchain-based CBDC. As compared with permissionless blockchain, permissioned blockchain is more fitting for CBDC, which describes the involvement of many countries in pertinent research. More than 46 central banks worldwide are viewing CBDC schemes with permissioned blockchain. As of 1 June 2022, 105 countries are researching a CBDC, which comprise over 95% of the global GDP. 50 countries are now in an advanced phase of exploration (launch, pilot, or development). A modest look at the country wise status of CBDC adoption through the CBDC tracker, a flagship project by the Atlantic Council Geoeconomics Centre is followed in next section.

COUNTRY-WISE CBDC

The development of CBDC across the world is a topic of much focus as it has the potential to change the way money can work across various sectors. The Atlantic Council Geoeconomics centre has developed a live CBDC tracker to track progress of CBDC in all countries worldwide. Figure 2 below gives the current status of CBDC progress worldwide.

Figure 2.

Country wise CBDC progress for the 109 countries exploring CBDC

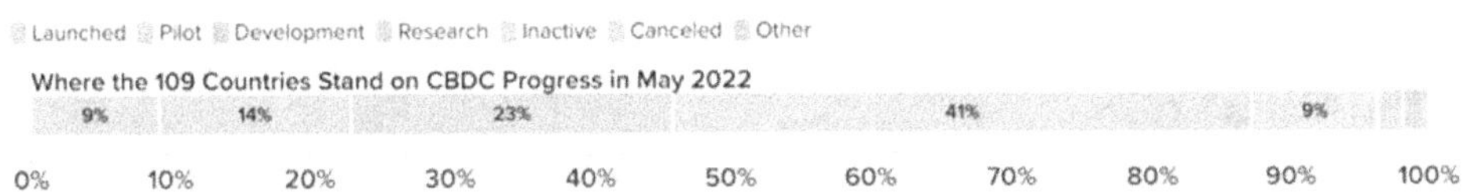

Source: CBDC Tracker, Atlantic Council Geoeconomics Centre, May 2022.

Key findings

- 105 countries, representing over 95 percent of global GDP, are exploring a CBDC. In May 2020, only 35 countries were considering a CBDC. A new high of 50 countries are in an advanced phase of exploration (development, pilot, or launch).
- 10 countries have fully launched a digital currency, with China's pilot set to expand in 2023. Jamaica is the latest country to launch a CBDC, the JAM-DEX. Nigeria, Africa's largest economy, launched its CBDC in October 2021.
- Of the G7 economies, the US and UK are the furthest behind on CBDC development. The European Central Bank has signalled it will aim to deliver a digital euro by the middle of the decade.
- 19 of the G20 countries are exploring a CBDC, with 16 already in development or pilot stage. This includes South Korea, Japan, India, and Russia. Each has made significant progress over past six months.

- Many countries are exploring alternative international payment systems. The trend is likely to accelerate following financial sanctions on Russia. There are 9 cross border wholesale CBDC tests and 3 cross-border retail projects. This includes cross-border tests not only between China, Thailand, and the United Arab Emirates but also between South Africa, Australia, Malaysia, and more.
- The creation of different CBDC models across different economies need a revisit to international standard setting as the existing financial system in the near future could possibly face a substantial interoperability issue.

Country-wise improvement in examining CBDC gives a clear view of the stress laid by central banks towards enforcing a successful digital currency. On the one hand, this would do away with the existing drawbacks of a fiat currency and shrink the development of private cryptocurrencies. However, many aspects, like AML, CFT, cross-border capital flows, and more structured planning and consensus.

RELIABILITY

The whole issue of reliability rests on the psychological aspect of trust. As mentioned earlier, the origin of private crypto (Bitcoin) found its basis in non-reliability in major currencies arising due to continued devaluation and, thus, lack of trust in the centralised system. Hence the idea of having a currency that could not be manipulated by other people/institutions. Central banks have the power to design policies and ensure monetary sovereignty, but with power comes a responsibility to uphold the trust of the people who rely on such powers/monetary sovereignty. The acceptance of private currency (cryptocurrency) by a large section of society has opened the eyes to the centralised system of currency regulation. People now have the power to choose their currency, and capitalism follows (Bitcoin case) to accept the payment method, so why it would matter to introduce CBDC remains a pertinent question. What makes a currency, commodity, or country reliable for citizens is a matter of more significant importance. A fall in the value of a currency monitored by central banks simultaneously coexisting with a considerable amount of black money can always raise questions about the integrity of a nation's monetary policy. It cannot be denied that considerations regarding security, resilience, identity management of CBDC users, governance, as well as regulatory standards (including AML/CFT), and interoperability with existing payment systems are becoming more complex with the involvement of several jurisdictions (BIS Report to G20, 2021). Hence, tackling money laundering (AML/CFT) through any innovation in the currency will be a welcome move, whether public or private. If CBDC can retain the reliability aspect of the proposed architecture, monetary sovereignty can be safeguarded. The evolution of currency from gold to gold-backed currency (gold standard) to paper and now to digital money has been a long journey and will continue indefinitely. With time comes technology and innovation and a regulatory system aimed at safeguarding the currency and preventing it from speculative attacks. Ponzi games would increase their reliability and effectiveness as a monetary alternative. CBDC may increase the traceability and reliability of transactions as information will be stored in the decentralised network. Hence it can be said that consumer protection, market conduct, data privacy and stability, coupled with operational resilience will be the best tests for reliability of any form of digital currency.

CONCLUSION

With increase in digital payment modes and online shopping, there is less reliance on cash. Wallets are gradually moving from pockets to smartphones and other electronic devices. Since any money issued by central banks is considered safe because of the credibility and authority of the central bank system, any money issued by intermediaries carries the underlying promise of one-to-one convertibility with central bank money. So, in a digital world, CBDCs are necessary to preserve the role of central bank money as a stabilising force at the heart of the payments system and to safeguard monetary sovereignty (Priyadarshini & Kar, 2021). However, at the same time, avoid risks to financial intermediation. There is no virtue in disabling digital innovations in private money. Instead, the Central bank currency—along with regulation, oversight, and surveillance—must persist in anchoring the solidity and efficiency of the payment system with privately-issued money, augmenting this foundation with innovation and diversity. Not to forget that confidence in any private means of payment is determined by the ability to convert it into safe public money (Panetta, 2022). This conviction, thus, should not be breached. As of now, privately-issued money has become an efficient payment mechanism to the degree that it can be redeemed into central bank currency. Hence, belief and confidence are essential parts of the entire payment mechanism. Private money having comparable confidence of redeeming in an acceptable form can hold substantial power. Thus, the option of redemption into central bank currency is essential for stability, interoperability, innovation, and diversity of privately-issued money, be it a bank account or another. Since non central bank money are liabilities of private issuers: their value is based on the soundness of the issuer and is underlined by the promise of one-to-one convertibility with central bank money. At this time of digital innovation, monetary sovereignty of central banks cannot be the only cause to hold back private cryptocurrencies, rather there need to be a consensus on the integration into a dual monetary system where the private and central bank offerings build on each other. Just as without the anchor of sovereign money, people would constantly have to monitor the soundness of private issuers, at the same time, non-acceptance of private money will only lead to riskier innovations and impact credibility of transactions. Thus, there is merit in so many countries pursuing the possibility of a CBDC as it looks like the best option for Central banks to ensure that their money can remain a payments anchor in a digital world. At the same time there is utmost need for international coordination for the successful implementation of world-wide CBDC and the Bank for International Settlements (BIS) are supporting international discussions, ensuring that central banks can continue learning from one another and can cooperate on key issues in design. In this way, central banks can work together to support digital money ready for the economy of the future.

REFERENCES

Auer, R. & Böhme, R. (2020). The technology of retail central bank digital currency. *BIS Quarterly Review*.

BIS Committee. (2021). Central Bank Digital Currencies for cross-border payments. *Report to the G20*.

Carstens, A. (2021). *Digital currencies and the future of the monetary system*. Bank for International Settlements, Hoover Institution policy seminar.

Committee on Payments and Market Infrastructure. (2018). Markets Committee Papers. Bank for International Settlements.

Committee on Payments and Market Infrastructures. (2016). *Fast payments – Enhancing the speed and availability of retail payments*. Bank for International Settlements.

Federal Reserve System. (2022). Money and Payments: The U.S. Dollar in the Age of Digital Transformation. Board of Governors of the Federal Reserve System.

Fiedler, S. (2019). The Future of Money. Study for the Committee on Economic and Monetary Affairs, Policy Department for Economic, Scientific and Quality of Life Policies, European Parliament, Luxembourg.

Koning, JP. (2016). Fedcoin: A Central Bank-issued Cryptocurrency. *R3 reports*.

Mancini-Griffoli, T., Martinez Peria, M. S., Agur, I., Ari, A., Kiff, J., Popescu, A., & Rochon, C. (2018). Casting Light on Central Bank Digital Currencies. IMF Staff Discussion Note, International Monetary Fund.

Nag, K. A. (2021). A Proposed Architecture for a Central Bank Digital Currency for India. *ORF Occasional Paper No. 340*, Observer Research Foundation.

Panetta, F. (2022). *Central bank digital currencies: defining the problems, designing the solutions.* Speech by Fabio Panetta to a panel discussion on central bank digital currencies at the US Monetary Policy Forum. https://www.ecb.europa.eu/press/key/date/2022/html/ecb.sp220218_1~938e881b13.en.html

Priyadarshini, D., & Kar, S. (2021). Central Bank Digital Currency (CBDC): Critical Issues and the Indian Perspective. *IRG working paper no.444.*

PwC (2021), Central Bank Digital Currency in the Indian context. PwC.

Sackheim, M. S., & Howell, A. N. (2018). *The Virtual Currency Regulation Review.* Law Business Research Ltd.

Sankar, R.T. (2021). Central Bank Digital Currency – Is This the Future of Money. Keynote address delivered by Shri T Rabi Sankar. *Vidhi Centre for Legal Policy*, New Delhi.

Chapter 5
Cryptocurrencies on a New Rise

Sadeesh J.
SRM Institute of Science and Technology, India

E. Suresh
University of Technology and Applied Sciences, Oman

ABSTRACT

Cryptocurrency is a widely used word. As e-commerce becomes increasingly important, more Techno-Indians are buying online. Bitcoin was created in 2009 as an internet currency. Financial institutions bridged the buyer-seller divide. They processed trustworthy e-payments. Even if the gap was filled, buyer and seller trade operations remained dependent. This research examines cryptocurrency's influence on Indians. This reliance helped create Cryptocurrency. This will help India advance in e-commerce. Cryptocurrency will help Indians, but not necessarily the country.

INTRODUCTION

Cryptocurrency doesn't depend on banks to validate transactions. It's a peer-to-peer payment system that anybody may use. Instead of tangible money transported and traded in the real world, bitcoin payments are digital entries in an online database. The public ledger records bitcoin transactions. Wallets hold cryptocurrency. Cryptocurrency verifies transactions via cryptography. This means storing and sending bitcoin data requires complex code. Encryption ensures security. Bitcoin, launched in 2009, is the first and best-known cryptocurrency. Speculators drive up cryptocurrency values by trading for profit.

DOI: 10.4018/978-1-6684-5691-0.ch005

Historical Perspective of Bitcoin and the Need Behind Bitcoin

Satoshi Nakamoto released "Bitcoin: A Peer-to-Peer Electronic Cash System" in 2008. Nakamoto's famous white paper described a digital currency that would allow secure peer-to-peer transactions without a government, bank, or company. These transactions would be recorded using a blockchain, a distributed ledger utilised by financial institutions, with all parties owning precise copy. Bitcoin won't surpass 21 million. Nakamoto created bitcoin to recapture money from banking elites. Nakamoto gave 10 Bitcoins to developer Hal Finney on Bitcoin's launch day. Laszlo Haneke bought two pizzas for 10,000 Bitcoin in 2010. Baldridge Bitcoin is a decentralised cryptocurrency with anonymous spending. Ripple, Litecoin, Monero, Neo, etc. Bitcoin is decentralised online currency. India has few bitcoin-accepting shops. Low-cost, anonymous crypto-currencies remove intermediate expenses.

Cryptocurrency

Ten years ago, bitcoin was unheard of. It refers to cryptographic digital or virtual money. Digital assets are inflation-resistant, portable, secure, and counterfeit-resistant. Popular cryptocurrency Bitcoin. Bitcoin, a decentralised cryptocurrency, was created in 2009. Paronym Satoshi Nakamoto. Several prominent scientists and engineers claim to have created bitcoin.

Bitcoin Mining

Bitcoin mining is how new bitcoins enter circulation and contributes to the upkeep and development of the blockchain ledger. Supercomputers are used to tackle complicated mathematical problems. Bitcoin mining is undertaken by high-powered computers that handle tough computational arithmetic tasks. These issues are too complicated to be solved manually and burden even the most advanced computers (Bitcoin Mining, 2021).

Bitcoin transactions are verified. This regulation safeguards Bitcoin. Mining prevents "double- spending" The same bitcoin is double-spent when spent twice. Once you give $20 bn to purchase vodka, you no longer have it, thus you can't buy lottery tickets next door (How Does Bitcoin Mining Work? 2021). Counterfeit money is different from double-dipping. Digital money holders may make a copy and transmit it to a merchant while keeping the original. Mining Bitcoin has two effects. Bitcoin network computers produce fresh bitcoin when they solve math problems (not unlike when a mining operation extracts gold from the ground). Bitcoin miners solve arithmetic problems to verify transaction data, securing the network. Bitcoin is transferred. In-store or online transactions are captured by banks, POS systems, and receipts. Nodes watch blocks so they may be verified later by Bitcoin miners.

Present and Future of Cryptocurrency in India

India doesn't regulate cryptocurrencies. Bitcoin exchanges like Unocoin, Zebpay, etc. have implemented KYC standards in the absence of legislation. In 2014, the Reserve Bank of India revealed interest in cryptocurrency's block chain technology to curb physical paper money circulation. The RBI studied private blockchain in 2015. ICICI bank and Emirates NBD adopted blockchain technology in 2016. RBI's IDRBT issued a white paper and pilot test in 2017. In his Union Budget 2018 statement, the finance minister said, "The government does not consider cryptocurrencies lawful money or currency and will abolish their use in supporting illicit activities or as a payment method." Blockchain can organise any data or transaction chain without intermediaries, according to the government. Blockchain technology will be studied for digital economy. Government is wary about cryptocurrencies but excited about blockchain.

Cryptocurrency sector argues blockchain and cryptocurrencies must go together. Until a decentralized system is created, it's tracking. Block chain technology establishes a centralized system that may be changed. India's experts and observers foresee phased cryptocurrency regulation. This boosts bitcoin's prospects. Private enterprises dealing in cryptocurrencies have established up the Digital Assets and Blockchain foundation to educate the people on the advantages and investment prospects in bitcoin by undertaking security checks using government- issued IDs, PANs, or Aadhaar IDs. Cryptocurrencies grew with the internet. India may develop virtual banks using internet and blockchain. To demonstrate, the RBI launched Lakshmi.

STATEMENT OF THE PROBLEM

Cryptocurrency's worth is defined by market participants' transactions; therefore, lack of trust may cause a collapse in trading and a reduction in value. Since cryptocurrencies aren't backed by any bank or organisation, if they fall, they all fall. As society evolves, criminals adapt. With the rise of cryptocurrencies, cybercrimes are becoming more common. Cryptocurrency uses encryption to maintain security and anonymity. This is risky for terror financing, smuggling, frauds, and money laundering. Encryption makes finding the sender and other facts harder.

OBJECTIVES OF THE STUDY

To study is focused on Crypto Policy and India.

To learn the impact of Union Budget 2022-23 on cryptocurrency.

RESEARCH METHODOLOGY

This work uses secondary data from journals, newspapers, internet, and statutory reports.

REVIEW OF LITERATURE

Kurihara and Fukushima, 2017 argued it's not digital cash that's worldwide. Bitcoin may be artificially inflated at whim, but its supply is fixed and cannot be altered.

Wonglimpiyarat, 2016 notes that lawless tender is a hurdle for Bitcoin, which seeks official approval. Bitcoin may alter banking in impoverished nations, but it's hard to replace cash.

Crypto Policy and India: The Spectacle Continue

India just voted to tax digital assets like cryptocurrency and non-fungible tokens (30% tax on transfer, 1% TDS on every transaction). This low-cost TDS, which won't feel pricey, offers a list of bitcoin traders. The action sparked a dispute over the legality of such assets and whether taxes legitimized them. Crypto assets aren't unlawful, but taxing them doesn't make them legitimate. For all the crypto industry operators' concerns about a high number of investors, the RBI has a counterargument: "November data tends to show that crypto investments by Indians is nothing near becoming substantial" (although the pace of growth could make it a concern in future). Four out of five investor accounts had less than INR10,000, on average INR1,566. If wealth loss occurs, it will harm a tiny percentage of these investors.

RESEARCH GAP

Accounting-Information Technology gap Bitcoin mixes cash and technology, bridging accountancy and IT. Virtual currencies provide technical elements that may be daunting for accountants, but the danger of financial fraud makes them worthwhile.

Cryptocurrency in India

In 2013-17, India's cryptocurrency craze began. During this period, India's cryptocurrency development was fraught with uncertainty. RBI warned about cryptocurrency in 2013. Consumers, holders, traders/agencies, etc. are considered "public." RBI has said it is actively watching Bitcoin (a prominent cryptocurrency) and other cryptocurrencies (Altcoins-An Altcoin is an alternative digital currency to Bitcoin). RBI informed the public again in February 2017 and again in the final quarter of 2017 that "virtual currencies/cryptocurrencies are not legal money in India." Due to several PILs filed in court as a response to RBI's warning, the Indian government has constituted a committee to look into cryptocurrency concerns and recommend further steps. No virtual currency bans occurred during this time.

In April 2018, the finance ministry of India developed a cryptocurrency law but "was not in favour of a prohibition."

2019 (Bitcoin ban): Below are key points.

In March 2020, the supreme court of India reversed RBI's prohibition on cryptocurrency.

Trading, mining, keeping, transferring, or using cryptocurrencies may result in a fine or 10 years in jail in India.

Any holder/user/person must declare/dispose of any cryptocurrencies within 90 days of this act's publication.

Cryptocurrency processes/technology may be used for academic research/ development. RBI may introduce digital rupee as legal money in India.

In public interest, India may loosen certain trade restrictions (if necessary).

Judgement: A bench of justices Rohinton Nariman, Aniruddha Bose, and V. Ramasubramanian passed a 180-page verdict claiming that: RBI has not mentioned any point regarding regulations of virtual currencies by nationalised banks/commercial banks/other financial institutions etc. and RBI has not yet mentioned any adverse effect directly or indirectly, completely/partially due to the exchange of virtual currencies.

Justice Balasubramanian stated the RBI's position was "disproportionate." The Supreme Court noted India's inability to develop a lawful digital rupee despite various legislation and committees.

2021: A high-level Inter-Ministerial Committee (IMC) is constituted to analyse cryptocurrencies and recommend further steps. Nirmala Sitharaman announced this in 2021. Anurag Thakur, minister of state for finance, stated the government would establish a cryptocurrency legislation. Finance minister Nirmala Sitharaman said the government wants to foster crypto research and innovation. In November 2021, the standing committee on finance, chaired by Jayant Sinha, met with crypto exchange officials and Blockchain and Crypto Assets Council (BACC) and decided to regulate cryptocurrencies in India. Then, RBI governor Shaktikanta Das warned unregulated cryptocurrencies might threaten the financial system and RBI intends to build its own digital currency (as a legal tender of course). Finance minister Nirmala Sitharaman said the government hasn't prohibited cryptocurrency marketing but would promote awareness through RBI and SEBI (Securities and Exchange Board of India).

Cryptocurrencies in India Have Few Limitations

1. Cryptocurrency is a platform for hackers, terror financing, drug transactions, and money laundering. This has exhausted the population because it diminishes security and confidence.
2. Cryptocurrencies are speculative and hazardous. Investing in cryptocurrency is risky. Demand and supply dictate bitcoin prices. Bitcoin price speculation introduces risk.
3. Cryptocurrency gains aren't taxed under income tax laws. The IRS may tax crypto profits. Investors may incur long-term or short-term capital gains taxes depending on how long they hold a cryptocurrency.
4. The Indian government is waiting to regulate cryptocurrencies, while other countries have moved. Bitcoin is unregulated. Fraud and investor protection threats increased.

The Digital Rupee

Deputy Governor of India's Reserve Bank, has noted, "Cryptocurrencies are decentralised systems where users validate transactions by consensus." They sidestep the financial system's restrictions. Governments can't track or seize them. Transactions are validated, but not intentions or counterparties.

The RBI will debut India's Digital Rupee in FY 2023, according to the current Union Budget. The RBI wants to know the objective of digital-asset transactions, not simply the parties. The digital rupee may not employ blockchain, according to one tech argument. Multiple nodes validate transactions on a permission-less blockchain network. The RBI would seek to manage the digital rupee and be the exclusive transaction validator. That makes digital rupees "permissioned," which is anti-blockchain. The RBI must add additional transaction nodes to make the digital rupee accessible to people. Without this, the digital rupee may be limited to the RBI and banks, which is useless. Crypto policy and legislation have witnessed both hope and cynicism. Exuberance has surrounded the development of a statute whose draught form has reportedly undergone several modifications but has never been made available for input. Hopefully, 'crypto-legality' will be settled shortly.

Union Budget 2022-23 on Cryptocurrencies in India

Transfers of virtual currency/cryptocurrency assets would be entitled to a 30% tax deduction, according to India's federal budget 2022-23. No loss may be carried forward. Gifts of virtual assets/cryptocurrencies are taxable to the recipient. RBI will issue a CBDC using Blockchain by 2023. 1% of digital asset transfers will be taxed at source.

Impact: This announcement may acknowledge cryptocurrency as a genuine asset and trading as a lawful activity. Tax slab clarity may promote industry size.

No carry forward losses will hurt investors since cryptocurrencies are volatile. This worry will keep individual investors from trading bitcoins. The high tax rate will reduce investors' net profits, and the 115BBH provisions on virtual currency income will take effect on 1 April 2023.

Dilemma: Taxing cryptocurrencies does not proclaim them lawful since India's income tax is based on assets, not the means of getting them.

Future: Based on past experience and current tax disclosures, it's doubtful that India would submit a measure to ban cryptocurrencies.

CONCLUSION

Cryptography is based on evading government authority. Cryptocurrencies circumvent the regulated financial system. These should prompt caution. We've seen that cryptocurrencies can't be defined as a money, asset, or commodity; they have no underlying cash flows or intrinsic value; they're like Ponzi schemes, or worse. These should exclude them from the legitimate financial system. They also weaken financial integrity, notably KYC and AML/CFT requirements, and may encourage anti-social behavior. If permitted, they may damage the currency system, monetary authority, banking system, and the government's capacity to oversee the economy. They jeopardize a country's financial sovereignty and render it vulnerable to strategic manipulation by private corporations or governments. These facts suggest that India should prohibit cryptocurrencies. None of the justifications for regulating cryptocurrencies pass basic inspection.

REFERENCES

Adhami, S., Giudici, G., & Martinazzi, S. (2018). Why Do Businesses Go Crypto? An Empirical Analysis of Initial Coin Offerings. *Journal of Economics and Business*, *100*, 64–75. doi:10.1016/j.jeconbus.2018.04.001

Afzal, A., & Asif, A. (2019). Cryptocurrencies, Blockchain and Regulation: A Review. *The Lahore Journal of Economics, 24*(1), 103–130. doi:10.35536/lje.2019.v24.i1.a5

Babkin, A. V., Burkaltseva, D., Pshenichnikov, W., & Tyulin, A. (2017). Cryptocurrency and Blockchain-Technology in Digital Economy: *Development Genesis. St. Petersburg State Polytechnical University Journal. Economics, 67*(5), 9–22.

Baldwin, J. (2018). In Digital We Trust: Bitcoin Discourse, Digital Currencies, and Decentralized Network Fetishism. *Palgrave Communications, 4*(1), 1–10. doi:10.105741599-018-0065-0

Berg, C., Davidson, S., & Potts, J. (2019). Blockchain Technology as Economic Infrastructure: *Revisiting the Electronic Markets Hypothesis. Frontiers in Blockchain, 2*, 22. doi:10.3389/fbloc.2019.00022

Bouri, E., Gupta, R., Lau, C. K. M., Roubaud, D., & Wang, S. (2018). Bitcoin and global financial stress: A copula-based approach to dependence and causality in the quantiles. *The Quarterly Review of Economics and Finance, 69*, 297–307. doi:10.1016/j.qref.2018.04.003

Briere, M., Oosterlinck, K., & Szafarz, A. (2013). Virtual currency, tangible return: Portfolio diversification with bitcoins ULB–Universite Libre de Bruxelles. *Working Papers CEB*, 13-031.

BritoJ.ShadabH. B.Castillo O'SullivanA. (2015). Bitcoin Financial Regulation: Securities, Derivatives, Prediction Markets, and Gambling. SSRN.

Burniske, C., & White, A. (2017). *Bitcoin: Ringing the bellfor a new asset class.* Ark Invest. https://Research.Ark-Invest.Com/Hubfs/1_Download_Files_ARK- Invest/White_Papers/Bitcoin-Ringing-The-Bell-For-A-New-Asset-Class. Pdf.

Button, S. (2018). Cryptocurrency and Blockchains in Emerging Economies. *Software Quality Professional, 20*(3).

Calcaterra, C., Kaal, W. A., & Rao, V. (2020). Stable Cryptocurrencies. *Washington University Journal of Law and Policy, 61*, 193–228.

Cennamo, C., Marchesi, C., & Meyer, T. (2020). Two Sides of The Same Coin? Decentralized Versus Proprietary Blockchains and The Performance of Digital Currencies. *Academy of Management Discoveries, 6*(3), amd.2019.0044. doi:10.5465/amd.2019.0044

Chohan, U. W. (2017). The Double Spending Problem and Cryptocurrencies. Scholarly Paper ID 3090174.

Clark, B., & Burstall, R. (2018). Blockchain, IP and The Pharma Industry-How Distributed Ledger Technologies Can Help Secure the Pharma Supply Chain. *Journal of Intellectual Property Law & Practice*, *13*(7), 531–533. doi:10.1093/jiplp/jpy069

Corbet, S., Lucey, B., Urquhart, A., & Yarovaya, L. (2019). Cryptocurrencies as a Financial Asset: A Systematic Analysis. *International Review of Financial Analysis*, *62*, 182–199. doi:10.1016/j.irfa.2018.09.003

Dashkevich, N., Counsell, S., & Destefanis, G. (2020). Blockchain Application for Central Banks: A Systematic Mapping Study. *IEEE Access: Practical Innovations, Open Solutions*, *8*, 139918–139952. doi:10.1109/ACCESS.2020.3012295

Demidenko, D. S., Malevskaia-Malevich, E. D., & Dubolazova, Y. A. (2018). ISO as a Real Source of Funding Pricing issues. 2018 International Conference on Information Networking (ICOIN), (pp. 622– 625). IEEE. 10.1109/ICOIN.2018.8343193

Dimitrova, V., Fernández-Martínez, M., Sánchez-Granero, M. A., & Segovia, J. E. T. (2019). Some Comments on Bitcoin Market (In)Efficiency. *PLoS One*, *14*(7), e0219243. doi:10.1371/journal.pone.0219243 PMID:31283773

Dodd, N. (2018). The Social Life of Bitcoin. *Theory, Culture & Society*, *35*(3), 35–56. doi:10.1177/0263276417746464

Dorfleitner, G., & Lung, C. (2018). Cryptocurrencies from The Perspective of Euro Investors: A Re- examination of Diversification Benefits and a New Day-of-The-Week Effect. *Journal of Asset Management*, *19*(7), 472–494. doi:10.105741260-018-0093-8

Dostov, V., & Shust, P. (2014). Cryptocurrencies: An unconventional Challenge to the AML/CFT Regulators? *Journal of Financial Crime*, *21*(3), 249–263. doi:10.1108/JFC-06-2013-0043

Duque, J. J. (2020). State Involvement in Cryptocurrencies. A Potential World Money? *Journal of Political Economy*, *46*(1), 65–82. doi:10.1080/2329194X.2020.1763185

Fadeyi, O., Krejcar, O., Maresova, P., Kuca, K., Brida, P., & Selamat, A. (2020). Opinions on Sustainability of Smart Cities in the Context of Energy Challenges Posed by Cryptocurrency Mining. *Sustainability*, *12*(1), 169. doi:10.3390u12010169

Fantacci, L. (2019). Cryptocurrencies and the Denationalization of Money. *International Journal of Political Economy*, *48*(2), 105–126. doi:10.1080/08911916.2019.1624319

Flori, A. (2019). Cryptocurrencies In Finance: Review and Applications. *International Journal of Theoretical and Applied Finance*, *22*(5), 1–22. doi:10.1142/S0219024919500201

Foley, S., Karlsen, J. R., & Putniņš, T. J. (2019). Sex, Drugs, and Bitcoin: How Much Illegal Activity Is Financed through Cryptocurrencies? *Review of Financial Studies*, *32*(5), 1798–1853. doi:10.1093/rfs/hhz015

García-Medina, A., & Hernández, J. B. (2020). Network Analysis of Multivariate Transfer Entropy of Cryptocurrencies in Times of Turbulence. *Entropy (Basel, Switzerland)*, *22*(7), 760–762. doi:10.3390/e22070760 PMID:33286532

Glaser, F., & Bezzenberger, L. (2015). Beyond Cryptocurrencies-A Taxonomy of Decentralized Consensus Systems. Scholarly Paper ID 2605803.

Gott, M., Ward, S., Gardiner, C., Cobb, M., & Ingleton, C. (2011). A Narrative Literature Review of The Evidence Regarding the Economic Impact of Avoidable hospitalizations Amongst Palliative Care Patients in the UK. *Progress in Palliative Care*, *19*(6), 291–298. doi:10.1179/1743291X11Y.0000000014

Harvey, J., & Branco-Illodo, I. (2020). Why Cryptocurrencies Want Privacy: A Review of Political Motivations and Branding Expressed in "Privacy Coin" Whitepapers. *Journal of Political Marketing*, *19*(1–2), 107–136. doi:10.1080/15377857.2019.1652223

Hashemi Joo, M., Nishikawa, Y., & Dandapani, K. (2019). Cryptocurrency, a Successful Application of Blockchain Technology. *Managerial Finance*, *46*(6), 715–733. doi:10.1108/MF-09-2018-0451

Hayes, A. (2015). A Cost of Production Model for Bitcoin. *Working Papers No. 1505*. New School for Social Research, Department of Economics.

Hu, A., Parlour, C. A., & Rajan, U. (2018). Cryptocurrencies: Stylized Facts on a New Investible Instrument. Scholarly Paper ID 3182113. doi:10.2139/ssrn.3182113

Hudson, R., & Urquhart, A. (2019). Technical Trading and Cryptocurrencies. *Annals of Operations Research*, *297*(1-2), 191–220. doi:10.100710479-019-03357-1

Keogh, J. G., Dube, L., Rejeb, A., Hand, K. J., Khan, N., & Dean, K. (2020). The Future Food Chain: Digitization as an Enabler of Society 5.0. In D. Detwiler (Ed.), *Building the Future of Food Safety Technology*. Elsevier. doi:10.1016/B978-0-12-818956-6.00002-6

Keogh, J. G., Rejeb, A., Khan, N., Dean, K., & Hand, K. J. (2020). Blockchain and GS1 Standards in the Food Chain: A Review of the Possibilities and Challenges. In D. Detwiler (Ed.), *Building the Future of Food Safety Technology*. Elsevier.

Kerr, J. (2018). How Can Legislators Protect Sport from the Integrity Threat Posed by Cryptocurrencies? *The International Sports Law Journal, 18*(1), 79–97. doi:10.100740318-018-0132-0

Larios-Hernández, G. J. (2017). Blockchain Entrepreneurship Opportunity in The Practices of The Unbanked. *Business Horizons, 60*(6), 865–874. doi:10.1016/j.bushor.2017.07.012

Lu, Q., Xu, X., Liu, Y., Weber, I., Zhu, L., & Zhang, W. (2019). uBaaS: A Unified Blockchain as a Service Platform. *Future Generation Computer Systems, 101*, 564–575. doi:10.1016/j.future.2019.05.051

Marian, O. (2013). Are Cryptocurrencies Super Tax Havens? *Michigan Law Review First Impressions, 112*(1), 38–48. https://repository.law.umich.edu/mlr_fi/vol112/iss1/2

Mendoza-Tello, J. C., Mora, H., Pujol-López, F. A., & Lytras, M. D. (2018). Social Commerce as a Driver to Enhance Trust and Intention to Use Cryptocurrencies for Electronic Payments. *IEEE Access: Practical Innovations, Open Solutions, 6*, 50737–50751. doi:10.1109/ACCESS.2018.2869359

Mendoza-Tello, J. C., Mora, H., Pujol-López, F. A., & Lytras, M. D. (2019). Disruptive Innovation of Cryptocurrencies in Consumer Acceptance and Trust. *Information Systems and e-Business Management, 17*(2), 195–222. doi:10.100710257-019-00415-w

Michelman, P. (2017). Seeing Beyond the Blockchain Hype. *MIT Sloan Management Review, 58*(4), 17–20.

Miller, P. (2016). The Cryptocurrency Enigma. In J. Sammons (Ed.), *Digital Forensics* (pp. 1–25). Syngress. doi:10.1016/B978-0-12-804526-8.00001-0

Milne, A. (2018). Cryptocurrencies from an Austrian Perspective. In A. Godart-van der Kroon & P. Vonlanthen (Eds.), *Banking and Monetary Policy from the Perspective of Austrian Economics* (pp. 223–257). Springer International Publishing. doi:10.1007/978-3-319-75817-6_12

Momtaz, P. P. (2019). The Pricing and Performance of Cryptocurrency. *European Journal of Finance*, 1–14. doi:10.1080/1351847X.2019.1647259

Omane-Adjepong, M., & Alagidede, I. P. (2020). High- and Low-Level Chaos in The Time and Frequency Market Returns of Leading Cryptocurrencies and Emerging Assets. *Chaos, Solitons, and Fractals, 132*, 109563. doi:10.1016/j.chaos.2019.109563

Omane-Adjepong, M., Alagidede, P., & Akosah, N. K. (2019). Wavelet Time-Scale Persistence Analysis of Cryptocurrency Market Returns and Volatility. *Physica A*, *514*, 105–120. doi:10.1016/j.physa.2018.09.013

Polasik, M., Piotrowska, A. I., Wisniewski, T. P., Kotkowski, R., & Lightfoot, G. (2015). Price Fluctuations and the Use of Bitcoin: An Empirical Inquiry. *International Journal of Electronic Commerce*, *20*(1), 9–49. doi:10.1080/10864415.2016.1061413

Pournader, M., Shi, Y., Seuring, S., & Koh, S. C. L. (2020). Blockchain Applications in Supply Chains, Transport and Logistics: A Systematic Review of the Literature. *International Journal of Production Research*, *58*(7), 2063–2081. doi:10.1080/00207543.2019.1650976

Raymaekers, W. (2015). Cryptocurrency Bitcoin: Disruption, Challenges and Opportunities. *Journal of Payments Strategy & Systems*, *9*(1), 30–46.

Rejeb, A., & Bell, L. (2019). Potentials of Blockchain for Healthcare: Case of Tunisia. *World Scientific News*, *136*, 173–193. doi:10.2139srn.3475246

Rejeb, A., Keogh, J. G., & Treiblmaier, H. (2019a). Leveraging the Internet of Things and Blockchain Technology in Supply Chain Management. *Future Internet*, *11*(7), 161. doi:10.3390/fi11070161

Rejeb, A., Sűle, E., & Keogh, J. G. (2018). Exploring new technologies in procurement. *Transport & Logistics: The International Journal*, *18*(45), 76–86.

Scharding, T. (2019). National Currency, World Currency, Cryptocurrency: A Fichtean Approach to the Ethics of Bitcoin. *Business and Society Review*, *124*(2), 219–238. doi:10.1111/basr.12169

Searing, J. M., & MacLeod, D. (2019). Cryptocurrency Gift Strategies for Not-for-Profits: Here's What Organizations Should Consider as They Ponder Whether and How to Accept Donations of Virtual Currency. *Journal of Accountancy*, *227*(2), 34–36.

Shahzad, F., Xiu, G., Wang, J., & Shahbaz, M. (2018). An Empirical Investigation on the Adoption of Cryptocurrencies Among the People of Mainland China. *Technology in Society*, *55*, 33–40. doi:10.1016/j.techsoc.2018.05.006

Sharma, A. K., & Kumar, S. (2010). Economic Value Added (EVA)-Literature Review and Relevant Issues. *International Journal of Economics and Finance*, *2*(2), 200–220. doi:10.5539/ijef.v2n2p200

Sudzina, F. (2018). Distribution of Foreign Aid in Cryptocurrencies: Initial Considerations. *International Advances in Economic Research*, *24*(4), 387–388. doi:10.100711294-018-9715-7

Symitsi, E., & Chalvatzis, K. J. (2018). Return, Volatility and Shock Spillovers of Bitcoin with Energy and Technology Companies. *Economics Letters*, *170*, 127–130. doi:10.1016/j.econlet.2018.06.012

Tama, B. A., Kweka, B. J., Park, Y., & Rhee, K.-H. (2017). A Critical Review of Blockchain and Its Current Applications. *2017 International Conference on Electrical Engineering and Computer Science (ICECOS)*, (pp. 109–113). IEEE. 10.1109/ICECOS.2017.8167115

Till, B. M., Peters, A. W., Afshar, S., & Meara, J. G. (2017). From Blockchain Technology to Global Health Equity: Can Cryptocurrencies Finance Universal Health Coverage? *BMJ Global Health*, *2*(4), e000570. doi:10.1136/bmjgh-2017-000570 PMID:29177101

Torre, C., Rocha, J. G., Falcão, M. I., Taniar, D., Apduhan, B. O., & Gervasi, O. (2014). *Computational Science and Its Applications*, 720–732. Berlin: Springer International Publishing.

Trautman, L. J. (2014). Virtual Currencies; Bitcoin & What Now After Liberty Reserve, Silk Road, and Mt. Gox? *Richmond Journal of Law and Technology*, *20*(4), 1–108.

Treiblmaier, H. (2018). The Impact of The Blockchain on The Supply Chain: A Theory-Based Research Framework and a Call for Action. *Supply Chain Management*, *23*(6), 545–559. doi:10.1108/SCM-01-2018-0029

Tucker, T. (2013). Bitcoin's Volatility Problem: Why Today's Selloff Won't Be the Last. *Bloomberg.Com.* https://www.bloomberg.com/news/articles/2013-12-05/bitcoins-volatility-problem- why-todays-selloff-wont-be-the-last

Uddin, M. A., Stranieri, A., Gondal, I., & Balasubramanian, V. (2019). A Lightweight Blockchain Based Framework for Underwater IoT. *Electronics (Basel)*, *8*(12), 1552. doi:10.3390/electronics8121552

Vandezande, N. (2017). Virtual Currencies Under EU Anti-money Laundering Law. *Computer Law & Security Review*, *33*(3), 341–353. doi:10.1016/j.clsr.2017.03.011

Vaz, J., & Brown, K. (2020). Sustainable Development and Cryptocurrencies as Private Money. *Economia e Politica Industriale*, *47*(1), 163–184. doi:10.100740812-019-00139-5

Vidal-Tomás, D., Ibáñez, A. M., & Farinós, J. E. (2019). Weak efficiency of the cryptocurrency market: A market portfolio approach. *Applied Economics Letters*, *26*(19), 1627–1633. doi:10.1080/13504851.2019.1591583

Vincent, O., & Evans, O. (2019). Can Cryptocurrency, Mobile Phones, and Internet Herald Sustainable Financial Sector Development in Emerging Markets? *Journal of Transnational Management*, *24*(3), 259–279. doi:10.1080/15475778.2019.1633170

Volosovych, S., & Baraniuk, Y. (2018). Tax control of cryptocurrency transactions in Ukraine. *Banks and Bank Systems, 13*(2), 89–106. https://www.ceeol.com/search/article-detail?id=696926

Wang, G. (2019). Marx's Monetary Theory and Its Practical Value. *China Political Economy*, *2*(2), 182–200. doi:10.1108/CPE-10-2019-0026

Chapter 6
Modeling Time-Varying Co-Movements Between Major Cryptocurrencies and Foreign Exchange Markets

Arifenur Güngör
Istanbul Topkapı University, Turkey

Mahmut Sami Güngör
Marmara University, Turkey

ABSTRACT

This chapter scrutinizes the dynamic linkages between major cryptocurrencies and fiat currencies of developed and emerging countries. To do this, the authors estimate the Scalar-BEKK GARCH models from September 2017 to January 2022. To shed light on the effects of specific events, the authors also estimate the models for the sub-periods: the great crypto crash, the Covid-19 pandemic, and the vaccination. Empirical results suggest that the time-varying relationships between the crypto- and fiat currencies highly depend on the country- and crypto-specific dynamics. By the decentralized nature of cryptocurrencies, it is not an easy venture to define the stylized facts on those dynamic relationships. The most striking result shows a sharp and massive decline in the conditional covariances between the cryptos and the fiat currencies of developed countries except the Japanese Yen at the onset of the Covid-19 pandemic.

DOI: 10.4018/978-1-6684-5691-0.ch006

INTRODUCTION

Just after the global financial crisis, the first decentralized cryptocurrency introduced in 2009 called Bitcoin, and since then, the literature has debated the notion of digital or virtual currency from various aspects. The success of Bitcoin has given rise to emerge many cryptocurrencies other than Bitcoin called altcoins. Cryptocurrencies are attractive for many users due to they provide pseudo-anonymity, low transaction costs, skyrocketing returns, and intraday hedging opportunities, and in addition, they are not required to be backed by any central authority for the legitimacy (Palazzi et al., 2021; Urquhart & Zhang, 2019; Yi et al., 2018). This attraction is not just related to the features of cryptos being monetary alternatives or investment opportunities but also the utilities of the Blockchain technology for the users (Chemkha et al., 2021). Thus, the literature focuses on the different aspects of cryptos (used interchangeably for cryptocurrencies throughout the chapter) to scrutinize their dynamics and characteristics (Elsayed et al., 2020).

The virtual currencies mainly aim to provide a new peer-to-peer payment system on the web without any necessity of a trusted financial institution (Chemkha et al., 2021). The literature defines a cryptocurrency as synthetic commodity money (Selgin, 2015) due to the crypto holds three functions of fiat money that are medium of exchange, store of value, and unit of account (Yermack, 2015), and its supply is scarce like commodity money despite no intrinsic value (Baur et al., 2018). The cryptos are also being considered a new investment opportunity for portfolio diversification because of their high returns, price volatilities, and low correlations between other financial assets (Yermak, 2015; Baur et al., 2018; Hsu et al., 2021); however, those have in-built economic risk during the bubble periods (Raza et al., 2022). Therefore, those currencies have been utilized for portfolio allocation besides fiat currencies or commodities for effective risk management and optimal hedging, especially during the turmoil periods (Hsu et al., 2021).

The markets for cryptos have continuously been encountering the boom and bust episodes somewhat similar to business cycles in macroeconomics. The cryptos have shown sharp fluctuations over time, especially in 2018, as risky assets due to those being a significant part of the investment market (Kostika & Laopodis, 2019). In this manner, Walther et al. (2019) put forward that the volatility of cryptocurrencies is mainly affected by global business cycles instead of country-specific dynamics. Moreover, foreign exchange markets are globally interconnected as cryptocurrency markets; thus, an impulse on the markets has the potential to create an immediate response on exchange rates.

The cryptos, particularly Bitcoin, have started to accept as the last resort against losing confidence in fiat currencies in economies like gold (Chemkha et al., 2021), furthermore Bitcoin is called as digital gold from time to time (Popper, 2016). Thus,

Bitcoin has outstanding potential to threaten the supremacy of fiat currencies as an alternative money. Independently of the discussion on whether crypto is either a currency or an asset or both, is it possible to find dynamic relationships between the crypto- and fiat currencies via various structural links (Palazzi et al., 2021)? Most of the literature focused on the markets for cryptocurrencies themselves and the dynamic linkages among the cryptos; however, there is relatively less attention on the time-varying relationships between the crypto- and fiat currencies (Kostika & Laopodis, 2019). Several studies have examined the time-varying linkages between the crypto- and fiat currencies using different sets of currencies and modeling strategies (e.g., Baumöhl, 2019; Kostika & Laopodis, 2019; Kristjanpoller & Bouri, 2019; Liu & Tsyvinski, 2021; Raza et al., 2022; Umar & Guberava, 2020).

The relationships between the crypto- and fiat currencies have quite complex dynamics in the financial system. Most studies have discussed contagion and spillover effects considering international portfolio allocation. Some studies emphasize the potential capabilities of cryptos to be used for hedging against foreign exchange risks (Umar & Guberava, 2020). During the last two years, the literature has also focused on the impact of the Covid-19 pandemic on cryptocurrency markets; however, early studies have compulsorily used very few observations to disseminate the preliminary results.

On this backdrop, this study investigates the dynamic co-movements between the major cryptocurrencies and the foreign exchange rates of selected developed and emerging countries against the U.S. dollar. To do this, the authors benefit from the Scalar-BEKK GARCH model with various specifications for different periods. The authors use a unique modeling approach that enables the models to consider the multilateral effects on the dynamic conditional correlations between the crypto- and fiat currencies considering indirect transmission mechanisms, unlike bivariate models. Aside from the full period from September 5th, 2017 to January 4th, 2022, this study also estimates the models for the sub-periods, which are the Great crypto crash, the Covid-19 pandemic, and the vaccination to investigate whether the specific events during the full period affect the time-varying linkages between the crypto- and fiat currencies. This study deepens the literature on the time-varying connectedness between the crypto- and fiat currencies by providing new empirical evidence with multivariate modeling.

The following section introduces the empirical methodology and the dataset. The third section gives the empirical results, and the last provides concluding remarks.

METHODOLOGY AND DATA

This study aims to investigate the dynamic linkages between major cryptocurrencies and foreign exchanges of selected developed and emerging countries. To do this, the authors benefit from a multivariate generalized autoregressive conditional heteroscedasticity (MGARCH) model. A multivariate approach provides a more convenient modeling framework than estimating separate univariate models (Bauwens et al., 2006). This section introduces a multivariate GARCH model estimated in the empirical analysis. In addition, it provides relevant information about the dataset.

Empirical Methodology: A Scalar BEKK Model

The authors use a Scalar-BEKK GARCH model, a multivariate extension of univariate GARCH models, to estimate time-varying conditional correlations between crypto- and fiat currencies. The BEKK model, the acronym that comes from Baba, Engle, Kraft, and Kroner in the early version of the seminal paper of Engle and Kroner, is proposed by Engle and Kroner (1995) to examine volatility spillover between financial markets. Bauwens et al. (2006) show that the model is a particular version of the vector error correction (VEC) model proposed by Bollerslev et al. (1988).

Equation 1 defines the conditional mean equation as follows:

$$r_t = \mu_t + \epsilon_t \tag{1}$$

where rt is an n×1 vector of multivariate stochastic process, and ϵ is the innovation process, $\epsilon_t \mid \Omega_{t-1} \sim N(0, H_t)$ where $\Omega_{t\text{-}1}$ and H_t denote the information set at time t–1 and the conditional variance-covariance matrix of ϵ_t,

$$H_t = Var(r_t \mid \Omega_{t-1}) = Var_{t-1}(r_t) = Var_{t-1}(\epsilon_t),$$

respectively. To assure positive definiteness, a new parameterization for H_t is proposed by Engle and Kroner (1995). The widely used specification is the multivariate GARCH (1,1) model (Tastan, 2006), which is the most appropriate way to depict conditional variances (Boffelli and Urga, 2016).

The BEKK-GARCH (1,1) model with no exogenous variables is defined in equation 2 as:

$$H_t = C_0^{'}C_0 + A_{11}^{'}\epsilon_{t-1}\epsilon_{t-1}^{'}A_{11} + B_{11}^{'}H_{t-1}B_{11} \tag{2}$$

where C_0, A_{11}, and B_{11} are $n \times n$ parameter matrices, however, C_0 is a triangular matrix. These matrices can be defined as

$$\psi = \left[vech\left[C_0\right]^{'}, \; vec\left[A_{11}\right]^{'}, \; vec\left[B_{11}\right]^{'} \right]^{'}$$

where *vech* is a vectorization operator, and *vec* uses to stack the columns of a matrix. The matrices A_{11} and B_{11} represent ARCH and GARCH effects, respectively. For the bivariate case, the BEKK-GARCH (1,1) model becomes as in equation 3:

$$H_t = C_0^{'} C_0 + \begin{bmatrix} a_{11} & a_{12} \\ a_{21} & a_{22} \end{bmatrix}^{'} \begin{bmatrix} \epsilon_{1t-1}^{2} & \epsilon_{1t-1}\epsilon_{2t-2} \\ \epsilon_{2t-1}\epsilon_{1t-1} & \epsilon_{2t-1}^{2} \end{bmatrix} \begin{bmatrix} a_{11} & a_{12} \\ a_{21} & a_{22} \end{bmatrix} + \begin{bmatrix} b_{11} & b_{12} \\ b_{21} & b_{22} \end{bmatrix}^{'} H_{t-1} \begin{bmatrix} b_{11} & b_{12} \\ b_{21} & b_{22} \end{bmatrix} \tag{3}$$

In the case of imposing no restrictions on the parameters (or estimating the Full-BEKK model), the number of ARCH and GARCH parameters required to be estimated by the BEKK (1,1) model is $n(5n+1)/2$ or $n(n+1)/2+2n^2$. To decrease the number of estimated parameters, one can impose either a Diagonal-BEKK model or a Scalar-BEKK model (Bauwens et al., 2006). The Scalar-BEKK model assumes that $A=aI$, and $B=bI$ where a and b are scalars. The foremost advantage of this model is to guarantee having positive definiteness while it needs to estimate fewer parameters, $(n(n+1)/2)+2$, than the Full-BEKK model (Degiannakis et al., 2014). The covariance stationarity condition is $\sum_{i=1}^{q} a_i^2 + \sum_{j=1}^{p} b_i^2 < 1$ for the Scalar-BEKK model without any explanatory variable.

Equation 4 provides the log-likelihood function as follows:

$$L(\psi) = \left(-\frac{Tn}{2}\right) + \ln(2\pi) - \left(\frac{1}{2}\sum_{t=1}^{T} \ln\left(\left|\mathrm{H}_t\right|\right) + \epsilon_t^{'} \left|H_t^{-1}\right| \epsilon_t)\right) \tag{4}$$

where T and n are the total numbers of observations and variables used in the model, respectively. ψ shows the vector of unknown parameters. The parameters of the Diagonal- or Scalar-BEKK models are estimated by using the quasi-maximum likelihood procedure imposing the covariance stationary condition. Those estimates are asymptotically normal and consistent; and thus, standard statistical tests are valid (McAller et al., 2008).

According to Bauwens et al. (2016), this model class provides relatively parsimonious specifications; however, these models are pretty restrictive on the cross-dynamics. Thus, they put forward that these models are much more suitable for examining the time-varying dynamics of variances and covariances rather than the volatility transmissions. The authors prefer to use the Scalar-BEKK model in the empirical analysis to overcome the curse of dimensionality due to this study focuses on examining the time-varying co-movements between crypto- and fiat currencies.

Dataset

In order to investigate the time-varying co-movement between crypto- and fiat currencies, this study makes use of the daily U.S. dollar price indexes of two major cryptocurrencies with respect to the market capitalization as of June 2022, namely Bitcoin (BTC/USD) and Ethereum (ETH/USD), for the period from September 5th, 2017 to January 4th, 2022. For robustness analysis, the authors also use the U.S. dollar price indexes for two well-known altcoins: Litecoin (LTC/USD) and Ripple (XRP/USD). Figure 1 provides the time series plots of the cryptocurrencies for the analysis period. For fiat currencies, this study uses the daily exchange rates against the U.S. dollar that are Euro (EUR/USD), Japanese Yen (JPY/USD), British Pound (GBP/USD) for developed economies, and Chinese Yuan (CNY/USD), Indian Rupee (INR/USD), Turkish Lira (TRY/USD) for emerging economies for the period as mentioned above. Figure 2 shows the time series plots of the fiat currencies from September 5th, 2017 to January 4th, 2022. The dataset used in the empirical analysis is taken from the database of Thomson Reuters Datastream.

Equation 5 provides the formula to calculate the return series of the exchange rates:

$$r_{it} = 100\times(\ln(cr_{it}) - \ln(cr_{it-1})) \tag{5}$$

where $i = \{ BTC, ETH, LTC, XRP, EUR, JPY, GBY, CNY, INR, TRY\}$, r_{it} is the logarithmic return, and cr_{it-1} is the daily U.S. dollar price indexes of cryptocurrencies or the daily exchange rates against the U.S. dollar at time t.

Table 1 shows the descriptive statistics for the logarithmic returns of the fiat currencies of several developed and emerging countries and selected cryptocurrencies. The log-returns of EUR, JPY, TRY, BTC, and ETH have negatively skewed (or left-tailed) distribution, while the ones of GBP, INR, CNY, LTC, and XRP have positively skewed (or right-tailed) distribution. All of the log-returns of the crypto- and fiat currencies have leptokurtic (or fat-tailed) distribution. In all cases, the results of the Jarque-Bera test reject the null hypothesis, which claims that the log-return of the currency (either fiat or crypto) is normally distributed. This study conducts an empirical analysis using 1131 daily observations for each crypto- and fiat currency. Figure 3 and Figure 4 represent the time series plots of the log-returns for the cryptocurrencies and the fiat currencies, respectively.

Table 1. Descriptive statistics for the returns of crypto- and fiat currencies

	Mean	Maximum	Minimum	Std. Dev.	Skewness	Kurtosis	J. Bera	# of obs.
Fiat Currencies								
EUR	0.0045	1.7539	-1.7528	0.3818	-0.0280	4.3564	86.861[0.000]	1131
JPY	0.0051	2.0219	-2.6938	0.4024	-0.4795	7.2921	911.50[0.000]	1131
GBP	-0.0037	2.8123	-3.1725	0.5509	0.0380	5.5431	305.06[0.000]	1131
INR	0.0134	1.8822	-1.4261	0.3291	0.5318	6.3934	595.98[0.000]	1131
CNY	-0.0020	1.3501	-1.4330	0.2480	0.0049	7.6216	1006.5[0.000]	1131
TRY	0.1214	14.879	-34.135	1.6870	-6.2936	161.91	11975[0.000]	1131
Cryptocurrencies								
BTC	0.2096	20.808	-49.396	4.9671	-0.9454	13.535	5399.3[0.000]	1131
ETH	0.2241	35.514	-57.559	6.3524	-0.7222	11.472	3481.1[0.000]	1131
LTC	0.0681	54.098	-45.740	6.7309	0.1134	12.458	4218.5[0.000]	1131
XRP	0.1222	62.361	-53.920	7.7872	1.0030	16.452	8718.2[0.000]	1131

Note: The significance levels of the Jarque-Bera test are given in square brackets.

Figure 1. Time series plots of the cryptocurrencies

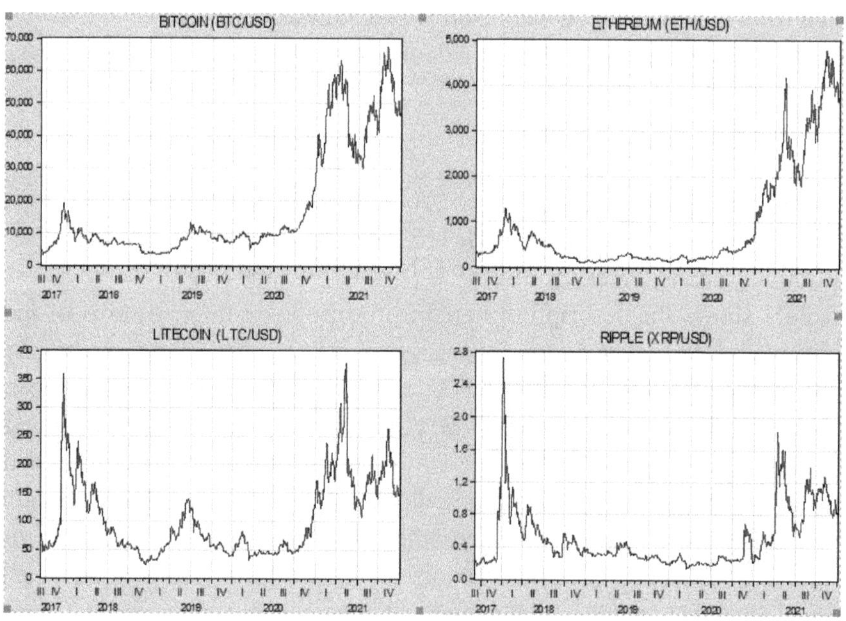

The authors conduct both the Augmented Dickey-Fuller (ADF) test and the Phillips-Perron (PP) test, with a trend and an intercept, for the log-return series of crypto- and fiat currencies to investigate whether the returns have unit roots or not. Table 5 provides the findings of the unit root tests in Appendix 1. These tests reject the null hypothesis of existing a unit root for the log-returns of crypto- and fiat currencies at a one percent significance level. As a result, the unit root tests show that the return series of the currencies are stationary in all cases.

Figure 2. Time series plots of the fiat currencies

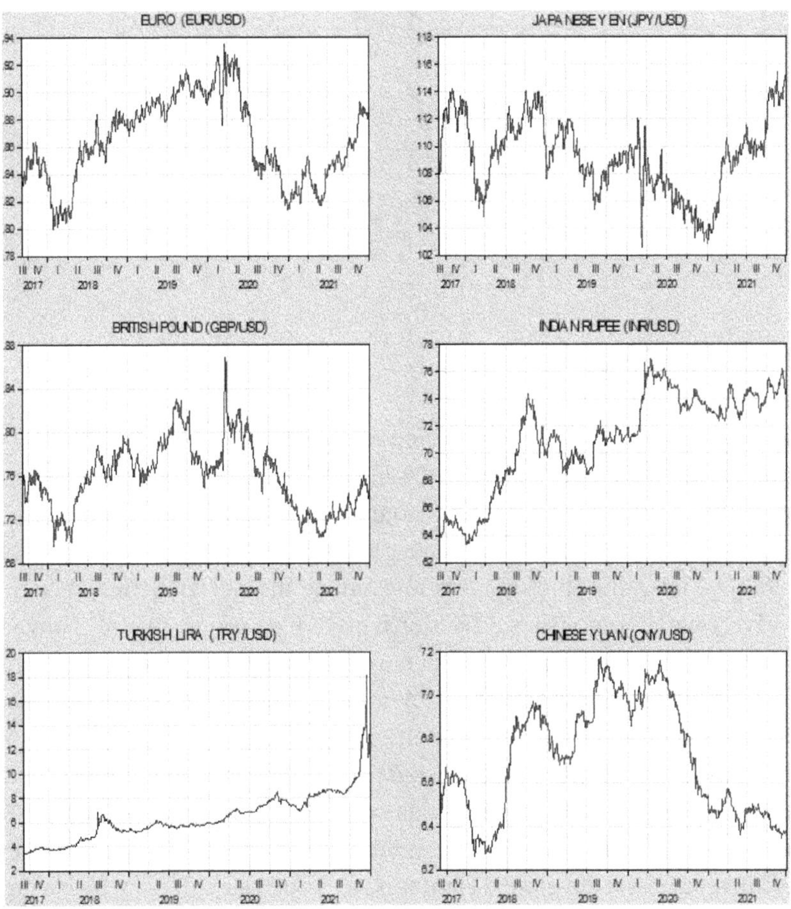

Figure 3. Time series plots of the returns of the cryptocurrencies

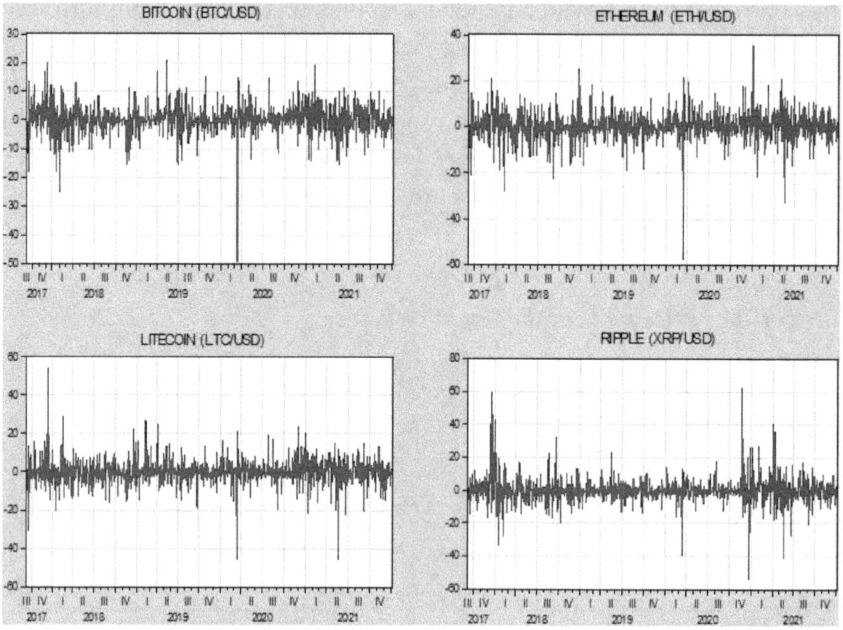

EMPIRICAL RESULTS

The authors examine the time-varying co-movements between the crypto- and the fiat currencies by using the Scalar-BEKK GARCH model. This model is commonly used when the number of series is up to four; otherwise, the curse of dimensionality occurs, and the model needs to estimate plenty of unknown parameters (Bauwens et al., 2006). Thus, this study prefers to estimate the Scalar-BEKK model, which has relatively parsimonious specifications, up to four series, two of them are from the cryptos and the others from the fiat currencies of a developed and an emerging economy. This modeling approach enables the Scalar-BEKK model to consider the multilateral effects on the dynamic conditional correlations between the crypto- and fiat currencies considering indirect transmission mechanisms, unlike bivariate models. As mentioned earlier, the authors focus on four crypto- and six fiat currencies. Therefore, the number of possible combinations that one can select two cryptos, one fiat currency for a developed economy, and one fiat currency for an emerging economy, are six, $C(4,2)$, three, $C(3,1)$, and three, $C(3,1)$, respectively. That means that 54 distinct Scalar-BEKK models that include four currencies can be alternately estimated to analyze the issue. To keep away from this laborious work, the authors choose four different models among all possible specifications to conduct the analysis.

Figure 4. Time series plots of the returns of the fiat currencies

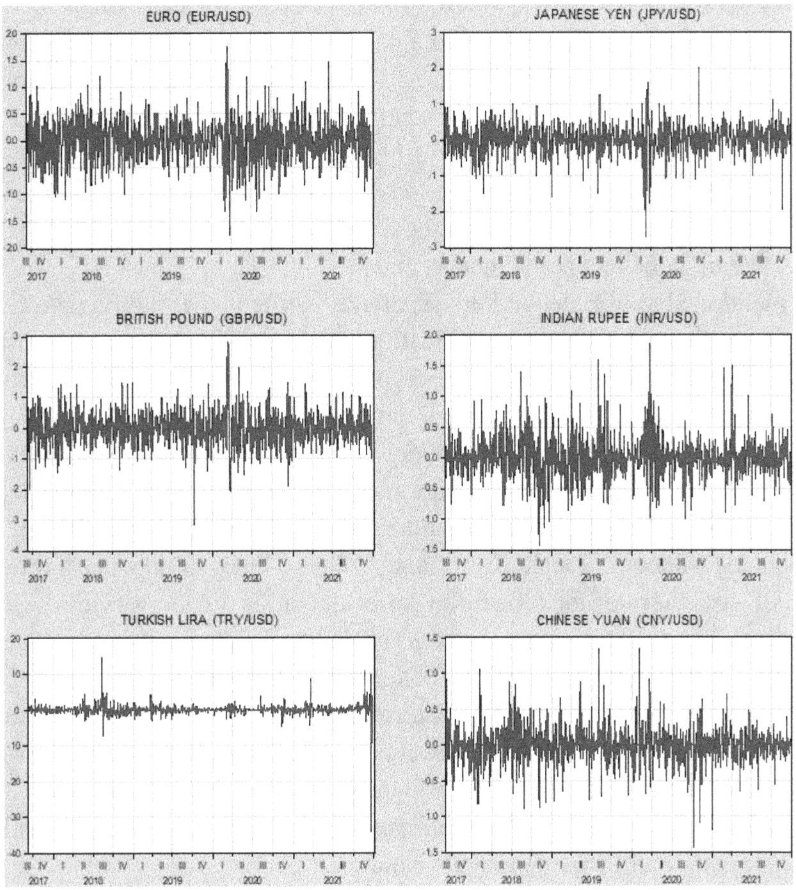

This study aims to estimate each model specification for four different periods. The first is the full period from September 5th, 2017 to January 4th, 2022. To examine whether the specific events during the full period affect the time-varying linkages between the crypto- and fiat currencies, the authors need to define sub-periods. For this purpose, the authors also estimate the Scalar-GARCH model for the 2018 cryptocurrency crash period, known as the Great crypto crash, between December 22nd, 2017 to November 15th, 2018. As might be expected, it is pretty tricky to define the turmoil period of an ongoing crisis, such as the Covid-19 pandemic. Some studies preferred to start the pandemic on March 11th, 2020, which is the date announced the outbreak of the Coronavirus pandemic by the World Health Organization (WHO). The others tend to use different dates rather than the date announced by the WHO. Afterward, many developed countries started the vaccination program against the Covid-19 on February 1st, 2021. The authors view the period from the announcement to the vaccination as the first phase of the Covid-19 pandemic. There was considerable uncertainty about the future of economies and financial markets worldwide during the first phase of the pandemic. Thus, the authors estimate the Scalar-BEKK model from March 11th, 2020 to February 1st, 2021 to examine the dynamic linkages between the crypto- and fiat currencies in the course of the first phase of the pandemic as well. Finally, this study also estimates the Scalar-BEKK GARCH model for the vaccination period, from February 1st, 2021 to January 4th, 2022 because the vaccination against the Covid-19 is expected to have the makings of a decline in global economic uncertainty.

As mentioned above, the authors separately estimate the multivariate GARCH model for both four different specifications and periods. The first specification includes Bitcoin and Ethereum as the cryptos and British Pound and Turkish Lira as the fiat currencies, the first for the developed economy and the latter for the emerging economy. Secondly, the model incorporates Bitcoin, Ethereum, Euro, and Indian Rupee. The third specification comprises Bitcoin, Ethereum, Japanese Yen, and Chinese Yuan. Lastly, the authors also estimate the Scalar-BEKK model that includes Litecoin, Ripple, Euro, and Chinese Yuan to conduct a robustness analysis. Due to the main focus being on the investigation of time-varying conditional correlations between the crypto- and the fiat currencies, the authors do not include any exogenous variables that might potentially affect those relationships or any endogenous variables that might be determined within the model. In addition, the authors include no regressor either in the conditional mean or the conditional variance in the Scalar-BEKK model. This study prefers to use the multivariate GARCH (1,1) specification, which is the most suitable way in the literature to estimate conditional variances because of its parsimonious nature.

Table 2 provides the estimation results of the Scalar-BEKK GARCH (1,1) model for Bitcoin, Ethereum, British Pound, and Turkish Lira. The estimates of the parameters are given for each period from the second to the fifth column. αi denotes a constant term in the conditional mean equation where i=1 for BTC, i=2 for ETH, i=3 for GBP, and i=4 for TRY. The off-diagonal element of the variance-covariance matrix, $Ci_{j,}$ shows the estimate of conditional covariance between the currencies of i and j. For instance, $C1_3$ represent the conditional covariance between Bitcoin and British Pound, and similarly $C2_4$ is the estimation of the conditional covariance between Ethereum and Turkish Lira. The diagonal elements of the variance-covariance matrix, $Ci_{t,}$ indicates the conditional variances. It is beyond the scope of this study to examine the dynamic conditional covariances just among the cryptos. The scope is limited to the time-varying co-movements between the crypto- and fiat currencies. Thus, the authors do not focus on the estimation results, which are not the center of interest. a and b represent ARCH and GARCH effects, respectively. The condition for covariance stationarity, $a2^{+}b2^{<}1$, is satisfied for all estimated models. The results of the McLeod and Li (1983) test cannot reject the null hypothesis of existing no serial correlation for all models. Thus, the estimated Scalar-BEKK models are based on convenient distributions and have no evidence for statistical misspecification. Besides, the estimates of the ARCH and GARCH parameters are statistically significant at the one percent level.

Table 2. The estimation results of the Scalar-BEKK GARCH (1,1) model for BTC, ETH, GBP, and TRY

	Full period	*Crash period*	*Pandemic period*	*Vaccination period*
$\alpha 1$	0.2834** (0.144)	-0.2990 (0.247)	0.6043** (0.299)	0.1822 (0.332)
$\alpha 2$	0.3191* (0.185)	-0.6810* (0.387)	1.0218** (0.450)	0.4605 (0.377)
$\alpha 3$	-0.0099 (0.016)	0.0091 (0.030)	-0.0497 (0.041)	0.0149 (0.024)
$\alpha 4$	0.0579** (0.030)	0.0071 (0.090)	0.0555 (0.061)	0.1073 (0.069)
C_{11}	1.4878*** (0.407)	1.0761*** (0.322)	1.1537*** (0.357)	2.6510*** (0.433)
C_{12}	1.6087*** (0.420)	1.5954*** (0.392)	1.3300*** (0.429)	2.4914*** (0.410)
C_{13}	-0.0211 (0.016)	0.0106 (0.020)	-0.0532** (0.022)	-0.0242 (0.023)
C_{14}	-0.0024 (0.016)	-0.0041 (0.045)	-0.0232 (0.029)	-0.0224 (0.061)
C_{22}	1.1504*** (0.293)	0.8662*** (0.245)	1.0647*** (0.312)	2.0023*** (0.382)
C_{23}	0.0026 (0.008)	0.0039 (0.023)	-0.0113 (0.014)	-0.0073 (0.019)
C_{24}	0.0047 (0.019)	0.0136 (0.035)	0.0097 (0.028)	0.0149 (0.049)
C_{33}	0.1701*** (0.042)	0.1397*** (0.027)	0.1604*** (0.046)	0.2391*** (0.033)
C_{34}	0.0281 (0.019)	0.0206 (0.041)	0.0254 (0.027)	0.1365** (0.055)
C_{44}	0.2783*** (0.072)	0.2862*** (0.084)	0.2404*** (0.073)	0.4420*** (0.064)
B	0.9023*** (0.036)	0.9174*** (0.026)	0.9306*** (0.028)	0.7727*** (0.051)
a	0.3483*** (0.058)	0.3549*** (0.079)	0.2466*** (0.050)	0.5178*** (0.086)
Log Likelihood	-9030.226	-1919.168	-1873.776	-1972.504
$Li-McLeod(20)$	257.255 [0.994]	332.345 [0.305]	350.460 [0.135]	313.835 [0.586]

Note: *Li–McLeod* is the Li and McLeod's multivariate portmanteau test on standardized residuals. *, **, and *** show the statistical significance level at ten, five, and one percent, respectively. The standard errors and p-values are given in parenthesis and square brackets, respectively.

Table 3 and Table 4 provide the estimation findings of the Scalar-BEKK GARCH (1,1) model for (i) Bitcoin, Ethereum, Euro, and Indian Rupee and (ii) Bitcoin, Ethereum, Japanese Yen, and Chinese Yuan, respectively. For robustness, Table 6 gives the estimation results of the Scalar-BEKK GARCH (1,1) model for Litecoin, Ripple, Euro, and Chinese Yuan in Appendix 1. All estimated models satisfy the condition for covariance stationarity, $a^2+b^2<1$. For all cases, the null hypothesis of no serial correlation cannot be rejected by the McLeod and Li test. These results mean that the estimated models are based on convenient distributions and do not indicate any evidence for statistical misspecification. Similar to the previous results, the estimates of the ARCH and GARCH parameters are also statistically significant at the one percent level.

Table 3. The estimation results of the Scalar-BEKK GARCH (1,1) model for BTC, ETH, EUR, and INR

	Full period	*Crash period*	*Pandemic period*	*Vaccination period*
$\alpha 1$	0.1677 (0.127)	-0.3850 (0.240)	0.5112* (0.298)	0.1292 (0.308)
$\alpha 2$	0.2212 (0.174)	-0.7521* (0.383)	0.8484** (0.424)	0.4281 (0.383)
$\alpha 3$	0.0113 (0.010)	0.0242 (0.026)	-0.0348 (0.030)	0.0298 (0.021)
$\alpha 4$	0.0085 (0.0009)	0.0516** (0.021)	-0.0173 (0.015)	0.0072 (0.019)
C_{11}	1.1293*** (0.197)	0.7337*** (0.198)	0.9328*** (0.235)	1.6812*** (0.440)
C_{12}	1.2226*** (0.206)	1.0820*** (0.241)	1.0612*** (0.266)	1.6626*** (0.429)
C_{13}	-0.0123 (0.008)	0.0085 (0.011)	-0.0394** (0.016)	0.0004 (0.009)
C_{14}	-0.0065 (0.005)	0.0031 (0.008)	-0.0008 (0.006)	-0.0085 (0.008)
C_{22}	0.8656*** (0.119)	0.6438*** (0.179)	0.8914*** (0.203)	1.3662*** (0.447)
C_{23}	0.0031 (0.005)	0.0038 (0.010)	-0.00001 (0.010)	-0.0061 (0.008)
C_{24}	-0.0034 (0.005)	-0.0117 (0.017)	0.0003 (0.005)	-0.0152** (0.007)
C_{33}	0.0885*** (0.012)	0.0841*** (0.014)	0.0945*** (0.022)	0.1224*** (0.032)
C_{34}	0.0152*** (0.005)	0.0163* (0.009)	0.0128 (0.008)	0.0222 (0.014)

continues on following page

Table 3. Continued

	Full period	Crash period	Pandemic period	Vaccination period
C_{44}	0.0747*** (0.010)	0.0717*** (0.012)	0.0563*** (0.015)	0.1030*** (0.026)
B	0.9455*** (0.010)	0.9622*** (0.010)	0.9501*** (0.018)	0.9188*** (0.039)
a	0.2364*** (0.022)	0.1953*** (0.039)	0.2160*** (0.051)	0.1649*** (0.056)
Log Likelihood	-7240.376	-1539.514	-1532.338	-1511.766
Li – McLeod(20)	337.255 [0.204]	340.342 [0.186]	322.452 [0.451]	329.989 [0.338]

Note: *Li–McLeod* is the Li and McLeod's multivariate portmanteau test on standardized residuals. *, **, and *** show the statistical significance level at ten, five, and one percent, respectively. The standard errors and p-values are given in parenthesis and square brackets, respectively.

Table 4. The estimation results of the Scalar-BEKK GARCH (1,1) model for BTC, ETH, JPY, and CNY

	Full period	Crash period	Pandemic period	Vaccination period
$\alpha 1$	0.1323 (0.131)	-0.4679* (0.244)	0.5809* (0.306)	0.1105 (0.309)
$\alpha 2$	0.1930 (0.177)	-0.7832** (0.388)	0.8975** (0.430)	0.3682 (0.368)
$\alpha 3$	0.0147 (0.113)	0.0134 (0.026)	0.0039 (0.028)	0.0399* (0.022)
$\alpha 4$	-0.0097 (0.007)	0.0157 (0.018)	-0.0387** (0.017)	-0.0043 (0.010)
C_{11}	1.1798*** (0.222)	0.7942*** (0.195)	1.3105*** (0.392)	1.2575 (0.769)
C_{12}	1.2768*** (0.229)	1.1664*** (0.224)	1.4919*** (0.488)	1.2679* (0.765)
C_{13}	-0.0049 (0.006)	0.0005 (0.010)	-0.036** (0.017)	0.0130 (0.010)
C_{14}	-0.0012 (0.003)	0.0015 (0.007)	-0.0081 (0.008)	-0.0004 (0.003)
C_{22}	0.8915*** (0.135)	0.6777*** (0.173)	1.2252*** (0.372)	1.0239 (0.699)
C_{23}	0.0033 (0.004)	-0.0048 (0.010)	0.0154 (0.010)	-0.0014 (0.007)
C_{24}	-0.0034 (0.005)	-0.0050 (0.007)	-0.0145 (0.015)	-0.0016 (0.006)
C_{33}	0.0962*** (0.013)	0.0871*** (0.013)	0.1268*** (0.037)	0.0950* (0.055)

continues on following page

Table 4. Continued

	Full period	*Crash period*	*Pandemic period*	*Vaccination period*
C_{34}	0.0018 (0.0037)	-0.0006 (0.007)	0.0022 (0.010)	0.0030 (0.004)
C_{44}	0.0614*** (0.008)	0.0585*** (0.010)	0.0849*** (0.025)	0.0448 (0.002)
B	0.9472*** (0.010)	0.9548*** (0.009)	0.9302*** (0.036)	0.9544*** (0.053)
a	0.2153*** (0.019)	0.2211*** (0.038)	0.1741*** (0.054)	0.1260* (0.068)
Log Likelihood	-7026.917	-1482.002	-1499.872	-1390.104
Li – McLeod(20)	339.126 [0.294]	328.094 [0.336]	343.151 [0.178]	353.870 [0.094]

Note: *Li – McLeod* is the Li and McLeod's multivariate portmanteau test on standardized residuals. *, **, and *** show the statistical significance level at ten, five, and one percent, respectively. The standard errors and p-values are given in parenthesis and square brackets, respectively.

Empirical findings show that the conditional covariance between the crypto- and fiat currencies differs by the crypto-fiat pairs and the periods. For instance, the models estimate negative conditional covariances between Bitcoin and the fiat currencies of the developed economies during the full period, while those covariances turn to be positive in the case of including Ethereum in the model rather than Bitcoin for the same period. Furthermore, for developed economies, there are negative conditional covariances between Bitcoin and the fiat currencies for the full period; however, those covariances also turn out to be positive in the course of the 2018 cryptocurrency crash and the vaccination period, except British Pound. The conditional covariances between Ethereum and the fiat currencies of the developed economies are negative only for the vaccination period. For emerging economies, the estimation results broadly mimic the empirical findings for the developed economies, with some exceptions. The conditional covariances between Bitcoin and the fiat currencies of the developed economies are estimated to be negative for the Covid-19 pandemic period; similarly, those covariances between Bitcoin and the fiat currencies of the emerging economies are also found to be negative for the same period. However, the first results are statistically significant at the one percent level while the latter results are not. To check the robustness of the results, the authors use Litecoin and Ripple in the model. The results of the Scalar-BEKK GARCH (1,1) model for Litecoin, Ripple, Euro, and Chinese Yuan are similar to the previous estimation results.

The authors provide the time series plots of the conditional covariances to explicitly put forward the time-varying linkages between the crypto- and fiat currencies. Figure 5 shows the conditional covariance between Bitcoin and the fiat currencies of the developed economies (in the left panel) and the covariances between Ethereum and those fiat currencies (in the right panel). The most striking result is a sharp and massive decline in the conditional covariances between the cryptos and the fiat currencies of the developed economies except the Japanese Yen at the onset of the Covid-19 pandemic. What is surprising is that the conditional covariances between the cryptos and the Japanese Yen exhibit a sudden increase at the beginning of the pandemic. A possible explanation for this result might be the appreciation of the Japanese Yen against the US dollar at the outset of the pandemic.

Figure 5. The conditional covariance between the cryptos and the fiat currencies for developed economies

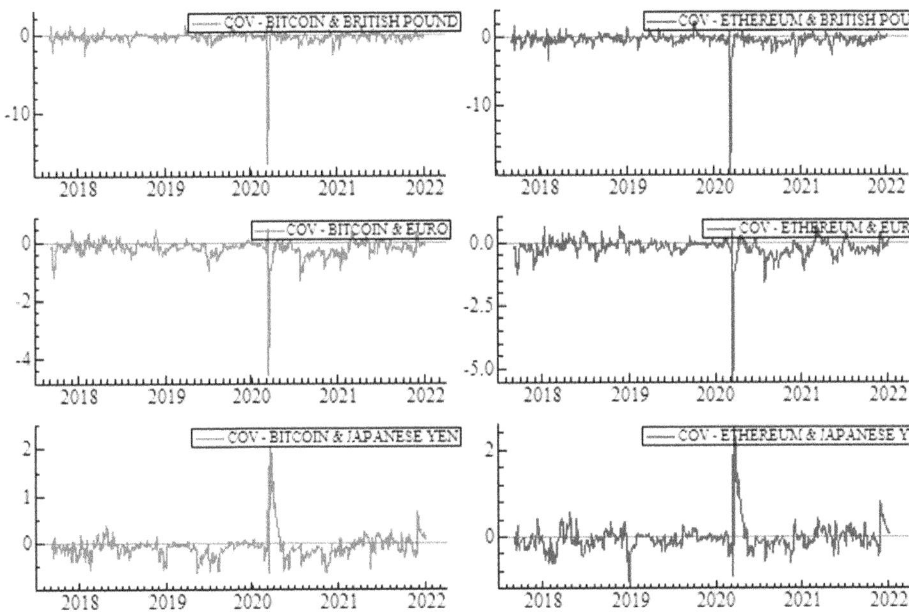

Figure 6 provides the conditional covariance between Bitcoin and the fiat currencies of the emerging economies (in the left panel) and the covariances between Ethereum and those fiat currencies (in the right panel). Similar to the results for the developed economies, there is also a sudden fall in the conditional covariances between the cryptos and the fiat currencies of the emerging economies at the onset of the pandemic. Compared to the developed economies, the conditional covariances for the emerging economies fluctuate more over time, and they do not exhibit stable patterns. It seems possible that this result is due to the fragile structure of the foreign exchanges of emerging economies. These results suggest that the course of the conditional covariance differs by the cryptocurrencies, and the country-specific dynamics are effective in the time-varying linkages between the crypto- and fiat currencies. For the interested readers, Figure 7 and Figure 8 provide the time series plots of the conditional correlations between the crypto- and fiat currencies for the developed and emerging economies in Appendix 2, respectively.

Figure 6. The conditional covariance between the cryptos and the fiat currencies for emerging economies

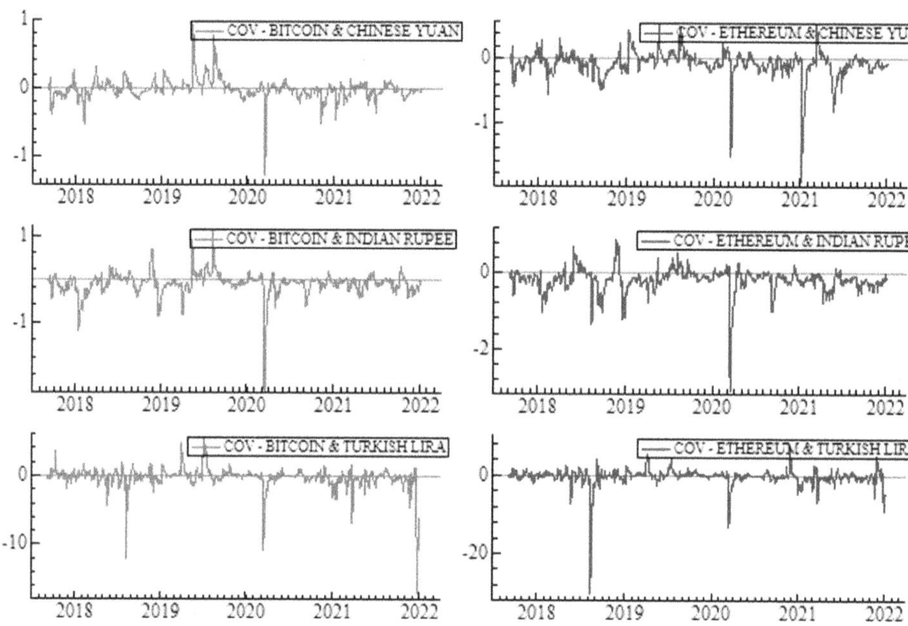

CONCLUSION

This study examines the dynamic connectedness between the major cryptocurrencies and the foreign exchange rates of selected developed and emerging countries against the U.S. dollar. For this purpose, the authors benefit from a Scalar-BEKK GARCH model, as a multivariate GARCH model, with various specifications for different periods. Aside from the full period, the authors also estimate the models for the sub-periods, which are the Great crypto crash, the Covid-19 pandemic, and the vaccination, to consider possible effects of specific events on time-varying linkages among cryptos and fiat currencies. Besides, this study uses two well-known altcoins, Litecoin and Ripple, instead of Bitcoin and Ethereum to check the robustness of the estimation results. Overall, empirical results show that the dynamic relationships between the crypto- and fiat currencies differ by the crypto-fiat pairs and the periods analyzed. Those relationships are highly dependent on both the country- and crypto-specific dynamics. The empirical findings suggest a sharp and massive decline in the conditional covariances between the cryptos and the developed economies' fiat currencies other than the Japanese Yen at the beginning of the Covid-19 pandemic. In addition, likely due to the fragile structure of the foreign exchanges of emerging economies, the conditional covariances between the cryptos and the emerging countries' fiat currencies fluctuate more over time. They do not exhibit stable patterns in comparison with developed economies. These findings should doubtless be much scrutinized; however, by the decentralized nature of the cryptocurrencies, it is not an easy venture to either define the stylized facts on the dynamic linkages between the cryptos and fiat currencies or ex-ante predict those time-varying relationships. It might be possible to use either a different set of currencies or other multivariate time-series models to scrutinize the dynamic linkages among cryptos and fiat currencies in future research. Further research might also incorporate several macro-financial control variables into empirical models to take into account probable direct and indirect effects of those on the time-varying connectedness among cryptos and fiat currencies. The empirical results of this study will benefit portfolio managers, global investors, hedgers, and policymakers seeking to understand the dynamic interactions between cryptocurrencies and exchange rates, especially during the recent crisis arising from the Covid-19 pandemic.

REFERENCES

Baumöhl, E. (2019). Are cryptocurrencies connected to forex? A quantile cross-spectral approach. *Finance Research Letters*, *29*, 363–372. doi:10.1016/j.frl.2018.09.002

Baur, D. G., Dimpfl, T., & Kuck, K. (2018). Bitcoin, gold and the US dollar – a replication and extension. *Finance Research Letters*, *25*, 103–110. doi:10.1016/j.frl.2017.10.012

Bauwens, L., Laurent, S., & Rombouts, J. V. (2006). Multivariate Garch Models: A survey. *Journal of Applied Econometrics*, *21*(1), 79–109. doi:10.1002/jae.842

Boffelli, S., & Urga, G. (2016). *Financial econometrics using stata*. Stata Press.

Bollerslev, T., Engle, R. F., & Wooldridge, J. M. (1988). A capital asset pricing model with time-varying covariances. *Journal of Political Economy*, *96*(1), 116–131. doi:10.1086/261527

Chemkha, R., BenSaïda, A., & Ghorbel, A. (2021). Connectedness between cryptocurrencies and foreign exchange markets: Implication for Risk Management. *Journal of Multinational Financial Management*, *59*, 100666. doi:10.1016/j.mulfin.2020.100666

Degiannakis, S., Duffy, D., & Filis, G. (2014). Business Cycle Synchronization in EU: A Time-varying approach. *Scottish Journal of Political Economy*, *61*(4), 348–370. doi:10.1111jpe.12049

Elsayed, A. H., Gozgor, G., & Lau, C. K. (2020). Causality and dynamic spillovers among cryptocurrencies and currency markets. *International Journal of Finance & Economics*, *27*(2), 2026–2040. doi:10.1002/ijfe.2257

Engle, R. F., & Kroner, K. F. (1995). Multivariate simultaneous generalized arch. *Econometric Theory*, *11*(1), 122–150. doi:10.1017/S0266466600009063

Hsu, S., Sheu, C., & Yoon, J. (2021). Risk spillovers between cryptocurrencies and traditional currencies and gold under different global economic conditions. *The North American Journal of Economics and Finance*, *57*, 101443. doi:10.1016/j.najef.2021.101443

Kostika, E., & Laopodis, N. T. (2019). Dynamic linkages among cryptocurrencies, exchange rates and global equity markets. *Studies in Economics and Finance*, *37*(2), 243–265. doi:10.1108/SEF-01-2019-0032

Kristjanpoller, W., & Bouri, E. (2019). Asymmetric multifractal cross-correlations between the main world currencies and the main cryptocurrencies. *Physica A*, *523*, 1057–1071. doi:10.1016/j.physa.2019.04.115

Liu, Y., & Tsyvinski, A. (2021). Risks and returns of cryptocurrency. *Review of Financial Studies*, *34*(6), 2689–2727. doi:10.1093/rfs/hhaa113

McAleer, M., Chan, F., Hoti, S., & Lieberman, O. (2008). Generalized autoregressive conditional correlation. *Econometric Theory*, *24*(6), 1554–1583. doi:10.1017/S0266466608080614

McLeod, A. I., & Li, W. K. (1983). Diagnostic checking ARMA time series models using squared-residual autocorrelations. *Journal of Time Series Analysis*, *4*(4), 269–273. doi:10.1111/j.1467-9892.1983.tb00373.x

Palazzi, R. B., Júnior, G. D., & Klotzle, M. C. (2021). The dynamic relationship between Bitcoin and the foreign exchange market: A nonlinear approach to test causality between Bitcoin and currencies. *Finance Research Letters*, *42*, 101893. doi:10.1016/j.frl.2020.101893

Popper, N. (2016). *Digital Gold: Bitcoin and the inside story of the misfits and millionaires trying to reinvent money*. Harper.

Raza, S. A., Ahmed, M., & Aloui, C. (2022). On the asymmetrical connectedness between cryptocurrencies and foreign exchange markets: Evidence from the nonparametric quantile on quantile approach. *Research in International Business and Finance*, *61*, 101627. doi:10.1016/j.ribaf.2022.101627

Selgin, G. (2015). Synthetic Commodity Money. *Journal of Financial Stability*, *17*, 92–99. doi:10.1016/j.jfs.2014.07.002

Tastan, H. (2006). Estimating time-varying conditional correlations between stock and foreign exchange markets. *Physica A*, *360*(2), 445–458. doi:10.1016/j.physa.2005.06.062

Umar, Z., & Gubareva, M. (2020). A Time–frequency analysis of the impact of the COVID-19 induced panic on the volatility of currency and cryptocurrency markets. *Journal of Behavioral and Experimental Finance*, *28*, 100404. doi:10.1016/j.jbef.2020.100404 PMID:32983899

Urquhart, A., & Zhang, H. (2019). Is bitcoin a hedge or safe haven for currencies? an intraday analysis. *International Review of Financial Analysis*, *63*, 49–57. doi:10.1016/j.irfa.2019.02.009

Walther, T., Klein, T., & Bouri, E. (2019). Exogenous drivers of Bitcoin and cryptocurrency volatility – a mixed data sampling approach to forecasting. *Journal of International Financial Markets, Institutions and Money*, *63*, 101133. doi:10.1016/j.intfin.2019.101133

Yermack, D. (2015). Is bitcoin a real currency? an economic appraisal. Handbook of Digital Currency, 31-43. doi:10.1016/B978-0-12-802117-0.00002-3

Yi, S., Xu, Z., & Wang, G. (2018). Volatility connectedness in the cryptocurrency market: Is bitcoin a dominant cryptocurrency? *International Review of Financial Analysis*, *60*, 98–114. doi:10.1016/j.irfa.2018.08.012

KEY TERMS AND DEFINITIONS

Altcoin: An abbreviation of the words of "alternative" and "coin" and used to define all cryptocurrencies other than Bitcoin.

Bitcoin: The most well-known and original cryptocurrency introduced by an anonymous person or group named Satoshi Nakamoto in 2009 as a "peer-to-peer electronic payment method".

Covariance: A measure of a directional relationship between two random variables. A positive covariance shows that those variables move together while a negative one indicates an inverse relationship.

Covid-19: A very contagious respiratory illness caused by the SARS-CoV-2 virus and discovered in December 2019 in Wuhan, China.

Cryptocurrency: A digital or virtual currency secured by cryptography, used encryption to verify transactions, and based on decentralized networks instead of reliant on any central authority.

Fiat Currency: A government-issued currency (or national currency) declared to be legal tender and not pegged to the price of any commodity such as gold or silver.

Pandemic: A spread of a new infectious disease across a large region or worldwide and affecting a plenty number of individuals, e.g. the Covid-19 pandemic.

Vaccination: An act of needle injection of a vaccine prepared with a killed microbe to stimulate or help the immune system against a disease.

APPENDIX 1

Table 5. The results of the Augmented Dickey-Fuller and Phillips-Perron unit root tests

	T-statistic	**Test critical value %1 level**	**Test critical value %5 level**	**Test critical value %10 level**	**p-value***
Trend and intercept in test equation (ADF)					
EUR	-30.2626	-3.96618	-3.41379	-3.12897	0.0000
JPY	-31.5232	-3.96618	-3.41379	-3.12897	0.0000
GBP	-32.9769	-3.96618	-3.41379	-3.12897	0.0000
INR	-33.6578	-3.96618	-3.41379	-3.12897	0.0000
CNY	-34.8165	-3.96618	-3.41379	-3.12897	0.0000
TRY	-21.8064	-3.96620	-3.41380	-3.12897	0.0000
BTC	-35.0670	-3.96618	-3.41379	-3.12897	0.0000
ETH	-22.8318	-3.96619	-3.41379	-3.12897	0.0000
LTC	-32.7507	-3.96618	-3.41379	-3.12897	0.0000
XRP	-32.4745	-3.96618	-3.41379	-3.12897	0.0000
Trend and intercept in test equation (PP)					
EUR	-30.1385	-3.96618	-3.41379	-3.12897	0.0000
JPY	-31.6505	-3.96618	-3.41379	-3.12897	0.0000
GBP	-32.9809	-3.96618	-3.41379	-3.12897	0.0000
INR	-33.6813	-3.96618	-3.41379	-3.12897	0.0000
CNY	-34.8443	-3.96618	-3.41379	-3.12897	0.0000
TRY	-32.6937	-3.96618	-3.41379	-3.12897	0.0000
BTC	-35.0481	-3.96618	-3.41379	-3.12897	0.0000
ETC	-35.8047	-3.96618	-3.41379	-3.12897	0.0000
LTC	-32.7951	-3.96618	-3.41379	-3.12897	0.0000
XRP	-32.7943	-3.96618	-3.41379	-3.12897	0.0000

Table 6. The estimation results of the Scalar-BEKK GARCH (1,1) model for LTC, XRP, Euro, and CNY

	Full period	*Crash period*	*Pandemic period*	*Vaccination period*
$\alpha 1$	-0.1092 (0.186)	-1.0131*** (0.362)	0.6834* (0.404)	0.0001 (0.437)
$\alpha 2$	-0.0884 (0.174)	-0.8415* (0.447)	0.1311 (0.338)	0.1485 (0.466)
$\alpha 3$	0.0130 (0.010)	0.0359 (0.026)	-0.0690** (0.028)	0.0251 (0.022)
$\alpha 4$	-0.0071 (0.006)	0.0161 (0.017)	-0.0600** (0.023)	-0.0053 (0.010)
C_{11}	1.5243*** (0.309)	1.6303*** (0.398)	5.8437*** (1.079)	1.2340*** (0.470)
C_{12}	1.2023*** (0.272)	1.6242*** (0.430)	3.8215*** (0.965)	1.0698** (0.454)
C_{13}	-0.0050 (0.005)	0.0078 (0.015)	-0.0957** (0.046)	-0.0027 (0.007)
C_{14}	-0.0036 (0.003)	0.0031 (0.009)	-0.0173 (0.022)	-0.0034 (0.003)
C_{22}	1.0315*** (0.334)	0.8980*** (0.258)	2.0134*** (0.387)	0.7377** (0.382)
C_{23}	0.0042 (0.005)	0.0024 (0.016)	0.0567 (0.045)	-0.0054 (0.005)
C_{24}	0.0048 (0.003)	0.0028 (0.008)	0.0332 (0.025)	-0.0012 (0.004)
C_{33}	0.0844*** (0.017)	0.1184*** (0.028)	0.3714*** (0.038)	0.0613** (0.024)
C_{34}	0.0149*** (0.005)	0.0255** (0.010)	0.0697*** (0.024)	0.0087 (0.007)
C_{44}	0.0563*** (0.011)	0.0686*** (0017)	0.2198*** (0.029)	0.0285** (0.012)
B	0.9430*** (0.016)	0.9260*** (0.027)	0.4318*** (0.115)	0.9700*** (0.018)
a	0.2625*** (0.035)	0.2955*** (0.070)	0.8826*** (0.206)	0.1699*** (0.048)
Log Likelihood	-7596.474	-1602.766	-1648.737	-1543.602
$Li-McLeod(20)$	323.426 [0.425]	337.996 [0.234]	343.675 [0.116]	310.613 [0.636]

Note: $Li-McLeod$ is the Li and McLeod's multivariate portmanteau test on standardized residuals. *, **, and *** show the statistical significance level at ten, five, and one percent, respectively. The standard errors and p-values are given in parenthesis and square brackets, respectively.

APPENDIX 2

Figure 7. The conditional correlation between the cryptos and the fiat currencies for developed economies

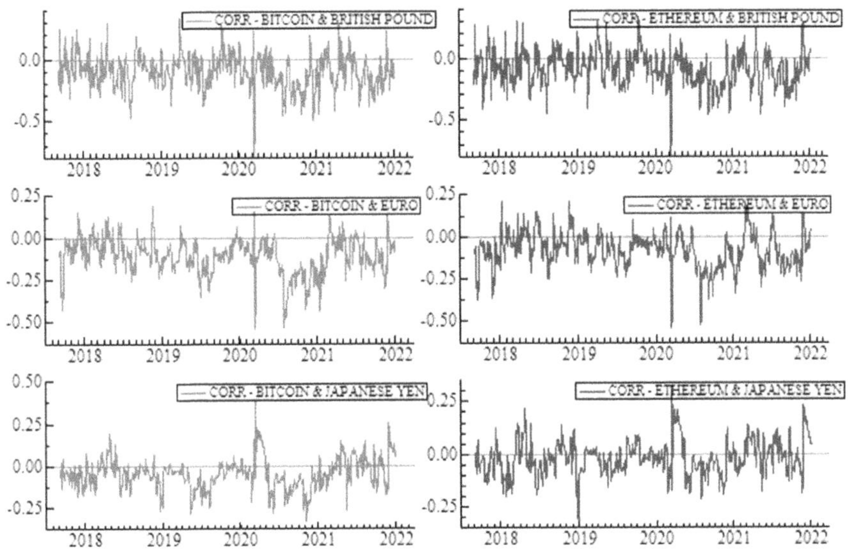

Figure 8. The conditional correlation between the cryptos and the fiat currencies for emerging economies

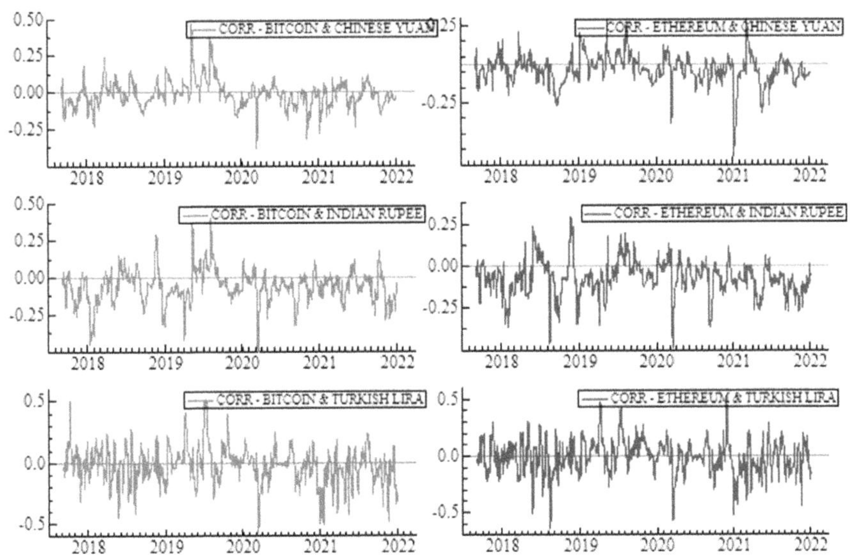

Chapter 7
Cryptocurrency May Prove Financial Crime:
A Conceptual Analysis

Sathish Kumar S.
SRM Institute of Science and Technology, India

S. Thowseaf
Centre for Distance and Online Education, India

ABSTRACT

Despite the rise in Bitcoin scams, there is a lack of thorough research on the subject. Sophisticated scammers and money launderers can take advantage of Bitcoin mixing services and exchanges. Bitcoin mixing services will send more coins to the customer's address after deducting the mixing cost. The frequency and amount of payments/fees may seem unpredictable, but this is the reality. Criminals use bitcoin mixing services to disguise the source of lost profits and pay securely through cryptocurrency exchanges for anonymous use. Bitcoin's normative unpredictability and organizational opacity attract people with shady intentions, such as supporting rebels or buying drugs. The results of this scoping study show that investigations into cryptocurrency fraud are increasing in scope and depth, but are in the early stages of examining future concerns and circumstances.

DOI: 10.4018/978-1-6684-5691-0.ch007

INTRODUCTION

Cryptocurrency Intelligence (2021) Bitcoin was launched in 2009. Because cryptocurrencies are new and unregulated, the government faces significant legal and financial issues. Establish effective defences against emerging online currency hazards or restrict their development and use? Few governments have proclaimed a legislative plan to include Bitcoin and other cryptocurrencies in the regulatory framework, despite doubt about the benefits and risks to the financial system's integrity. Bitcoin traders should be aware of its risks and volatility.

Cryptocurrencies are encoded digital money that prevents counterfeiting and duplicate payments. Blockchain technology is a distributed ledger managed by a network of computers. As cryptocurrencies aren't issued by governments, they may be immune to official influence and manipulation.

Bitcoin's characteristics may make it difficult to tackle money laundering and terrorist financing if they aren't controlled. rather than assessing the hazard. While widespread bitcoin abuse is unlikely, there are signs it may be occurring more often. As more customers are pushed into stealing important information or paying a Bitcoin ransom, the absence of proper regulation makes procedures rigid.

In light of this, it's simple to see why governments should be pro-Bitcoin. By applying current rules to cryptocurrencies or establishing new legislation to oversee the virtual market, keeping the public in the dark about Bitcoins might leave governments woefully unprepared to defend their economies from the perils of handling uncontrolled and unconfirmed cash.

A Primer on Cryptocurrencies

Trozze, Arianna, and Kamps (2022) Decentralization, pseudo-anonymity, and openness are the three pillars on which cryptocurrencies like Bitcoin and others are built. They are considered decentralised since, rather than being governed by a single organisation, they are administered through a peer-to-peer network. Most participants in this network are required to come to an agreement regarding which transactions and sections of a distributed virtual ledger (the "blockchain") are authentic. The reason for this is because Bitcoin employs hashes of public keys to identify users rather than usernames or account numbers. This provides a mechanism for "decentralised identity management" that is independent from users' actual identities in the real world.

Even though cryptocurrencies are no longer directly connected with particular people or organisations, they are nevertheless referred to as having a pseudonym since the transactions involving them are completely open and transparent (Meiklejohn et al., 2016). Transparency is achieved as a consequence of the fact that every transaction that has ever taken place is recorded on the blockchain and made available to the public.

Miners, a subset of peers with specialised expertise, gather contemporaneous transactions into a 'block' They compete to find an input to a hash feature that produces a given outcome. After trying various inputs, a miner broadcasts the right one. This is called Proof of Work (PoW) because the challenge demands the miner to squander computer resources.

Fraud Detection and Anti-Money Laundering (AML)

Nhien-An. (2021) Cipher Trace predicts $432 million in crypto thefts, hacks, and scams by April 2021. DeFi (Decentralized Finance) hacks, which were rare before 2019, account for 60% of hacking and larceny. Cryptocurrency might be used for money laundering and terrorism. Iran, which faces economic sanctions, was linked to 72,000 IP addresses. Cipher Trace provides cases of scams, hacks, illicit money transfers, and money laundering. More machine learning and deep learning research identifies connected owners' wallets.

Researcher argued against combining the GCN and random forest approaches. This gives an Elliptic dataset of Bitcoin transactions with a time series graph of over 200k transactions. The abundance of Bitcoin network data makes deep learning and machine learning difficult. Since blockchain is public, a wealth of information is available. Since the Elliptic dataset only provides a snapshot of the blockchain, studying a single wallet's transactions would need access to the whole network.

Cybercriminals mix or tumble cryptocurrencies to obscure where the money comes from. This may be done by having a trustworthy third party accept bitcoin from a smart address and then sending the initial coins to a user-found address. Multiple addresses may be used to make it difficult to locate a person's original address. Figure depicts how a deep autoencoder mixes bitcoin. Experiment has four stages. First, a group action graph was built from 10,000 bitcoin transactions. When two users transact, an edge is created between them. Next, a deep autoencoder is utilised to embed graph nodes into the transaction graph.

The final phase employs clump classification, or fast unfolding, to locate groupings in the graph. Researchers can locate a node willing to mix transactions using an outlier detection step. Overall, it was proven that it is feasible to construct community structures in bitcoin group action graphs, locate bitcoin intermixture services using deep learning approaches, and go beyond previous methods to recognise bitcoin communities. Elliptic has revealed how to follow wallets across the Darknet and combine currency to create new wallets.

Figure 1. Deep Autoencoder Mixes Bitcoin

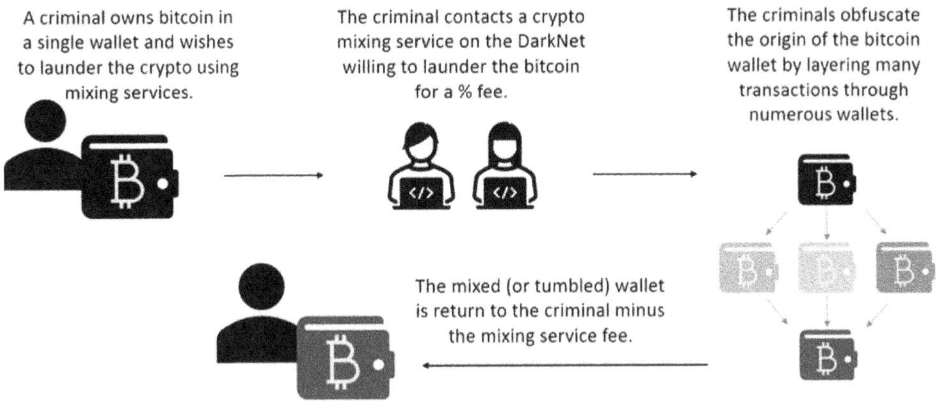

How to Track Patterns in Bitcoin Laundering

Tookitaki (2020) As a crypto-currency that is not a "fiat money," Bitcoin is potentially not subject to the legal requirements of the AML laws. This prevents Bitcoin dealers from being registered as money transmitters, making transactions difficult to trace and monitor for money laundering purposes. In addition, the complexity of Bitcoin protocols and the obscurity of the network are very tempting to individuals with nefarious purposes, such as financing terrorism or purchasing illicit substances.

Occasionally, Bitcoin has been linked to illegal activity. Satoshi Dice is only one example of a tool that facilitates online gambling with bitcoins. In the Gregorian calendar month of 2013, Satoshi Dice was responsible for over half of all Bitcoin transactions. When it came to using bitcoin to purchase illegal drugs, another website known as trade route was a huge assistance (only mode of payment therein website). Despite the fact that the original Silk Road was shut down in 2013, there are still several unregulated markets available via the TOR Browser (or through DarkNet) for these illegal uses of Bitcoins.

Mt Gox, one of the largest Bitcoin exchanges in the world, which processed 70-85% of all Bitcoin transactions in 2013, is a further case of Bitcoin fraud. In February 2014, the company ceased all commercial operations, shut down its website and exchange service, and filed for bankruptcy. In April 2014, it was reported that around 850,000 Bitcoins with a total value of $450 million were stolen from clients.

Bitcoin transactions might be an extremely complex and daunting undertaking. Bitcoin identities do not appear to be explicitly related to real-world individuals or institutions. Similar to cash, Bitcoin transactions do not expressly identify the payer or the recipient and are irreversible. The majority of anti-money laundering specialists say that a major "benefit" of Bitcoin for criminals is that "law societal control confronts challenges in policing questionable behaviour, differentiating users, and obtaining trading records."

Nonetheless, it is crucial that banks and alternative money facilities determine if a client's exchange of Bitcoins for fiat currency corresponds to information recorded from the transaction or other information accessible from public or private databases. Additionally, all Bitcoin ATM suppliers are required to identify and track users that conduct Bitcoin transactions through their systems. This may be done to ensure that consumer transactions adhere to AML and KYC regulations. When their clients engage with Bitcoins (either buying or selling), financial institutions should conduct a client (or improved) due diligence procedure so that possible concealment using Bitcoins may be detected and prevented. These precautions can dissuade Bitcoin consumers and sellers from engaging in money laundering and illegal activity via Bitcoin circulation.

Criminals Use Cryptocurrencies for Money Laundering

Mangion (2022) Criminals use bitcoins to hide unlawful payments. All of these techniques recognise cryptocurrency's flaws while applauding its pseudonymity, cross-border transactions, and peer-to-peer payments. Cryptocurrency hiding is a three-step procedure.

1. **Placement**

In this phase, illegal funds enter the economy via financial institutions, exchanges, stores, and casinos. Cryptocurrencies may be bought using cash or other cryptocurrencies. Bitcoin exchanges allow it. Criminals employ low-AML exchanges for this

2. **Layering**

In this phase, thieves employ structured transactions to hide seizeable cash. This makes tracking illegal currency harder. By manipulating cryptocurrency exchanges, criminals may convert one cryptocurrency into another or participate in an ICO in which one digital currency is paid for with another. Criminals may even move cryptocurrencies abroad.

3. **Integration**

Here, illegal monies are given a basic status. Criminals often utilise over-the-counter (OTC) agents as middlemen between bitcoin buyers and sellers. OTC agents provide cash-laundering services for high commissions.

Crypto Mixing

Mixing services, often called tumblers, allow cryptocurrency users to mix their coins with others'. A typical blending service accepts client cryptos, distributes them to various addresses, then recombines them to create "clean" cryptos.

Peer-to-Peer Crypto Networks

Criminals use decentralised networks to move monies to a distant location, usually outside the country with lax anti-money laundering legislation. These exchangers convert bitcoin to currency to buy luxury goods.

Crypto ATMs

These ATMs let users buy bitcoin using credit or debit cards or currencies. Some ATMs provide crypto-to-coin exchanges. In certain countries, KYC requirements for using these devices are lax.

Money Laundering Using Cryptocurrencies

The expanding use of cryptocurrencies and their unregulated or less-regulated status in a lot of countries is a cause for worry in the money industry. In the digital era, cryptocurrencies are becoming important methods of thinking exchange. Several significant organisations accept digital money for products and services, while others are investigating blockchain technology. Bitcoin might replace paper and plastic money. It's important to analyse the weaknesses that enable these currencies to be exploited for concealment and to develop countermeasures.

Legitimate Uses for Cryptocurrency

Virtual currencies minimise transaction costs and improve payments and transfers. Bitcoin is a worldwide currency that doesn't suffer exchange expenses, is processed cheaper than credit and debit cards, and might enhance online payment systems like PayPal.

Virtual currencies may make micropayments easier and enable companies to monetize extremely cheap internet products and services, such one-time games or music downloads. By eliminating the higher transaction fees associated with typical credit and debit cards, it enables sales at an adequately low per-unit cost.

Additionally, virtual currencies enhance financial inclusion in various ways and enable international remittances. One illustration is the creation of online goods and services to meet the requirements of unbanked people.

Criminals are Exploiting Cryptocurrencies

Joshi, C. M. (2021) Criminals have traditionally been among the first to adopt new technologies, and this is true of cryptocurrencies. As a result, bitcoin is rapidly being used in practically all illicit activities relevant to AML experts.

Fraud: The vast majority of cryptocurrency-related crimes are scams, with criminals making over $2.6 billion in only 2020. Most bitcoin frauds operate similarly to classic investment frauds or Ponzi schemes that exist in the realm of fiat money.

Trafficking: Cryptocurrency is used by dark web marketplaces to make it easier to sell illegal substances, unlicensed weapons, stolen information, and hacking tools.

Terrorism: Terrorist groups have started utilising cryptocurrencies to ask for donations. Additionally, they employ cryptocurrencies to circumvent restrictions.

Extortion: The use of ransomware increased in 2020, with hackers demanding over $400m (£293m) in bitcoin.

Crypto Money-Laundering Stages

Entry: Criminals purchase a basic cryptocurrency, frequently through a middleman with a clear criminal history and verifiable job. By employing pseudo-anonymous e-wallets, utilising pseudonyms, log-less virtual private networks (VPNs), and blockchain-optimized devices, they further separate themselves from the purchase.

Conversion: After the transaction has been confirmed, monies are placed to acquire primary currencies like Bitcoin using fiat cash. These are then used to buy alternative coins on a sophisticated exchange. Some alternative currencies provide a higher level of privacy.

Masking: Then, to deceive the blockchain and obstruct audit traceability, criminals switch main currency addresses for temporary digital wallet addresses using mixing services like Bitmixer.

Washing: Then, to successfully clean up their illicit funds for reintegration into the conventional financial system, thieves overlay many privacy coins, exchanges, and digital addresses.

Withdrawal: Once monies have been cleaned up, criminals remove them, often utilising one of these techniques:

- Burst-out integration is the process by which privacy coin holdings are exchanged for main coins and subsequently converted into a base currency that can be transferred to a linked bank account.
- Digital assets are moved to a physical cryptocurrency wallet or printed out QR codes that may be delivered to anybody in the globe.

Rise of Financial Crimes in Cryptocurrencies

Financial and monetary systems (2021) Rising attractiveness of cryptocurrencies and the privateness blessings that cryptocurrencies are offering, are not hidden from criminals. They use cryptocurrencies which include Bitcoin for numerous purposes. Some of them consist of laundering grimy money, defrauding investors, monetizing ransomware, or shopping for illicit goods.

For years, reviews have additionally advised that famous terrorist corporations have been the usage of cryptocurrencies you acquire funding. In fact, the sale of unlawful tablets and different sorts of lawbreaking on so-known as darkish markets and procuring them in cryptocurrencies, has skyrocketed over the previous couple of years.

Essentially, this entire improvement across the upward thrust of cryptocurrencies in valid and illegit companies' way that irrespective of wherein you presently take a seat down in today's enterprise world, you're impacted through the economic crime dangers round cryptocurrencies in a few ways.

Bitcoin have become maximum famous, whilst it got here to crime along the emergence of darkish net marketplaces like Silk Road and cybercrime hobby like Ransomware. New sorts of crime required a brand-new technique of fee for working over internet. Bitcoin crammed this gap. In addition, the era is evolving in favour of the customers. These technologies consist of anonymizing technology, mixers and privateness cash that make it more difficult to hint the path of cryptocurrency transactions.

Cryptocurrency Financial Crime Risk Mitigation

Financial and monetary systems (2021) One of the untold tales withinside the universe of cryptocurrencies is simply how powerful AML controls may be almost in mitigating and dealing with risks. Over the beyond few years there was a dramatic lower in the proportion of Bitcoin transactions related to illicit entities.

It is thought that the primary motive for this is the stepped forward great of AML controls and the growing presence of policies associated with cryptocurrencies. So lengthy tale short, the use case of cryptocurrencies is inevitable in today's global and the want for monetary crime hazard and compliance companies to catch-up and overtake cryptocurrency criminals omnipresent.

The first-class and maximum obvious manner to do this, is to teach the modern era of monetary crime experts and provide them the competencies they want to get a maintain of this complicated new universe to in the end increase quite sound AML compliance packages and to higher combat cryptocurrency monetary crimes.

CONCLUSION

Financial and monetary systems (2022) Over $1 billion was lost by 46,000 people in crypto-scams in the 14 months ending in Q1 2022, according to the Federal Trade Commission. The decentralised blockchain infrastructure that cryptocurrencies are largely founded on provides a great playground for currency laundering and cybercriminal exercise because to its privacy-enhancing properties. The number of ransom payments made in cryptocurrency is tracked by the blockchain analytics firm Chain analysis. A total of over $692 million was extorted by ransomware in 2020, according to the company's report for 2022, almost double the amount from the previous year.

A total of around $900 million was found to have been laundered using decentralised finance (DeFi) protocols, and this growth in cryptocurrency laundering by way of these systems was documented by chain analysis. There are benefits to regulation even if cryptocurrency is never used for illicit purposes.

Exciting new information about the current state of regulations and cryptocurrencies was revealed at a recent DIFC Fintech conference.

Approximately 95% of governing bodies currently have a team dedicated to crypto regulations.

The crypto company is campaigning to push for clean regulations, since it regards rules as a high-quality enhancement with a view to accelerate the enterprise.

Over 96% of Finance's user base passed the know-your-consumer (KYC) verifications that were instituted after the global cryptocurrency exchange began requiring them.

The SEC levied around $2.35 billion in general economic repercussions in opposition to virtual asset marketplace participants in 2021.

Sixty-five percent of the SEC's 20 enforcement actions that year had allegations of fraud, eighty percent involved allegations of unregistered securities imparting violations, and 55 percent involved allegations of both.

As it stands, the Financial Action Task Force (FATF) defines "digital asset carrier providers" to include cryptocurrency exchanges, strong coin issuers, DeFi protocols, and NFT markets.

This definition lets set the tone for regulation, with legislative rules and directives following. Therefore, the global prognosis for crypto regulations in the present day is bright and expanding. The United Kingdom and the United States, for instance, are aggressively expanding regulations to oversee cryptocurrencies.

According to the UK's HM Treasury, "HM Treasury expects economic crime and anti-cash laundering requirements to follow to all wallets and issuers, and that those may even have to check in beneath AML [anti-money laundering] registration for their or her activities in terms of all types of crypto-assets." The desire to mainstream bitcoin is likely to spur research towards lowering the cost of storing renewable energy.

Furthermore, the first measures being done by various governments to bring bitcoin into the light should undoubtedly culminate in well-considered legislation for mining cryptocurrencies and punishing violations of environmental standards. To address cryptocurrency sceptics, one oft-repeated argument is that traditional currencies have a high carbon impact as well.

Fiat money has a secondary impact by keeping a large number of financial institution offices, people that use fossil-gas primarily based wholly shipping to go to those places of work, and over five million ATMs worldwide that consume power 24 hours a day, seven days a week. The fact that bitcoin is a much younger generation is typically disregarded in the debate. Bitcoin, like other cryptocurrencies, is evolving, and maturation may take years. It will progressively become more environmentally friendly, owing to the enthusiasm around recent breakthroughs.

Finally, the era will reach equilibrium, resulting in a greater appeal and prompting regulators to integrate it with established financial institutions. We might be only a few regulatory steps away from seeing an increase in the usage of renewable energy for cryptocurrency. Similarly strong is the desire to fundamentally legalise cryptocurrencies. It is already a low-cost alternative for international transactions, and some large banks are leading the way by enabling bitcoin exchanges to act as "remittance and transfer services."

In June, China, which contributed 75% of the world's bitcoin mining capacity, banned the practise. One explanation for the crackdown, according to analysts, is that China is risk-averse and may wish to prevent anything that impedes the spread of the digital yuan on a permissioned blockchain (meaning, the authorities come to a decision who can use the virtual yuan). The most probable reason is that bitcoin mining is impeding China's objective of being carbon-neutral by 2060.

This is spreading across the world. Tata Steel, a big Indian metal conglomerate, is collaborating with HSBC to test smart contracts on the blockchain, moving raw materials all over the globe while shortening contract agreement periods from weeks to days. Consider how much power is packed into the method. The Carbon Utility Token (CUT) is an example of a new class of green assets designed to help businesses manage their carbon permits. Each CUT token sold contributes to investments in carbon capture and offsetting activities, bringing the cryptocurrency ecosystem one step closer to carbon neutrality. As more businesses incorporate Bitcoin and other cryptocurrencies to their balance sheets, it is important to remember that CUT offers a way to entirely offset the carbon footprint associated with each currency.

While there will be hurdles, crypto and blockchain can bring us to a significantly greener society, with discussions about crypto and energy motivating us to speed our transition to renewable energy sources and providing us with the means to do so.

REFERENCES

CCI. (2021). *Cryptocurrency Crime and Anti-Money Laundering Report.* Ciphertrace Cryptocurrency Intelligence.

CRSIL. (2017). *Bitcoin: Currency of the future or money laundering vehicle*. Lead Analyst, Financial Crime and Compliance Analytics.

How blockchain and cryptocurrency can create a greener future. (n.d.). World Economic Forum. https://www.weforum.org/agenda/2021/06/how-blockchain-and-cryptocurrencies-can-help-build-a-greener-future/

How to make cryptocurrency sustainable. (n.d.). World Economic Forum. https://www.weforum.org/agenda/2021/11/how-to-make-bitcoin-and-cryptocurrency-sustainable-renewable-energy-blockchain-crypto-mining/

Joshi, C. M. (2021, March 18). Crypto Currency Financial Crime Risk. *Indiaforensic*. https://indiaforensic.com/certifications/crypto-currency-financial-crime-risk/

Mangion, D. (2021). Cryptocurrency Money Laundering Risks. Cryptocurrency Money Laundering Risks. *Skillcast*. https://www.skillcast.com/blog/cryptocurrency-money-laundering-risks

Money Laundering via Cryptocurrencies: All You Need to Know. (2020). Tookitaki. https://www.tookitaki.com/blog/news-views/moneylaundering-via-cryptocurrencies

Nicholls, Jack & Kuppa, Aditya & Le-Khac, Nhien-An. (2021). *Financial Cybercrime: A Comprehensive Survey of Deep Learning Approaches to Tackle the Evolving Financial Crime Landscape.* IEEE Access. . doi:10.1109/ACCESS.2021.3134076

Trozze, A., Kamps, J., Akartuna, E., Hetzel, F., Kleinberg, B., Davies, T., & Johnson, S. (2022). Cryptocurrencies and future financial crime. *Crime Science*, *11*(1), 1. doi:10.118640163-021-00163-8 PMID:35013699

Why the crypto industry needs to be AML and KYC compliant. (2022). World Economic Forum. https://www.weforum.org/agenda/2022/09/why-crypto-businesses-need-anti-money-laundering-regulations/

Chapter 8
Digital Currencies and Their Relationship Towards Economic Instability

Naveenraj X.
https://orcid.org/0000-0003-2681-5964
SRM Institute of Science and Technology, India

Ramya J.
SRM Institute of Science and Technology, India

ABSTRACT

The widespread rise in popularity of cryptocurrencies over the past few years has the potential to have sparked new revolutions in the global ecosystem. The investors face both new opportunities and challenges as a result of this ecosystem. The modern era makes it simple for people to make financial decisions regarding investments, payments, and other financial services via the internet. This development in technology makes it easier for inventors to create and process crypto currencies around the world. Decentralization is the fundamental principle of digital currency. Financial regulations and control are virtually non-existent for digital currencies. As a result, investors are increasingly using it as a decentralized financial instrument. Investors can use it to conduct unregulated financial transactions from one location to any location worldwide. Digital currencies also cause financial instability, despite growth and gains. Every nation in the world faces a serious threat as a result of financial instability.

DOI: 10.4018/978-1-6684-5691-0.ch008

INTRODUCTION

The global interest in Central Bank Digital Currencies, or CBDCs, is now widespread. They have emerged as an essential component of the conversation regarding the digitalization of financial prudence, which includes the rapid shifts in the background of payments and the character of money itself. CBDCs are increasingly being viewed as the succeedingphase in the evolution of (fiat) money - from shells and cowries to coins and paper money and now digital demonstrations of fiat currencies. (Barontini & Holden, 2019) BIS's 2020 Annual Economic Report. The introduction of CBDCs is being considered by numerous central banks worldwide. Some of them have made significant progress. Digital versions of their respective sovereign currencies have been piloted by Sweden and China, both of which are major advanced economies and major emerging markets and developing economies (EMDEs). The Bahamas became the first nation in the domain to produce a digital currency for retail use from its central bank the "Sand Dollar" in October 2020. The Eastern Caribbean Currency Union was the primary currency amalgamation central bank to issue DCash, a blockchain-based digital variety of the Eastern Caribbean Dollar.

The ramifications of CBDCs generally were briefly discussed in a report from an Inter-Ministerial Committee in India, which included the central bank of India among its members. (Report of the Interministerial Committee, 2019) While noting that the benefits of adopting CBDCs in the context of India were unknown, it nevertheless advised keeping an open mind about doing so in the future. Additionally, the Reserve Bank of India (RBI), the country's central bank, is apparently developing a model for CBDCs and a gradual rollout.(Sankar, 2021). The RBI is also expected to issue an Indian CBDC, or a "digital rupee", in the financial year 2022-23. (Moneycontrol, 2022). However, there is relatively less information available in public domain about RBI's detailed thinking on this subject. It is in this background that this chapter scrutinize the outline of bring together a CBDC in India.

What are CBDCs?

In order to define CBDCs, the Bank for International Settlements (BIS) compares them to several types of central bank money that are currently in use. in contrast to the balances in conventional reserve or settlement accounts, as "a digital form of central bank money."

Based on the issuer's identity (central bank vs. private enterprises) and form, the aforementioned broad definition (digital vs. physical). In addition to this broad description, the BIS goes on to categorise various CBDCs based on two other criteria: technology (account or token based) and accessibility (limited, like current central bank reserves, or unrestricted access, like cash). They are:

- A token-based "general purpose" CBDC that is primarily used for retail transactions but might be used for other purposes as well.
- A token-based "wholesale" CBDC that is only utilised for wholesale settlement and payment transactions.
- An easily accessible account-based "general purpose" CBDC.

The criteria that these other definitions of CBDCs highlight depend, among other things, on the focus of their research and experimentation or the centrality of certain features to the definition of CBDCs. These definitions are in addition to the BIS definition. CBDCs, for instance, are "an electronic form of central bank money that could be used by households and businesses to make payments and store value," according to the Bank of England. That is, retail access is the sole focus (Bank of England, 2020).CBDCs are referred to as "a legal tender and a central bank liability in digital form, denominated in sovereign currency and appearing on central bank balance sheet," as defined by the RBI. According to them (RBI, 2021), CBDCs are a type of electronic currency that can be exchanged for cash in a similar amount and conventional central bank deposits.

The International Monetary Fund (IMF) addressed concerns regarding CBDCs' potential to disintermediate the banking system in yet another definition or design. The synthetic CBDC, or CBDC, basically replicates or maintains the current two-tier architecture of the monetary and payments system by allowing private sector entities to issue the currency or payment instruments (like stable coins) that represent their liabilities and backing them with central bank reserves. However, the BIS and seven other central banks, including the Federal Reserve and the European Central Bank, rejected a CBDC as a genuine CBDC in a report published last year. Instead, they define CBDCs solely as a digital payment instrument that is a direct liability of the central bank and is denominated in the national unit of account and the Bank of Canadaal., 2020) CBDCs could be constructed in any of the following ways:

- A direct CBDC, where the central bank is entirely in charge, from issuance to maintenance of ledger and compliance with laws.
- A hybrid CBDC, where the CBDC represents a direct claim on the central bank, like cash, and the private sector would continue to focus on offering customer-facing services such as on boarding, KYC, execution of payments etc. The central bank would retain a copy of all retail CBDC holdings and also have both the technical and legal ability to transfer customers from one PSP to another in cases of insolvency or other failures. (Annual Economic Report, BIS, 2020)
- An intermediated CBDC, a nuanced variation of the hybrid model in which the private sector would retain full ownership of the retail ledger and the

central bank would have no access to it. In addition, CBDCs could either carry no interest like cash or interest like stocks and bonds. Finally, regardless of whether the underlying technology is proposed to be block chain-based, the majority of research at this point appears to be technology agnostic.

As a result, CBDCs do not yet have a common design or definition across jurisdictions. In order to either capitalize on potential innovations (such as interest-bearing CBDCs that can help transmit monetary policy transmission directly) or mitigate potential disruptions (such as indirect or synthetic CBDCs that replicate existing two-tier architecture), definitions or descriptions of CBDCs differ based on certain core features like issuing authority, access, technology, or design elements. The aforementioned discussions make it abundantly clear that the CBDCs are in fact an institutional design. In addition, depending on the particulars of the design, they will alter the nature of money and, not surprisingly, have a number of effects on the economy. Evidently, policymakers are deeply concerned about whether CBDCs should be implemented.

History of CBDC

Over the period with the development of technology and augmented practice of the electronic money, Central Bank is confronted with a choice to announce a CBDC to reinforce their monetary power. They have been underneath heaviness to answer back to the encounters posed by cryptocurrency and to progress the effectiveness of the prevailing payment system (Ward and Rochemont, 2019). Interest in CBDC was born in 2008 with the financial predicament and the occurrence of cryptocurrency and the decline in the practice of cash. Many countries have started exploring the CBDC area and have launched pilot programs like Sweden's central Bank has launched a digital currency named e-Krona, when it saw a decline in the use of the cash. Moreover in 2018 only 6 percentage of the total household payments were made in cash. In order to keep pace with the changes in the payments space due to the technological changes and the innovations has made the central banks around the world to think whether they can use the fiat currency in the digital form or not (Javaid). The Cryptocurrency and Regulation of Official Digital Currency Bill, 2021 will provide the Reserve Bank of India (RBI) with legal powers to develop CBDC. On January 25th RBI stated that it is trying to find out if there is a need to introduce a Central Bank Digital Currency (CBDC) in India. If there is a need then the central bank might look for ways to operationalize this.

There are two types of CBDC:

1. **Wholesale CBDC:** Financial Institutions will use this CBDC. It could reduce settlement risk and provide 24/7 availability and reduce cross-border payment costs. Since cross border payments involves many intermediaries, significant cost and add a level of complexity. Wholesale CBDC could help in simplifying the process and aiding in automation (Deloitte, n.d.). These can be used for domestic payments and as well as for cross border payments.
2. **Retail CBDC:** Individuals, household and corporations will use this. It is available to the public and is widely accessible and digital form of fiat currency. If a CBDC is well designed then it could enhance the financial integrity in comparison to cash. According to an article (Today, 2017) it is said that the RBI and other commercial bank spends about 21,000 crore every year on cash management. A researcher of repute (Kosse et al., 2017) mentions that the cost of cash usage in Canada was 0.5 per cent of GDP but another author (BANKA, 2018) had reported that Albania used 1 per cent and Guyana used 2.5 per cent of GDP. In Uruguay private cost of using cash was 0.6 per cent of GDP (Álvez et al., 2020). By devising an effective retail CBDC a decline in cash usage cost could be achieved.

CBDCs From an Indian Perspective

The previous discussions have made it abundantly clear that the establishment of a CBDC is an institutional change that will fundamentally reshape the monetary and financial sector and have repercussions for nearly every sector of the economy. In this context, it is essential to comprehend that such significant institutional changes are gradual and ongoing processes rather than one-time policy changes. Furthermore, path-dependence and "transitional institutions" experimentation have been the foundation of every successful institutional change.

In the Indian framework, gradualism, the use of transitional institutions, and path dependence suggest that rather than making an allowance for an unexpected institutional change to a CBDC-based system, nation need to understand the current institutional preparations, particularly in terms of digital payment systems, and whether there are solid arguments to move ahead to CBDCs, given the strong point and faults of the current system.

The Indian financial and monetary systems were primarily bank-based, with cash and bank deposits serving as forms of currency. Bank-generated money served as the foundation for digital transactions. In the past ten years or so, this payments infrastructure has undergone significant transformation, with India emerging as a leader in the development of digital payment systems. In 2007, the National Payments Corporation of India (NPCI), a not-for-profit organization supported by a large number of private and public sector banks, was established. The NPCI developed a number of products that aid in retail payment for a variety of transactions because it was aware of the economy's diverse requirements. The Universal Payment Interface (UPI), a real-time payments system that enables the instantaneous transfer of funds between two banks using a mobile device, has been the game-changer in this sector. Apps like Google Pay, Paytm, and PhonePe have greatly increased the use of digital payments thanks to this platform. The RBI has also been motivated to implement a more market-based "for-prof it" addition to the NCPI as a result of its rapid success in the digital payments sector. This is expected to be a group of private businesses known as the New Umbrella Entity (NUE) that will bring more innovation to the payments industry. It is evident that the Indian Central Bank has been actively supporting the growth of the digital payments sector even without the CBDCs.

An important feature is that this initiative is clearly market-oriented and aims to grow through the dynamism of the private sector. In countries like China, where CBDCs are supposed to provide a mechanism for the state to control large private payment companies, this vision creates a dilemma for the payment industry to adopt CBDC. In short, the question for India is whether a CBDC is needed if private parties in the payments industry and the banking sector can work together to create an efficient payment system. It is interesting to note that two important reasons for India's CBDC come from outside our domestic context. First, in most countries, the development of national CBDCs and their interoperability are considered to be the main drivers of international trade and payments in the near future. to the main economies of the world. Even the Bank for International Settlements (BIS) is actively interested in countries considering an international perspective when designing their CBDCs. The current cross-border payment system based on the SWIFT platform is increasingly seen as expensive and time-consuming. While India's private sector-based payments system may function adequately, a sovereign-backed digital currency will be the only one that can be reliable in a worldwide system for at least foursome time.

Another important external factor for India is China's strong push to introduce the digital yuan not only as a domestic currency, but also for use in cross-border payments to its trade and investment partner countries. Once the digital yuan is accepted as a global currency, it is only a matter of time before they start flowing into the Indian economy.

This not only raises the possibility of a problem similar to dollarization in the traditional sense, but it also raises serious concerns about data vulnerability. It is in India's best interest to limit this possibility given the contentious relationship that India has with China. Establishing global protocols for the growth of CBDC cross-border use is the most effective strategy for addressing this issue. India will benefit greatly from having a reputable and operational CBDC. An Indian CBDC can also assist with domestic digitalization. In order to have a say in the development of these international standards and collaborations to develop cross-border use cases for CBDCs, India will need to have a CBDC that is credible and operational. Despite the fact that the current UPI-based digitalization drive has been extremely successful, a digital divide is still possible. Private sector banks have participated very little in the current financial inclusion efforts, with the majority of the burden falling on public sector banks, resulting in significant losses for the latter.

The or-prof it NUE mechanism may exacerbate the divide because it is also bank-account-based. India's inclusive digitalization project will be challenging as a result of this. By working outside of the banking industry, such as through the postal system, CBDCs may be able to provide an alternative to the NUE in this instance. The banks will not bear the losses caused by these activities because the RBI could directly regulate and pay for the logistics of these accounts. Our public sector banks will also be able to become more professional as a result of this. Of course, the volume of such activities needs to be deliberately limited in order to avoid significant disintermediation of the banking sector. The advantages of an Indian CBDC are compelling, but neither are the drawbacks. As was previously mentioned, the introduction of CBDCs has the potential to disintermediate the banking system and lead to bank runs if savers consider them to be superior financial assets to bank deposits (Kar & Priyadarshini, 2022).

As long as the banking system is in good working order, there are, of course, certain design solutions that can reduce this risk. These design decisions must also take into account the major structural weaknesses of the Indian banking system, which are reflected in the large volumes of non-performing assets (NPAs) and the possibility of insolvency. Although liquidity and solvency are two distinct issues, it is common knowledge that they complement one another. Due to India's weak banking sector, banks will require significantly more assistance in the event of systemic disintermediation or a bank run caused by CBDCs. In addition, although it is intended that a CBDC would offer a safer alternative to private virtual currencies, the method by which this will be accomplished is still unknown. Due to their anonymous, decentralized, and borderless structure, it may be difficult or even counterproductive to prohibit such currencies. For instance, the IMC India Report, which advocates for the prohibition of private cryptocurrencies, also makes the observation that there may be ways to circumvent the prohibitions by making use of unregistered virtual private networks (VPNs) or by taking advantage of the fragmented regulatory environment to shift to jurisdictions that are more accommodating. Additionally, it has been argued that prohibiting the activities would conceal them, making it difficult to monitor them, particularly for use in illegal activities. (2018, Nishith Desai Associates)

Likewise, while China, the only major frugality to enjoin crypto currency related conditioning like trading and original coin immolations, has arguably been fairly successful in administering them, it's worth noting that similar conditioning have continued to live, egging yet another crackdown lately, several times after the original nonsupervisory conduct in 2013 and 2017. Easily, any verdict to introduce CBDCs in India will have to take into account all of these considerations. In order to remain internationally competitive and to insure digital and fiscal security, we may have to borrow and develop CBDCs sooner rather than latterly. There are, still, genuine enterprises over disintermediation and fiscal insecurity, and all preventives need to be taken to minimize and control these problems.

Private Cryptocurrencies and Economic Instability

When private cryptocurrencies were to find widespread economic use, either coexisting with or fully displacing fiat money, the result would be increased financial instability, inequality, and social instability. Cryptocurrencies are controversial. Advocates see them as a better form of money that imparts freedom, useful economic functions, fabulous riches, and hedges against bad government policies. The sceptics worry about investor protection and environmental impact. Cryptocurrencies today do not pose much threat to financial stability, as noted by den Haan et al. (2017) and a recent Financial Stability Board report (Financial Stability Board, 2018). That will change if cryptocurrencies find widespread economic use, either coexisting with or fully displacing fiat money. They will then have a strong and negative impact on financial stability, equality and social cohesion. Some cryptocurrencies promise to replace fiat money with private money whose integrity is underpinned by algorithms, not government guarantees. This includes the most prominent, Bitcoin, and many of the cryptocurrencies aiming to improve on Bitcoin. The majority of observers disagree. Since cryptocurrencies are primarily held for speculative purposes and have little economic value outside of that, an asset class with less than $200 billion is quite small in comparison to the overall asset markets. Currently, cryptocurrency does not pose a threat to financial stability. However, assuming that cryptocurrencies like Bitcoin achieve success in the money market and become widely used in everyday economic transactions. The current fiat system is affected by the same forces of financial instability as a cryptocurrency-based monetary system (the "cryptosystem"), as well as new forms of instability. Almost every financial crisis is caused by the same fundamental forces, excessive endogenous risk, regardless of the underlying monetary system (gold, fiat, or cryptocurrency) that goes unnoticed until it's too late, only to show up when a crisis starts and it's too late to do anything but react.

Endogenous risk refers to the interaction of human beings within the financial system, which is the source of all serious financial risk. They are susceptible to acting like a pro-cyclical herd and are affected by a variety of constraints and biases that have an impact on decisions and, consequently, outcomes. Behaviour is more erratic during times of prosperity than during times of crisis, when self-preservation instincts kick in. Prices move up and down an escalator or elevator because booms build slowly and deflate quickly.

Money creation is fundamental to financial instability. Base money is created by the central bank in the current fiat system, while M1 and M2 are created by the financial system. When rapid deleveraging causes the process to reverse, financial crises cause the most damage. Cryptosystems can be said to be the same. The supply of money is crypto M1 and M2, and just like with fiat, the creation of such money is under no one's control. The mining process only controls the creation of base money, which is the number of coins. Although some proponents of the cryptocurrency claim that this would not occur because a cryptosystem would be a full reserve system, this is highly unlikely. There will be people who want to lend coins to others and people who want to borrow coins. If these claims are traded, crypto M1 and M2 are created. In a similar vein, some crypto banks will find that continuing to operate as fractional reserve banks is more profitable. A cryptosystem, on the other hand, carries additional kinds of systemic risk that are absent from fiat systems. The claims on coins make up the majority of a cryptosystem's money, including crypto M1 and M2. Economic agents will run their financial institutions if they begin to worry that their money is not equivalent to coins during times of crisis when confidence evaporates.

There is a safety valve in fiat systems, which are affected by the same endogenous risk. Since the fiat framework can make limitless measures of liquidity when required, the national bank can ensure spectacular exhibition. It is able to demonstrate to the financial markets that it is able to satisfy any demand for liquidity, minimizing deleveraging, sustaining the economy, and avoiding the disastrous failures of the financial institutions without which the economy cannot function. A credible demonstration of this kind is stabilizing on its own. A crisis can be mitigated once the markets are aware that the central bank will do whatever it takes; that was demonstrated by the ECB's 2012 declaration that it would "do whatever it takes." A financial crisis and economic recession became a depression due to the Federal Reserve's failure to do the same during the Great Depression. In the autumn of 2008, the globally coordinated creation of liquidity prevented that crisis from developing into a depression. This ultimately indicates that a well-managed fiat system would face greater systemic risk than a monetary system based on private cryptocurrencies of today.

Someone will achieve profit if privately issued cryptocurrencies successfully challenge fiat currency. All cryptocurrencies have a current market value of around $200 billion; in the economies of the G20, M1 has a total value of $31 trillion. A profit of $31 trillion, or almost as much as the annual GDPs of the United States and China combined (at $34.5 trillion), will be transferred to a small group of crypto-speculators if we completely replace fiat money with cryptocurrencies. That is the limit above; with the possibility of private cryptocurrencies coexisting with fiat currency, the market value of cryptocurrencies could range anywhere from $200 billion to $31 trillion. Private cryptocurrency success indicates a significant transfer of a public good to private speculators. It would dwarf the largest previous expropriations of public property, such as the Highland Clearances in Scotland, the confiscation of Native American land in the United States and Aboriginal land in Australia, the Inclosure Acts in England and Wales, which resulted in the transfer of 2,800,000 hectares of common land to private ownership, and the more recent privatizations carried out by Russia and China.

The sovereign initiated the wealth transfers in the preceding examples, which purposefully enriched some citizens while impoverishing others. Transfers to crypto-speculators, on the other hand, are currently entirely voluntary. However, the sovereign must consent to the deliberate decision that Bitcoin should be used alongside or in place of dollars in order for cryptocurrencies to replace fiat currency. As a result, the transfer of up to $31 trillion to a handful of private speculators would dwarf any historical precedents to become the largest expropriation of a public good in human history. The reason for this is that fiat money is legal tender and the sovereign needs to allow the displacement of fiat. Crypto advocates strongly refute this, arguing that such notions are Marxist and do not recognize the just return for entrepreneurs who take risks. These counterarguments are irrelevant. The idea that an entrepreneur should not be expropriated but rather benefit from the results of their labour in a competitive market is well-supported. Crypto-fortunes, in contrast to entrepreneurial wealth, would be generated by enclosing a public good, so it would be fundamentally unfair to transfer the supply of public money to crypto-speculators.

Central Bank Digital Currencies (CBDCs) and Economic Instability

CBCDs are set to be an integral part of the future of finance. The way people pay is changing as the economy continues to become more digital. The pandemic has significantly accelerated the decline in the use of cash, the only form of public money issued by the central bank. With over 6,000 cryptocurrencies currently in use worldwide and one in ten people investing in them, central banks can no longer ignore demand for digital currencies. Central banks all over the world are stepping up to create their own digital currency options because they are confronted with a parallel monetary system that is completely out of their control. These CBDCs are a natural digital evolution of conventional monetary systems and have a lot in common with cash compared to the majority of major cryptocurrencies. CBDCs are created and offered directly by central banks, in contrast to other speculative crypto currencies and tokens, and are typically backed in a manner analogous to cash whether that be in the form of reserves or gold, thereby establishing trust and guaranteeing consumer safety.

CBDCs give customers convenient digital payment options without exposing them to cryptocurrencies' volatility. They have the potential to make payments faster, cheaper, safer, and more frictionless while addressing some of the dependencies in the current payment network and systems. They were created as a means of spending money. However, one of the hardest groups to convince of the value of CBDCs will continue to be retail customers who are concerned about data privacy and have already experienced real-time payments. Also, the needs of customers who aren't tech savvy should be carefully thought about because adoption might be especially hard for them, which could make society more tech-deprived.

CBDCs have the potential to cut costs, time, and settlement risk associated with international payments, and corporate customers are aware of the benefits and excited about this. CBDCs could be used to automatically pay taxes or other payments to the government as part of routine transactions by allowing the use of smart contracts. Digital audit trails also have the potential to streamline and simplify financial compliance. However, the shift will have a significant impact on how businesses interact with one another and conduct business. As they adjust to doing business with CBDCs, corporate customers will face a period of change, evolution, and confusion at various levels of the company. The perceptions of CBDCs among domestic banks are not quite as favourable. Domestic banks lose their essential roles as deposit takers and intermediaries when central banks directly issue digital currencies and pay interest on them. A decrease in deposit taking results in a reduction in the resources available for work, which in turn limits a domestic bank's capacity to offer credit to customers. In this sense, the expansion of CBDCs poses a real threat to the current operating models of domestic banking. Because their customer base is very cash-oriented and will take a long time to adjust to using CBDCs as their primary currency, credit unions and co-operative banks in particular will probably have a hard time adapting to this change.

CBDCs have the eventuality to fully transfigure the part of transnational banks, especially when it comes to transnational and cross currency trade. Transnational banks need to step up to re-invent their part in a CBDC driven frugality. Creating the structure demanded to support transnational CBDC transfers at scale carries a significant resource and invention burden in the short period.

For central banks themselves, CBDCs constitute a large shift in operations. They can substantially lessen the fees of printing, transporting and dealing with cash, liberating up sources to fulfil the brand-new demanding situations of CBDC management. And they can combat fraud automatically, way to guidelines embedded inside foreign money and transaction code. Desire to transport quick and capture first-mover advantage, the introduction of a brand new worldwide reserve foreign money and addressing the accelerated threat of disruption with the aid of using decentralized finance gamers should all fundamentally rework the worldwide monetary and political landscape. CBDCs have implications for each information-pushed detail of finance. From dealing with know your customer information to monitoring unlawful hobby throughout billions of transactions, the unique audit path that includes a virtual foreign money can assist address a number of primary banks' largest demanding situations. However, the ones advantages call for a steep prematurely cost. Securing buy-in from all stakeholders won't be easy – particularly on the customer level. Retraining and re-schooling may be necessary, new infrastructure will want to be established and primary banks will ought to outline and grasp a brand new technology of virtual finance wherein cyber struggle and threats may be of pinnacle concern.

CONCLUSION

This is a lengthy journey, but it can only begin with the correct planning and allies. The transition to CBDCs is without a doubt a challenging task for central banks. But it's an essential step to support the development of our society and monetary system, much like the switch to cash. Here are a few impact areas that CBDC strategists need to be aware of and handle using a multidisciplinary approach. Central banks look for solutions to crucial concerns such whether they should prioritise retail or wholesale money first, whether to offer interest on CBDCs, whether to provide anonymity, and whether to set transaction thresholds and limitations using robust simulation models (agent-based modelling), in addition to the hypothesis-based field test, central banks are trying to answer important questions such as whether to focus on retail or wholesale money first, whether CBDCs should offer interest, whether to offer anonymity, whether transaction limits and thresholds should be set, and whether cash and CBDC should to coexist or not. These tools and approaches may not provide definitive answers, especially for large-scale solutions, but they provide central banks with strong pointers to help make the transition much less of a bound into the unidentified.

REFERENCES

Álvez, M., Lluberas, R., & Ponce, J. (2020). The Cost of Using Cash and Checks in Uruguay. *Journal of Central Banking Theory and Practice*, *9*(2), 109–129. doi:10.2478/jcbtp-2020-0016

Banka, H. (2018). *Initial findings from the implementation of the Practical Guide for Measuring Retail Payment Costs.* World Bank Private Sector Development Blog. https:// blogs.worldbank.org/psd/initial-findings-implementa tion-practical-guide-measuringretail-%0Apayment-costs

Buisness Today. (2017). RBI, commercial banks spend Rs 21,000 crore on currency management. *Business Today.* https:// www.businesstoday.in/current/economy-politics/rbi-ba nks-spend-currency-management-cash/ story/ 251299.html

Danielsson, J (2018a). *Cryptocurrencies don't make sense.* VoxEU.org.

Danielsson, J (2018b). *Cryptocurrencies are lousy investments.* VoxEU.org.

Danielsson, J. (2018c). Cryptocurrencies: Policy, economics and fairness. *LSE Systemic Risk Centre Discussion Paper 86.*

Danielsson, J, Shin, H. S., & Zigrand, J.-P. (2009). *Modelling financial turmoil through endogenous risk.* VoxEU.org.

Den Haan, W., Ellison, M., Ilzetzki, E., McMahon, M., & Reis, R. (2017). *Economists relaxed about bitcoin: New CFM-CEPR expert survey on cryptocurrencies, the ðnancial system, and economic policy.* VoxEU.org.

Financial Stability Board. (2018). Crypto asset markets. *Potential channels for future ðnancial stability implications, technical report.* www.fsb.org/wp-content/ uploads/P101018.pdf

Javaid, A. (n.d.). *CBDC in India: What is Central Bank Digital Currency (CBDC)?* Jahran Josh. https://www.jagranjosh.com/general-knowledge/central-bank-digital-currency-cbdc-1612241965-1 5.

Kosse, A., Chen, H., Felt, M.-H., Jiongo, V., Nield, K., & Welte, A. (2017). *The Costs of Point-of-Sale Payments in Canada.* Discussion Papers.

Todd, R. & Rogers, M. (2020). *A Global Look at Central Bank Digital Currencies.* The Block Research.

Ward, O., & Rochemont, S. (2019). *An addendum to "A Cashless Society-Benefits, Risks and Issues (Interim paper)" Understanding Central Bank Digital Currencies (CBDC) By Orla Ward Sabrina Rochemont.* Actuaries.org. https:// www.actuaries.org.uk/system/files/field/document/Un derstanding CBDCs Final - disc.pdf

Chapter 9
Exploring the Feasibility of a Decentralized Autonomous Organization (DAO) as a New Model for Economic Governance in the Blockchain Era

Raja V.
SRM Institute of Science and Technology, India

Subashree S.
SRM Institute of Science and Technology, India

ABSTRACT

Decentralized autonomous organizations (DAOs) are a new type of organization that are run using blockchain technology and are designed to operate without the need for traditional management structures. In this research project, the authors explored the feasibility of using DAOs as a new model for economic governance in the blockchain era. The authors examined the key features and functions of DAOs, assessed the potential benefits and challenges of using these organizations as a model for economic governance, and considered the legal and regulatory implications of DAOs. The authors also examined case studies of existing DAOs and analyzed their successes and failures in order to identify best practices for implementing and operating DAOs effectively. The findings suggest that DAOs have the potential to disrupt traditional models of economic governance by providing a new way for organizations to operate and make decisions in a transparent and decentralized manner. However, there are also challenges and limitations to using DAOs as a model for economic governance.

DOI: 10.4018/978-1-6684-5691-0.ch009

BLOCKCHAIN TECHNOLOGY

Blockchain technology has become an attractive concept among the various researchers and developers. as it is continuously growing set of records. These records are grouped together into blocks, together with other information. The blocks are chained together through the application of cryptography as shown in figure 1. Every block contains hash of previous block, timestamp data and transactional data represented in the form of a merkle tree as shown in figure 2. A blockchain is called a decentralized ledger, as it saves all the transactions made in the peer-to-peer network. Blockchain eliminates the role of intermediaries, thereby making it secure, because of its features it is being used in a wide variety of applications in industries, financial sectors, health care systems and supply chain management systems.

FEATURES OF BLOCKCHAIN TECHNOLOGY

Blockchains apart from eliminating third parties also offer many other important features. Blockchain is a decentralized technology which enhances security by eliminating the centralized authority system. It is tampering proof, as the information is stored as cryptographic hash. The block diagram for the following features is as shown in figure 3.

Figure 1. Representation of Blockchain

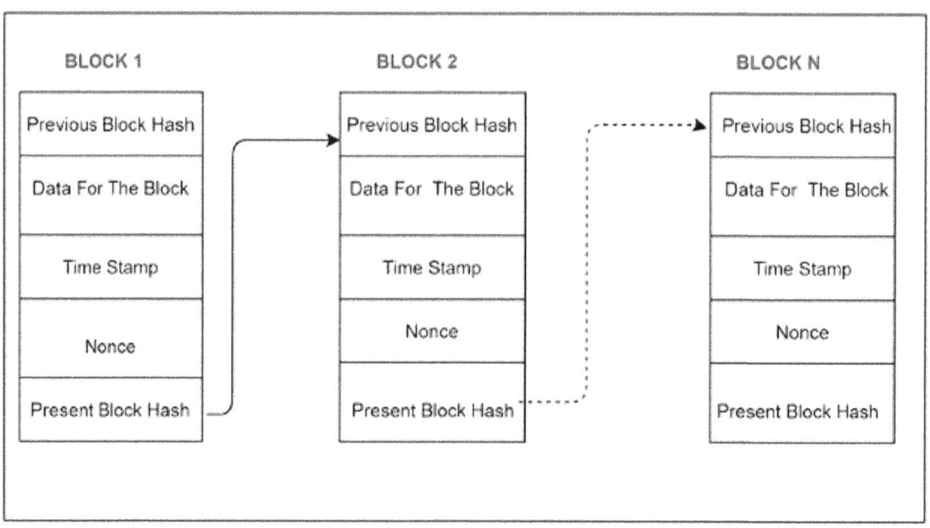

Figure 2. Merkle Tree of Transactions in a block

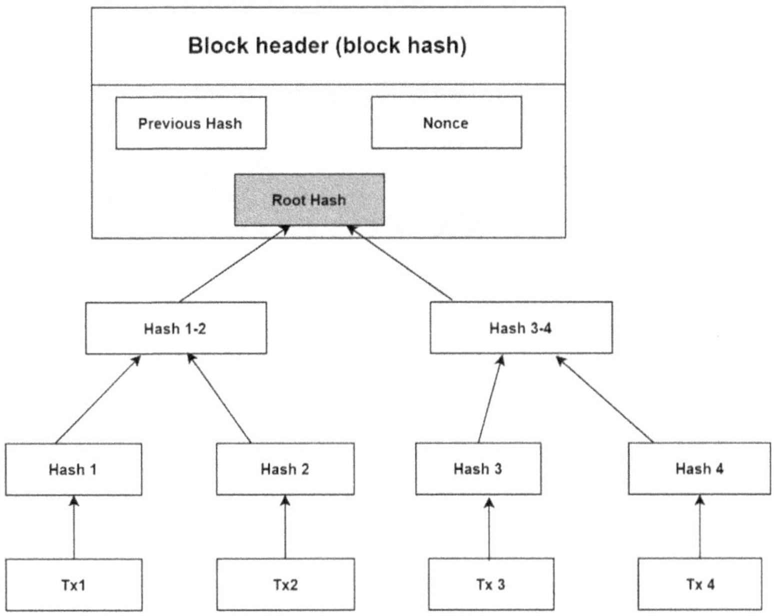

Some of the important features are:

Decentralized Ledger

Blockchain as a network, connects the users of the organization without third party interference. The transactions initiated in the network are shared to all the users in the peer-to-peer network. Every user in the network has the copy of the ledger in their node and sends that data to other nodes. Basically, it eliminates the central authority system like in banks and trusted intermediaries such as third-party service providers to exchange the value. It also reduces the resistance in the current transaction and creates a faster value exchange in real-time. Availability of the decentralized ledger across the network makes the system robust as there is no single point of failure occurring due to break down or collision. Hence, it increases the quality, reliability, and availability of service without any interruption.

Figure 3. Properties of Blockchain

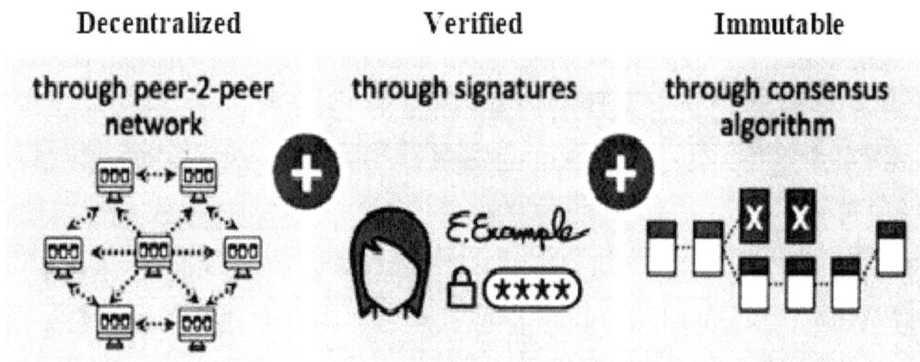

Transparency in Blockchain

All the transactions are visible to everyone available in the network. It does not allow any unauthorized transactions to be embedded in to the blockchain. However, the participants in the network can select which information should be made publicly available during the initiation of the transaction. Hence, every user in the network is provided with a digital signature also called the private key, i.e., proof of recognition for the node and the same is used to validate the transactions. However, the private key of the user is not to be disclosed to others. It is bundled with the public key to provide extra security to other users in the network.

Immutable Records

Blockchain use consensus algorithms to verify the trans- actions in a block and to embed them into the blockchain. If the majority of the participants in the network validate the group of transactions, then the transactions are included into the block to form a blockchain. Suppose, if any participant in the network tries to alter the ledger, he fails as it has to be validated by a consensus. And every new block created is cryptographically linked to the previous block. Soon after new block is updated, all the nodes in the blockchain will get the copy of the updated ledger. Hence changing the block in the blockchain is impossible. So, this feature makes the records in blockchain immutable.

ARCHITECTURE OF BLOCKCHAIN TECHNOLOGY

The blockchain architecture comprises of the following core components:

Node: A peer node is a computer which equipt with special software that maintains a blockchain. All nodes in the network can initiate transactions and exchange messages over a network.

Transaction: Transactions comprise of the smallest building entities participating in a blockchain system. Transactions are made up of nonce, gas price, gas limit, from address, to address, value and data. These transactions are responsible for altering the state of blockchain. They are grouped together and sent to every node to form a block. The processing and verification of these state changers are done independently in the peer-to-peer network. The format of a transaction consists of input, output and a script signature. The input parameter holds a link to the previous node's output providing uninterrupted service whereas out- put field consists of data and the cost. The script signature is embedded into the input data structure. This signature is generated using the Elliptic Curve Digital Signature Algorithm. This script signature consists the signature of the owner in the previous node and also the current node's owner proving that the owner has designed the transaction to give his own input.

Block: Blocks are data structures whose prime purpose is to hold a group of transactions, which are bundle together by the miner after verification. Blocks structure mainly consists of block header which is the metadata and the trans- actions. Block header helps the miners to check the validness of the block. It consists of six fields namely – version, Previous Hash, Merkle root hash, Times- tamp, Difficulty value and the nonce. Each of the above-mentioned metadata plays a vital role in the block's validation. Version holds the current version of the block structure; previous root hash refers the address of the previous node. Merkle root hash consists of the cryptographic hash of all the transactions embedded into the node; the time of creation is stored in timestamp; Difficulty value is the result of the mathematical puzzle's solution, number used only once is the random value embedded into the block.

Blockchain: It is chain of blocks, which are cryptographically linked to each other. Blockchain consists of various kinds of blocks – key chain blocks (nodes in current chain), lateral chain blocks (Nodes extending in the side chains) and the bereave blocks (these are left over nodes not known to processing). Lateral chain blocks and bereave blocks refer to the nodes in the key chain nodes.

Genesis Block: It is the first block in the blockchain, which define the initial configuration.

Network: It provides cooperation among all the nodes, so that they can execute and communicate with each other.

Miner: Miners collect transactions from mining pool send by various nodes in the network, solves the mathematical puzzle, verifies the cryptographic hash, thereby embedding them into a block. Miner can run on Ethereum node.

Mining: It is a process of a including a block by using proof-of-work, which will solve the complex mathematical puzzle.

Gas: It is the amount of the ether paid to run an EVM code on an EVM. Its price is set by the user. Miner will select the transaction based on gas price.

Call: Call to a function of an existing contract will execute the function code.

Consensus Mechanism: These act-like protocols ensuring synchronization of all the available nodes and to verify the common agreement among all nodes in the blockchain. To facilitate the distributed operation, and cooperation among the nodes. There may be faults occur in the system, which can be solved by using consensus. There are various kinds of consensus mechanisms working on various principles – Proof of Work (PoW), Proof of Stake (PoS), Delegated Proof of Stake (DPoS), Proof of Burn (PoB), Proof of Capacity (PoC), Proof of Elapsed Time (PoET), Consensus as a Service (CaaS) etc.

Hash function: Here the hash function accepts input as a combination of human readable characters comprising alphabets, numbers, special characters and can also accept various other files or media. The length of the output can vary between 32 – bit, 64 – bit, 128 – bit or 256 – bit, but all the generated outputs are of fixed bit length. This fixed length output can be generated depending on the encoding functions used. This is called hash code of that input sequence. There are many types of cryptographic functions available like Cyclic redundancy checks, Checksums, Universal hash function families, non-cryptographic hash functions, Keyed cryptographic hash functions, Unkeyed cryptographic hash functions. Out of which blockchain makes use of SHA-256 algorithm which belongs to Unkeyed cryptographic hash functions. This algorithm operates as a one-way function, producing unique fixed length outputs as shown in figure 2.4. The working of SHA – 256 algorithm differs from other encryption algorithms which uses keys to encrypt and decrypt text, in a way that it generates a message digest which is one – way. The message digest generated here cannot be decrypted by any of the decryption algorithms as it is only one – way code. As a result of this hashing any modification done to any of the blocks will generate a new hash code, breaking the chain. Hence to embed this new node into the chain all the node's hash values have to be altered making it almost impossible for a miner. This property of blockchain makes the data immutable.

Ethereum Virtual Machine (EVM): This is a computing machine, which provides an environment for the execution of EVM byte code. It has a limitation on number of computational steps, which is defined as gas.

Ethereum Network: It is a peer-to-peer network, which contains Ethereum nodes.

Ether: It is crypto currency used in the Ethereum platform to incentivize computation. Ethereum is popular and mature platform for developing smart contract.

Smart contract: It codifies the rules and regulations of organizations.

Contract Account: It is controlled by its contract code and can be initiated by an EOA using a call or function.

Go-Ethereum (Geth): It provides a command line interface to run an Ethereum node implementation in GO language. Geth functions can be accesses over a HTTP using JSON-RPC protocol.

State: Which is used to map between addresses and account states.

Account State: It consists of a nonce, balance, and storage root and hash value. Nonce represents the number of transactions sent from the account. Whereas the balance is the ether value owned by an account and storage root is the 256-bit hash of the root node in the hash tree. The EVM code is executed, when the account receives a message call.

Externally Owned Account: It is controlled by an external actor with the private key. But it does not have any associated EVM code. EOA can issue a transaction to transfer ether or to initiate a contract account.

Solidity: It is a programming language used for writing the smart contract. The syntax is similar to the JavaScript and it is developed to target the Ethereum platform. The miner, groups the transactions together in the form of blocks in the blockchain. The blockchain consist of data structure, which will link the block of transactions together, and these blocks will be stored as a database. Every block connected to the previous block in the form of chain starting from the gene- sis block, the current block stores the hash of the previous block. The block in the blockchain is indicated by the hash of the block header, Hash is generated using SHA-256. The figure 2.1 shows how the blocks are linked by using the previous block hash in the current block header.

The Structure of a Block: The block header consist of one parameter is hash of the previous block, and also hash of the Merkle root of the transactions to, time stamp of the block, difficulty target of the block, and nonce.

Verification of Transaction: Immediately after user initiates a transaction, the transaction is broadcast to the neighboring nodes of Ethereum blockchain until it is received by everyone in the network. According to the protocol, every node requires validating the originality of a transaction prior to the forwarding to the neighboring nodes, and making sure that the transaction forwarded is a valid one and added in a block (at the same time fake transaction is discarded by node). Similarly, every node verifies each transaction based on a list of criteria as mentioned below:

- Data structure and transaction syntax must be perfect.
- All the list of inputs and outputs must be filled.

- Transaction size must not exceed block size.
- The total value and the output must be below the specified range.
- No hash value of the input is equal to 0, N=1.
- The n Lock Time is below or equal to *INT MAX.*
- Transaction size must not exceed more than or equal to 100 bytes.
- The total number of signature operations consist in transaction must be less than the maximum signature operation limit.
- Only matched transaction must be in the group, or in the block
- To every input, if there is any referenced output existed in any other transaction in the group, that transaction must be rejected.

The miner individually verifies all the transactions, which are received before broadcast to the nodes in the network. Hence, each miner prepares a group of valid transactions. Immediately, the validated transactions are included in the memory pool, it is where transactions are stored and waiting until miner added in to the block (mined block).

Mining and Proof-of-Work: Mining is the process of adding blocks to the blockchain; block uses a proof-of-work concept, where miner participating in the Ethereum network uses software and hardware to solve the mathematical puzzle. The function of a Mining is to oversee to manage the ethers in the Ethereum and it takes care the security of the transactions against attacker, known as double-spending. The miner who solved the mathematical puzzle to include the block in the blockchain rewarded with Ether (1 Ether = 546.85 USD) and also miner will gain the transaction fee of transactions added in the block. The entire mining process is in centivizes miner to perform mining and validate the transactions.

Proof - Of - Work Algorithm: Mining process use the POW algorithm, which consist of performing a SHA-256 to the block header continuously, randomly changing the parameter (nonce) till the final hash reach the difficulty target. SHA is a one-way hash function, so that the resulting block header hash cannot mean sure priory, as every hash is independent from each other. Hence, the final answer needs "brute force" answer, i.e., miner search and test for a nonce continuously. Generally, nonce is incremented by one for each answer.

SHA-256 algorithm is generating a fixed length of output for the variable length of input. The output of hash algorithm is same for the particular input always, so it can be easily measured and verified by anyone using the hash algorithm. Whereas, it is impossible to determine the input for a given output. SHA-256, output is always 256-bit long. The below example shows the randomness of the algorithm. During the mining the integer appended is a nonce and is used to change the final hash values appended to it. In case of mining, the hash value is observed by a parameter known as difficulty target, which is accepted by miner. Difficulty is measured as the difficulty of building the present block compared to the genesis block, which is calculated as follows. Difficulty = difficulty 1 target / current target.

TYPES OF BLOCKCHAIN

Blockchain categories are public, private, consortium.

Public: In a public blockchain every participant in the network can read, send transaction and also perform the consensus process to determine the block, which can be added to the blockchain network. The user having a computer and internet can participate and perform the consensus. Public blockchain allows the all the users to participate in the process. It is suitable for a fully decentralized network. It is slow and more energy consume in the form of power.

Private: It is completely private network, read permission is open but write permissions are maintained centrally by one organization. As only one organization can write and verify the transactions. So, its efficiency is more than the public blockchain. And is also very fast processing. But it does not offer same decentralized security as public blockchain.

Consortium: The consortium blockchain is controlled by the pre - selected nodes to control the consensus mechanism. Instead of all nodes allowed to participate in the blockchain or few nodes allowed for consensus process in private blockchain, only few nodes, which are control the consensus process. It is considered as partially decentralized network. So, it is more suitable application for business collaborations. For example, it can be used for business collaboration contains five organizations, each one maintains a separate node. Read permissions are public or restricted to few nodes. Suppose one organization does not want to participate in the consensus mechanism, but still it is part of the business partner, then it is allowed for read permissions.

DECENTRALIZED AUTONOMOUS ORGANIZATION (DAO)

In recent years, the emergence of blockchain technology has led to the development of a new type of organization known as a decentralized autonomous organization (DAO). A DAO is a digital organization that is run using blockchain technology and is designed to operate without the need for traditional management structures. Instead, decision-making power is distributed among the members of the DAO, who are often referred to as "stakeholders." DAOs are based on smart contracts, which are self-executing contracts with the terms of the agreement between buyer and seller being directly written into lines of code. These smart contracts facilitate the automation of processes and decision-making within the DAO.

DAOs have the potential to disrupt traditional models of economic governance by providing a new way for organizations to operate and make decisions in a transparent and decentralized manner. By eliminating the need for traditional management structures and central decision-making authorities, DAOs have the potential to increase efficiency, reduce the risk of corruption, and foster greater collaboration among stakeholders. However, there are also challenges and limitations to using DAOs as a model for economic governance, and the legal and regulatory implications of these organizations are still unclear in many jurisdictions.

In this research project, we will explore the feasibility of using DAOs as a new model for economic governance in the blockchain era. We will examine the key features and functions of DAOs and assess the potential benefits and challenges of using these organizations as a model for economic governance. We will also consider the legal and regulatory implications of DAOs and explore potential frameworks for governing and regulating these organizations. Finally, we will examine case studies of existing DAOs and analyze their successes and failures in order to identify best practices for implementing and operating DAOs effectively. Through this research, we hope to gain a better understanding of the potential of DAOs as a model for economic governance and their potential to disrupt or transform traditional models of economic governance.

BLOCKCHAIN AND ENHANCED SECURITY

The hazards associated with holding data centralised are eliminated by the block chain by keeping data across its network. Its network doesn't have any concentrated areas of weakness that hackers may use. Everyone is familiar with the security issues on the internet today. Everybody relies on the 'username/password' method to safeguard their online identity and belongings. Encryption technology is used in block chain security techniques. The so-called public and private 'keys' are the foundation for this. A user's block chain address is represented by a public key a lengthy string of digits that are created at random. The network records any bitcoins sent to or from that address. Similar to a password, the 'private key' grants its owner access to their digital assets, such as Bit coins. Your data will not be harmed if you save it on the blockchain. This is true, but maintaining the security of your digital assets also necessitates printing off your private key and making a 'paper wallet' to store it in.

OBJECTIVES OF DECENTRALIZED AUTONOMOUS ORGANIZATION

1. To understand the key features and functions of DAOs, and how they differ from traditional organizations.
2. To assess the potential benefits and challenges of using DAOs as a model for economic governance, including their ability to facilitate decentralized decision-making, increase transparency, and promote greater accountability.
3. To examine case studies of existing DAOs and analyze their successes and failures in order to identify best practices for implementing and operating DAOs effectively.
4. To evaluate the legal and regulatory implications of DAOs and explore potential frameworks for governing and regulating these organizations.
5. To consider the potential impact of DAOs on traditional models of economic governance and assess their potential to disrupt or transform existing systems.

Functions of DAOs, and How They Differ From Traditional Organizations

A decentralized autonomous organization (DAO) is a type of organization that is run using blockchain technology and is designed to operate without the need for traditional management structures. DAOs are based on smart contracts, which are self-executing contracts with the terms of the agreement between buyer and seller being directly written into lines of code. These smart contracts facilitate the automation of processes and decision-making within the DAO.

One key feature of DAOs is that they are decentralized, meaning that they are not controlled by any single individual or entity. Instead, decision-making power is distributed among the members of the DAO, who are often referred to as "stakeholders." Decision-making within a DAO is based on the consensus of the stakeholders, who may vote on proposals or participate in other forms of decentralized governance. This is in contrast to traditional organizations, which often have a hierarchical management structure and a central decision-making authority. In addition to being decentralized, DAOs are also transparent. All transactions and decisions made within the organization are recorded on the blockchain and can be publicly audited. This increases accountability and helps to build trust among stakeholders.

DAOs have the potential to disrupt traditional models of economic governance by providing a new way for organizations to operate and make decisions in a transparent and decentralized manner. By eliminating the need for traditional management structures and central decision-making authorities, DAOs have the potential to increase efficiency, reduce the risk of corruption, and foster greater collaboration among stakeholders. However, it is important to carefully consider the potential benefits and challenges of using DAOs as a model for economic governance, as well as the legal and regulatory implications of these organizations.

Potential benefits and challenges of using DAOs as a model for economic governance, including their ability to facilitate decentralized decision-making, increase transparency, and promote greater accountability:

One potential benefit of using DAOs as a model for economic governance is that they facilitate decentralized decision-making. Because decision-making power is distributed among the stakeholders of a DAO, rather than being concentrated in the hands of a single individual or group, there is a greater level of participation and inclusivity in the decision-making process. This can lead to more diverse perspectives being considered and can ultimately result in better decision-making.

Another potential benefit of DAOs is that they increase transparency. Because all transactions and decisions made within a DAO are recorded on the blockchain and can be publicly audited, there is a higher level of accountability and transparency within the organization. This can help to build trust among stakeholders and can also reduce the risk of corruption.

In addition to facilitating decentralized decision-making and increasing transparency, DAOs have the potential to promote greater accountability. Because stakeholders have a direct say in the decision-making process and can hold each other accountable, there is a greater level of accountability within a DAO compared to a traditional organization.

While there are many potential benefits to using DAOs as a model for economic governance, it is important to also consider the challenges and limitations of these organizations. For example, DAOs may struggle to reach consensus on complex or controversial issues, and the decentralized nature of these organizations can make it more difficult to make rapid decisions or respond to changing circumstances. Additionally, the legal and regulatory status of DAOs is still unclear in many jurisdictions, which can create uncertainty and hinder the adoption of these organizations.

Case studies of existing DAOs and analyse their successes and failures in order to identify best practices for implementing and operating DAOs effectively:

One way to understand the potential benefits and challenges of using DAOs as a model for economic governance is to examine case studies of existing DAOs. By analyzing the successes and failures of these organizations, we can identify best practices for implementing and operating DAOs effectively. Some potential areas to consider when examining case studies of existing DAOs include: the governance structure of the organization, the types of decisions that are made within the DAO, the mechanisms for reaching consensus among stakeholders, and the processes for resolving disputes or handling conflicts. By understanding how these different aspects of DAO operations have worked in practice, we can identify patterns and trends that can inform the design and implementation of future DAOs.

It is also important to consider the context in which each DAO operates, as this can have a significant impact on its success or failure. For example, the legal and regulatory environment, the level of technological infrastructure, and the level of adoption and understanding of blockchain technology among stakeholders can all play a role in the effectiveness of a DAO. Overall, by examining case studies of existing DAOs and analyzing their successes and failures, we can gain a better understanding of the potential of these organizations as a model for economic governance and identify best practices for implementing and operating DAOs effectively.

Case 1

The DAO was a pioneering decentralized autonomous organization (DAO) that was launched in 2016 with the goal of using smart contracts to fund projects that aligned with its mission of decentralization. The organization raised over $150 million in a crowd sale, making it one of the largest crowdfunding campaigns in history at the time. However, just a few weeks after its launch, The DAO was hacked, resulting in the loss of millions of dollars' worth of cryptocurrency.

The case of The DAO highlights a number of key challenges and risks associated with using DAOs as a model for economic governance. One of the main challenges was the issue of security. Because DAOs rely on smart contracts and are operated using blockchain technology, they are vulnerable to hacking and other forms of cyber-attacks. The hack of The DAO illustrates the importance of having robust security measures in place to protect against these types of attacks.

Another challenge highlighted by the case of The DAO was the issue of conflict resolution. Because DAOs are decentralized and do not have traditional management structures, it can be difficult to resolve disputes or handle conflicts that may arise within the organization. The hack of The DAO led to a dispute over whether to attempt to recover the lost funds or to let the hack stand, and this dispute ultimately led to the creation of two separate versions of the Ethereum blockchain. The case of The DAO illustrates the importance of having clear procedures for resolving disputes or handling conflicts within DAOs in order to avoid these types of issues.

Overall, the case of The DAO demonstrates the potential risks and challenges of using DAOs as a model for economic governance. However, it also illustrates the potential for these organizations to disrupt traditional models of economic governance and to create new, more transparent, and decentralized ways of organizing and conducting business.

Case 2

Ocean Protocol is a decentralized data exchange platform that aims to create a fair and transparent marketplace for data. The organization is governed by a decentralized autonomous organization (DAO), which allows stakeholders to participate in decision-making and to hold the organization accountable. The DAO is responsible for making decisions on key issues such as the allocation of funds, the development of new features, and the direction of the organization.

The case of Ocean Protocol demonstrates the potential of DAOs to facilitate decentralized decision-making and to promote greater transparency and accountability within organizations. By allowing all stakeholders to participate in decision-making, DAOs have the potential to create more collaborative and inclusive models of governance. This can help to ensure that the interests of all stakeholders are taken into account and that decisions are made in a more transparent and accountable manner.

Additionally, the use of a DAO to govern Ocean Protocol allows the organization to operate in a more decentralized manner, reducing the risk of corruption and increasing the efficiency of decision-making. By eliminating the need for traditional management structures and central decision-making authorities, DAOs have the potential to increase efficiency and reduce the risk of corruption.

Overall, the case of Ocean Protocol illustrates the potential of DAOs as a model for economic governance, particularly in terms of facilitating decentralized decision-making and promoting greater transparency and accountability within organizations.

Case 3

Aragon is a platform for creating and managing decentralized autonomous organizations (DAOs). The organization is itself governed by a DAO, which allows stakeholders to participate in decision-making and to hold the organization accountable. The DAO is responsible for making decisions on key issues such as the allocation of funds, the development of new features, and the direction of the organization.

The case of Aragon illustrates the potential of DAOs to disrupt traditional models of economic governance and to create new, more collaborative and transparent ways of organizing and conducting business. By eliminating the need for traditional management structures and central decision-making authorities, DAOs have the potential to increase efficiency, reduce the risk of corruption, and foster greater collaboration among stakeholders.

Additionally, the use of a DAO to govern Aragon allows the organization to operate in a more decentralized manner, reducing the risk of corruption and increasing the efficiency of decision-making. By allowing all stakeholders to participate in decision-making, DAOs have the potential to create more inclusive models of governance that take into account the interests of all stakeholders.

Overall, the case of Aragon demonstrates the potential of DAOs as a model for economic governance, particularly in terms of disrupting traditional models and creating more collaborative and transparent ways of organizing and conducting business.

Legal and regulatory implications of DAOs and explore potential frameworks for governing and regulating these organizations

One of the challenges of using DAOs as a model for economic governance is that the legal and regulatory status of these organizations is still unclear in many jurisdictions. As a result, it is important to evaluate the legal and regulatory implications of DAOs and explore potential frameworks for governing and regulating these organizations.

Some potential areas to consider when evaluating the legal and regulatory implications of DAOs include:

- Classification of DAOs: It is important to determine how DAOs should be classified under existing legal frameworks. For example, are they considered to be partnerships, corporations, or something else entirely? This classification will have implications for the legal rights and responsibilities of the stakeholders within the DAO and for the way in which the DAO is regulated.
- Liability: It is also important to consider the liability of the stakeholders within a DAO and how this should be allocated in the event that something goes wrong within the organization.
- Regulatory oversight: The level of regulatory oversight that is appropriate for DAOs will depend on the nature of the organization and the types of activities it engages in. It is important to determine the most appropriate level of oversight and to establish clear guidelines for the regulation of DAOs.

Overall, it is important to carefully consider the legal and regulatory implications of DAOs and to explore potential frameworks for governing and regulating these organizations in order to ensure that they can operate effectively within the legal and regulatory environment.

LEGAL IMPLICATIONS

1. Definition of a DAO: There is currently no clear legal definition of a DAO, and it is not always clear how existing laws and regulations apply to these organizations.

2. Classification as a legal entity: DAOs are typically not considered legal entities in the same way that corporations or other traditional organizations are. This can make it difficult to determine how to hold these organizations accountable and how to enforce contracts or other agreements involving DAOs.
3. Jurisdiction: Because DAOs are decentralized and operate online, it is often unclear which jurisdiction they fall under. This can make it difficult to determine which laws and regulations apply to these organizations and how to enforce them.
4. Taxation: It is not always clear how DAOs should be taxed, and the tax treatment of these organizations varies significantly from one jurisdiction to another.
5. Regulation: There is currently no specific regulation of DAOs in many jurisdictions, and it is not clear how existing laws and regulations apply to these organizations.
6. Securities regulation: Some DAOs have been structured as securities offerings, and as such, they may be subject to securities regulations. However, the application of these regulations to DAOs is not always clear.
7. Consumer protection: DAOs may be subject to consumer protection laws, but it is not always clear how these laws apply to these organizations.
8. Money transmission: Some DAOs may be considered money transmitters, and as such, they may be subject to money transmission regulations. However, the application of these regulations to DAOs is not always clear.
9. Data protection: DAOs may be subject to data protection laws, but it is not always clear how these laws apply to these organizations.
10. Intellectual property: The ownership and licensing of intellectual property within DAOs can be complex, and it is not always clear how existing laws and regulations apply to these issues.

Potential impact of DAOs on traditional models of economic governance and assess their potential to disrupt or transform existing systems

DAOs have the potential to disrupt traditional models of economic governance by providing a new way for organizations to operate and make decisions in a transparent and decentralized manner. By eliminating the need for traditional management structures and central decision-making authorities, DAOs have the potential to increase efficiency, reduce the risk of corruption, and foster greater collaboration among stakeholders.

However, it is important to consider the potential impact of DAOs on traditional models of economic governance and assess their potential to disrupt or transform existing systems. For example, if DAOs become more widely adopted, they may challenge the dominance of traditional organizations and potentially lead to a shift in the balance of power within the economy. It is also important to consider the potential unintended consequences of using DAOs as a model for economic governance. For example, if a significant proportion of economic activity is facilitated through DAOs, it may become more difficult for governments to collect taxes or regulate economic activity. Additionally, if the use of DAOs becomes widespread, it may have implications for employment and the distribution of wealth within society. Overall, it is important to carefully consider the potential impact of DAOs on traditional models of economic governance and assess their potential to disrupt or transform existing systems in order to understand the full implications of these organizations.

CONCLUSION

DAOs are a new type of organization that are run using blockchain technology and are designed to operate without the need for traditional management structures. In this research project, we explored the feasibility of using DAOs as a new model for economic governance in the blockchain era. We examined the key features and functions of DAOs, assessed the potential benefits and challenges of using these organizations as a model for economic governance, and considered the legal and regulatory implications of DAOs.

Our findings suggest that DAOs have the potential to disrupt traditional models of economic governance by providing a new way for organizations to operate and make decisions in a transparent and decentralized manner. DAOs have the potential to facilitate decentralized decision-making, increase transparency and promote greater accountability within organizations. However, there are also challenges and limitations to using DAOs as a model for economic governance, and the legal and regulatory implications of these organizations are still unclear in many jurisdictions.

Overall, our research suggests that DAOs have the potential to be a disruptive force in the world of economic governance, but more work is needed to understand the full range of benefits and challenges that these organizations present. Further research is needed to identify best practices for implementing and operating DAOs effectively and to develop regulatory frameworks that can support the growth and development of these organizations while also protecting the interests of stakeholders.

ADDITIONAL READING

Böhmecke-Schwafert, M., Wehinger, M., & Teigland, R. (2022). Blockchain for the circular economy: Theorizing blockchain's role in the transition to a circular economy through an empirical investigation. *Business Strategy and the Environment*, *31*(8), 3786–3801. doi:10.1002/bse.3032

Çetin, S., Gruis, V., & Straub, A. (2022). Digitalization for a circular economy in the building industry: Multiple-case study of Dutch social housing organizations. *Resources. Conservation & Recycling Advances*, *15*, 200110. doi:10.1016/j.rcradv.2022.200110

Chauhan, A., Jakhar, S. K., & Chauhan, C. (2021). The interplay of circular economy with industry 4.0 enabled smart city drivers of healthcare waste disposal. *Journal of Cleaner Production*, *279*, 123854. doi:10.1016/j.jclepro.2020.123854 PMID:32863607

Cheah, C. G., Chia, W. Y., Lai, S. F., Chew, K. W., Chia, S. R., & Show, P. L. (2022). Innovation designs of industry 4.0 based solid waste management: Machinery and digital circular economy. *Environmental Research*, *213*, 113619. doi:10.1016/j.envres.2022.113619 PMID:35700763

Chen, Q., Feng, H., & de Soto, B. G. (2021). Revamping construction supply chain processes with circular economy strategies: A systematic literature review. *Journal of Cleaner Production*, *335*, 130240. doi:10.1016/j.jclepro.2021.130240

Chiaroni, D., Fraccascia, L., Giannoccaro, I., & Urbinati, A. (2022). Enabling factors for the diffusion of circular economy and their impacts on sustainability. *Resources. Conservation & Recycling Advances*, *15*, 200101. doi:10.1016/j.rcradv.2022.200101

Dantas, T. E. T., de-Souza, E. D., Destro, I. R., Hammes, G., Rodriguez, C. M. T., & Soares, S. R. (2021). How the combination of Circular Economy and Industry 4.0 can contribute towards achieving the Sustainable Development Goals. *Sustainable Production and Consumption*, *26*, 213–227. doi:10.1016/j.spc.2020.10.005

Demestichas, K., & Daskalakis, E. (2020). Information and communication technology solutions for the circular economy. *Sustainability*, *12*(18), 1–19. doi:10.3390u12187272

Dutta, P., Chavhan, R., Gowtham, P., & Singh, A. (2022). The individual and integrated impact of Blockchain and IoT on sustainable supply chains: A systematic review. In *Supply Chain Forum: An International Journal* (pp. 1-24). 10.1080/16258312.2022.2082851

Eraky, M., Elsayed, M., Qyyum, M. A., Ai, P., & Tawfik, A. (2022). A new cutting-edge review on the bioremediation of anaerobic digestate for environmental applications and cleaner bioenergy. *Environmental Research*, *213*, 113708. doi:10.1016/j.envres.2022.113708 PMID:35724728

Fernando, Y., Rozuar, N. H. M., & Mergeresa, F. (2021). The blockchain-enabled technology and carbon performance: Insights from early adopters. *Technology in Society*, *64*, 101507. doi:10.1016/j.techsoc.2020.101507

Figueiredo, K., Hammad, A. W., Haddad, A., & Tam, V. W. (2022). Assessing the usability of blockchain for sustainability: Extending key themes to the construction industry. *Journal of Cleaner Production*, *343*, 131047. doi:10.1016/j.jclepro.2022.131047

Hennemann Hilario da Silva, T., & Sehnem, S. (2022). The circular economy and Industry 4.0: Synergies and challenges. *Revista de Gestão*, *29*(3), 300–313. doi:10.1108/REGE-07-2021-0121

Igalavithana, A. D., Yuan, X., Attanayake, C. P., Wang, S., You, S., Tsang, D. C., Nzihou, A., & Ok, Y. S. (2022). Sustainable management of plastic wastes in COVID-19 pandemic: The biochar solution. *Environmental Research*, *212*, 113495. doi:10.1016/j.envres.2022.113495 PMID:35660402

Imoniana, J. O., Silva, W. L., Reginato, L., Slomski, V., & Slomski, V. G. (2020). Sustainable technologies for the transition of auditing towards a circular economy. *Sustainability*, *13*(1), 1–24. doi:10.3390u13010218

Jin, S., & Chang, H. (2022). The trends of blockchain in environmental management research: A bibliometric analysis. *Environmental Science and Pollution Research International*, 1–18. doi:10.100711356-022-19856-x PMID:35349072

Khan, S. A. R., Shah, A. S. A., Yu, Z., & Tanveer, M. (2022). A systematic literature review on circular economy practices: Challenges, opportunities and future trends. *Journal of Entrepreneurship in Emerging Economies*, *14*(5), 754–795. doi:10.1108/JEEE-09-2021-0349

Khan, S. A. R., Zia-ul-haq, H. M., Umar, M., & Yu, Z. (2021). Digital technology and circular economy practices: An strategy to improve organizational performance. *Business Strategy & Development*, *4*(4), 482–490. doi:10.1002/bsd2.176

Kristoffersen, E., Blomsma, F., Mikalef, P., & Li, J. (2020). The smart circular economy: A digital-enabled circular strategies framework for manufacturing companies. *Journal of Business Research*, *120*, 241–261. doi:10.1016/j.jbusres.2020.07.044

Kushwah, S., Dhir, A., Sagar, M., & Gupta, B. (2019). Determinants of organic food consumption. A systematic literature review on motives and barriers. *Appetite*, *143*, 104402. Advance online publication. doi:10.1016/j.appet.2019.104402 PMID:31421197

Lind, C. H., Kang, O., Ljung, A., & Rosenbaum, P. (2022). Involvement of multinational corporations in social innovation: Exploring an emerging phenomenon. *Journal of Business Research, 151*, 207–221. doi:10.1016/j.jbusres.2022.07.003

Martinez-Marquez, D., Florin, N., Hall, W., Majewski, P., Wang, H., & Stewart, R. A. (2022). State-of-the-art review of product stewardship strategies for large composite wind turbine blades. *Resources. Conservation & Recycling Advances, 15*, 200109. doi:10.1016/j.rcradv.2022.200109

Nandi, S., Sarkis, J., Hervani, A., & Helms, M. (2021). Do blockchain and circular economy practices improve post COVID-19 supply chains? A resource-based and resource dependence perspective. *Industrial Management & Data Systems, 121*(2), 333–363. doi:10.1108/IMDS-09-2020-0560

Narayan, R., & Tidström, A. (2020). Tokenizing coopetition in a blockchain for a transition to circular economy. *Journal of Cleaner Production, 263*, 121437. doi:10.1016/j.jclepro.2020.121437

Rehman Khan, S. A., Yu, Z., Sarwat, S., Godil, D. I., Amin, S., & Shujaat, S. (2022). The role of block chain technology in circular economy practices to improve organisational performance. *International Journal of Logistics Research and Applications, 25*(4-5), 605–622. doi:10.1080/13675567.2021.1872512

Chapter 10
Cryptocurrencies:
Changing the Face of Online Gaming

Srimathi T.
SRM Institute of Science and Technology, India

Bharathi R.
St. Joseph's College of Engineering, India

ABSTRACT

In this digital age, the rise of new technologies has caused a significant change in how we go about our daily business. The invention and adoption of cryptocurrencies have been one of the most significant recent developments. Given the surge in smartphone usage, cryptocurrency has had a big impact on a number of industries, including the mobile gaming sector. The use of cryptocurrencies has dramatically increased in recent days, with a wide range of uses including investments and transactions in the online gaming sector. With a billion-dollar market cap, the gaming sector is booming and not expected to stop. Every year, new systems and video games are released, giving players fresh things to look forward to. How players pay for their gaming is one area where the i-gaming industry has failed in making changes. The majority of the time, gamers have been forced to use conventional means like credit card payments or Google wallet. But what if a better option existed? What if cryptocurrency could be used by gamers to purchase their games?

DOI: 10.4018/978-1-6684-5691-0.ch010

INTRODUCTION

Cryptocurrency is a form of digital currency which requires cryptography for added security during financial transactions. Cryptocurrency is outsourced, which implies it is not controlled by a government or a financial institution. The first and most widely well-known crypto, Bitcoin, was established in 2009. Since then, a huge number of additional cryptocurrencies have been developed. Cryptocurrency has the potential to have a major impact on the videogame industry. For starters, it may make game buying safer. The widespread issue of credit card fraud in the gaming industry may be ameliorated by the use of cryptocurrency. Also, the use of cryptocurrency could facilitate the buying and selling of video games. Purchasing and selling games can be difficult right now. However, with cryptocurrency, it would become simple to purchase and sell video games online without the need for a third-party provider such as Xbox Live or Steam. Cryptocurrency could make micro-transactions more common in games. Microtransactions are small purchases that players can make inside a game. They are often used to purchase items or upgrades that make the game easier or more fun to play.

WHAT IS CRYPTOCURRENCY?

A cryptocurrency is a digital asset that is protected by cryptography. Using blockchain technology, guarantees decentralization, openness, and immutability. Because cryptocurrency is issued by no centralized authority, it is resistant to government meddling and manipulation. Bitcoin is the most well-known block chain-based crypto. In addition to Ethereum, Cardano, and EOS, other competing cryptocurrencies include Litecoin, Peercoin, and Namecoin.

The Potential of Cryptocurrency in Gaming

The gaming industry could be transformed by cryptocurrency, making it much more fair, clear, and secure. With cryptos, gamers can be confident that they are receiving what people paid for, and development teams can be confident that they are being fairly compensated for one‘s efforts. Furthermore, cryptocurrency can aid in the prevention of cheating and other types of fraud in gaming. However, some obstacles must be overcome before cryptos can actually take off in the video games industry. For starters, there will need to be a greater understanding of cryptocurrency and how it works. Furthermore, more businesses must begin accepting bitcoin and other cryptocurrencies as payment. When these issues are resolved, cryptocurrency will undoubtedly have a massive effect on the gaming industry.

Ins and Outs of Using Cryptocurrency in Video Games

There are several substantial benefits to using bitcoin and other cryptocurrencies in gaming. For starters, it can aid in the creation of a more engaging and realistic gameplay experience. For example, if a game is laid in something like a post-apocalyptic planet in which traditional currency no longer exists, incorporating cryptocurrency into the game could perhaps add an extra layer of reality. Another benefit is that it can aid in the prevention of fraud. When gamers use actual money, there is always the possibility that fraudsters will take advantage of them.

But with cryptocurrencies, every transaction is documented on a public ledger, making it much more difficult for scammers to exploit online players.

Cryptocurrency can also assist in cost reduction. For example, when gamers use traditional payment methods like credit cards or Google pay to make purchases, game makers must pay fees to all these companies. When gamers use cryptocurrency, however, there are no charges.

The term "electronic commerce" refers to the sale of electronic goods. One significant disadvantage is that it can be quite volatile. This implies that there can be significant daily fluctuations in the value of cryptocurrencies. If a player wants to buy an item in-game with cryptocurrency but their currency has lost value by the time they go to make the purchase, they may be in a bind.

One additional drawback is that not every game can be played using cryptocurrency. As a result, gamers who wish to use crypto in their favorite games might not be able to accomplish their goals.

The security of using cryptocurrencies for gaming has raised some concerns. Despite the high level of security offered by blockchain technology, there have been some well-publicized exchange hacks in which users lost their cryptocurrencies.

IS CRYPTOCURRENCY THE FUTURE OF GAMING?

Cryptocurrency is undeniably on the rise, with an increasing number of people investing in various cryptocurrencies. Although some industry watchers see cryptocurrency as gaming's inevitable future, this has yet to be proven. Cryptocurrency has revolutionized the gaming industry by providing a new way for players to spend and earn cash.

Gamers, for example, could be compensated in cryptocurrency for achieving specific tasks or accomplishments within a game. They may use this currency to buy in-game products or to play other games. Nevertheless, there are some disadvantages to using cryptocurrencies for gaming. For one thing, it is still a relatively brand-new technology, but there are often threats to investing in emerging technologies.

Furthermore, the value of cryptocurrency fluctuates significantly, making it challenging to utilize as a stable currency in games. The only thing that can tell us for sure is time: will virtual currencies become the norm in the gaming industry in the future? It is still an appealing option for those who want to invest in the video games industry. The cryptocurrency sector has the potential to transform the gaming industry by decentralizing it and giving users more control over their in-game assets.

In recent years, cryptocurrencies have spread throughout the world. The convenience of cryptocurrency benefits a variety of industries, one of which is online gaming. According to a Wax report, approximately 75% of players in online games want to transfer their virtual investments for a currency that can be used to buy and sell on other platforms. Cryptocurrencies allow players to gather and trade virtual assets that can be exchanged and traded anywhere in the globe. As a result, it provides the gaming industry with a safe and simple way to make money.

ONLINE GAMING AND CRYPTOCURRENCY: HOW DOES IT WORK?

Cryptocurrencies can be purchased or sold using exchanges from wallets. For instance, a user sends cryptocurrency units to some other user's digital wallet when they want to exchange them. In-app advertising, affiliate marketing, and in-app purchases are all examples of monetization strategies used in online gaming. Players can purchase items such as coins, additional lives, and unique characters through in-app purchases. In online bit coin games, players purchase items with cryptocurrency or purchase cryptocurrency itself. In-app advertising in online games takes the form of rewarded ads, which require players to complete particular things, watch video advertisements, and fill out surveys in order to earn cryptocurrencies. Affiliate marketing is a relatively new market phenomenon in which players must click affiliate links and banner ads in order to refer a friend, earn rewards, or sign up for a free offer. Nowadays, players can gamble at or keep trading in digital assets at online Gambling sites that have accepted cryptocurrency payments.

How Does Crypto Gaming Work?

Traditional online gaming typically uses affiliate program, in-app buying, and in-app adverts as monetization strategies. Additionally, in-game coins like those found in smartphone games like CandyCrush and Monopolistic are very common among today's gamers. But it's terrible that these coins haven't had any value outside of the game for so long.

Because it enables users to increase the value of their purchases, cryptocurrency gaming stands out in this regard. In crypto games, store vouchers, such as game-specific items, are frequently kept on a shared database over a crypto network. The blockchain, a distributed ledger, makes it possible to exchange game items for cryptos, which can then be exchanged for real money.

Players can purchase items like coins, additional lives, personalisation, outfits, gadgets, etc. right from the game to in-app purchases. Applying this to cryptocurrency gameplay, in-app purchases occur when users purchase goods with cryptocurrency or virtual currency itself. In contrast, classical games typically purchase their assets from a core programmer store, making the developers the true winners of these games rather than the players.

Additionally, players cannot alter the game's life cycle in conventional games. Unused virtual assets will be removed by the operator when the server is shut down, and the player will no longer have access to them. Only the game's operator, not the player, is the true owner of any commodities in the game.

Modern games do support digital ownership, but they lack the value or shareholdings that crypto games do. Users might be able to own in-game items, but you are not allowed to sell them to other players. From the possession of investments to its decentralized procedure to the fact that players' securities are globally scattered and not constrained, the entire idea of crypto games is very different in comparison. Additionally, players cannot alter the game's life cycle in conventional games. Unused virtual assets will be removed by the operator when the server is shut down, and also the player would no longer have access to them. Only the game's controller, not the player, is the true owner of any goods in the game.

Make money playing crypto games.

Essentially, crypto games are video games that use a distributed ledger architecture and run on a cryptocurrency network to give players proveable possession over the virtual items they can access in the games. Players can exchange virtual goods for cryptos, which can then be exchanged for real money, as a result.

For the longest time, only the game's creators or game studios were involved. Since these investments had only a purely cosmetic value, only the game's developers or game studios were able to profit from the digital money that were managed to sell to players or users. This meant that despite users paying real money to buy them, almost everything that one could buy in a play (such as skins, armor, improvements, etc.) had only a small value.

Liquidity in the crypto video game market

It's crucial to discuss the market liquidity in these markets given how crypto video game are incredibly reliant on the gaming industry. Liquidity, in its simplest form, refers to the largest number of items that can be purchased and sold at any given time on the game market. Liquidity is a reliable indicator of any industry because the more liquidity there is, the safer the market is.

The crypto game market may include both NFT and FT holdings to improve liquidity. While NFT assets can be utilized more for their rareness, which typically has high value but low supply, FT assets can be tried to scale to be have high liquidity marketplaces and therefore be used for utility assets in the game.

Benefits of Cryptocurrency in Online Gaming:

Cryptocurrency is being used in online games to solve problems with transactions and fraud that players encounter while playing online games. Some of the benefits are streamlined payments, the real ownership of players, the decentralisation of payments, and cross-game compatibility.

Some advantages of using cryptocurrency in online games.

1- Instant Transaction

Cryptocurrency removes bureaucratic authority and inefficient intermediaries from the process, allowing players to enjoy their favourite games more quickly.

It makes the process of exchanging crypto units instant and efficient.

Another issue that game developers frequently face is the inability to sell their software outside of app stores. These developers can use blockchain to process nano-payments and receive payment instantly.

2- Playing Ability to Play Anywhere

The use of cryptocurrency allows gamers to play across borders without worrying about security or exchange rates.

It allows gamers to play without confirming their identity or email address. It enables gamers to pay and withdraw funds more quickly and without restrictions from anywhere in the world.

3- Secured and Reliable

When making frequent transactions in computer games, security is essential because so many gaming websites lack credibility. Blockchain technology stops the illegal trading of digital assets in online games. By establishing an immutable record, it also ends key duplication as well as hacking and theft of keys. It helps players maintain their trust in the smart contracts that make sure their payments are safe and secure.

4. Better Value for Each Cash

Compared to PayPal, bank transfers, and credit cards, cryptocurrencies are more affordable. There are no additional costs associated with using bitcoins, and it is not necessary to wait for money to transfer. Because peer-to-peer transactions between users eliminate middlemen, the usage of cryptocurrency in online games also eliminates processing and exchange fees. Players and game makers can use the concept more effectively as a result. Players receive greater value for their cash and developers earn more money.

5- Disguise One's Identity

Personal information might not always be protected when users engage in online games, even while the money might be safe. Online bitcoin gaming are the ideal to choose if you don't feel comfortable or keen in disclosing any personal information.

Additionally, unless a user chooses to openly publish interactions, crypto purchases are private. It's because each time a consumer makes a purchase, a new anonymous bitcoin address is established.

CRYPTO CHALLENGES IN THE GAMING SECTOR?

It poses numerous future problems to the video games industry. One of the first issues being considered is whether a house threshold on winnings in events based on this should be implemented.

The issue concerns the fact that any house constraint could possibly encourage collusion among gamers using real money to bet in order to guarantee a particular result.

1. Fluctuation: Cryptos are very prone to sudden drops in value, which can result in sizable losses.
2. Safety: Since cryptocurrency transactions are irreversible, users who make mistakes or fall prey to forgery cannot get one's cash back.
3. Trading Fees: Based on the cash and the sum being transferred, transaction fees for cryptocurrency transactions can be quite high.
4. Lack of Oversight: Users are unprotected in the occasion of theft or fraud because cryptocurrencies are not governed by any governmental body or financial firm.
5. Limited Acknowledgement: Due to the lack of cryptocurrency acceptance on many i-gaming platforms, users may need to convert their cryptocurrency.

Due to the inherent volatility of these digital tokens, a further issue is how specific game platforms should express their terms & conditions, as well as how they generate User Agreements for gameplay that do use them. The fundamental block chain has the potential to significantly disrupt the gaming industry in a variety of ways. Primarily, gamers can already transact virtual goods and cryptos for real-world goods and services. This opens the door for game developers to develop new small transaction-based business strategies that could boost game revenue. Furthermore, it has the potential to decrease fraud gaming activities including deception or game object theft. Finally, blockchain could aid in the resolution of long-standing disputes between game developers.

Cryptocurrencies are poised to dominate online games according to the data.

One may be surprised to learn that, compared to just 5% of all millennials, 55% of millennial gamers possess cryptocurrencies. The findings of a recent survey demonstrate how eager players are to use cryptocurrencies to improve their gaming experience.

A poll of 1,000 American gamers who have previously acquired, sold, or exchanged virtual goods online was conducted by the Worldwide Asset eXchangeTM. According to the study, 75percent of participants stated they would like to be able to trade their virtual items for money to buy or resell on other channels. Approximately 5% of millennials, based on a recent London Block Exchange survey, have made investments in different cryptocurrencies. Amazingly, 55 percent of today's millennial players have already used cryptos, according to WAX.

According to WAX, more than 50% of American gamers of all ages currently hold bitcoin. Nevertheless, 86 percent of those who have, have never utilized it in gaming and 80 percent of those who are interested have never done so. Nearly two-thirds wished they had more chances to do so. The acceptance rate of cryptos inside gaming should only rise over time due to the worldwide nature of the gaming world and the tech-savvy millennial population.

According to William Quigley, "the broad use of crypto in online video games is impending." "Video gamers are technologically sophisticated members of a worldwide community who seek to conduct frequent, brief cross-border trades. The study's findings are crystal clear: online gaming want to be capable of making inexpensive transactions connected to gaming using bitcoin.

High prices and currency exchange, ineffective middlemen, and lengthy transaction times are problems that could be resolved by the general acceptance of a crypto which is designed specifically for the marketplace of virtual game goods. Over 75% of players cite better usability as a major benefit, among the many possible advantages of using cryptocurrencies in gaming. Moreover, 66 percent said they were 49 percent of participants would like the higher processing speeds, and keen in the increased security. Additionally, 44 percent want lower transaction fees, while 42 percent like why cryptocurrency dramatically lowers exchange rates.

The World's First Crypto Prize Pool Continues Cryptocurrency's Tremendous Growth in e - Sports and Videogames

Similar to cryptocurrency traders, gamers who trade in-game virtual goods known as skins. They deal in electronic information with significant real-world value, face attack threats when trading with strangers all over the world, and have similar worries about the safety of their merchant accounts and exchanges. They also face the challenges of trading digital goods inside a fiat-centric planet, such as currency exchange service charges and a lack of readily available options for converting fiat into valuable online material. The transactions range in value from cents to thousands of dollars. The Worldwide Asset exchange was created by the team behind OPSkins. com in response to this. Gamers will be capable of purchasing and selling digital in-game items more quickly, safely, affordably, and conveniently thanks to WAX. WAX aims to bring cryptocurrency to the masses among such 400 million players, making the long-promised widespread acceptance of cryptocurrencies a reality – all beginning with skin.

Cryptocurrencies will be widely adopted thanks to video games. The recent statement of a cryptocurrency prize money for a CS: GO competition, the most well-known Steam game with in-game item trade, solidifies the partnership between these two sectors.

India's Current Crypto Gaming Regulations

According to current Indian regulations, crypto is neither forbidden nor regarded an asset. The most recent regulations concern cryptocurrency tax implications.

As of April 1, 2022, cryptocurrency will be subject to a 30% tax imposed by the government on digital assets. The recently passed legislation covers all in-app transactions and reward points provided by cryptocurrency gaming apps. Additionally, the government has suggested charging a 1% (TDS) on transactions involving virtual digital assets. Additionally, TDS would be levied through in purchases and benefits from cryptocurrency gaming apps, and since the players would be responsible for paying it, their income would be reduced.

The murkiness surrounding the imposition of TDS for in-app purchases of gaming items in cryptocurrency games is the problem. An in-depth analysis of the legal system would be necessary for complete clearness regarding taxes in cryptocurrency gaming. Users are uncertain regarding whether the tax fee will be charged once or every time they buy a particular asset. The regulations can have a significant positive effect in a number of ways if they are implemented correctly:

More Employment: Legal enrollments in India would help many businesses that are currently acting from various parts of the universe while conducting business in India to create themselves. The number of jobs in this industry would increase as a result.

More Income for the Nation: Taxing and governing sports betting will bring in 1000s of crores of rupees for the nation, boosting its economy and doing away with the requirement for a black market as a whole.

Convenient: Companies that are registered in India give authorities the ability to monitor operations and make sure everything is legal. All transactions, from investments to cashouts, can be monitored to make sure no fraud is occurring. Users frequently encounter scams where victims are unable to withdraw money or where credit or debit card information is obtained through the cloning of personal information. Having a place to instruct their concerns would significantly raise users' trust in the industry.

Regulatory oversight: A crackdown on the other businesses that operate unlawfully will be necessary if regulations are passed and gaming enterprises are able to legitimize themselves by submitting license applications and paying taxes. Legitimate companies would need assurances from the authorities that every attempt would be made to keep unauthorized operators out.

Taxation is a significant part where the government must do it correctly. High taxes on betting companies will probably encourage them to carry on with their current illegal operations. The ideal situation would be for cryptocurrency to be accepted as a valid form of payment, enabling people when using their digital currencies as a means of exchange or bond. To enable calculated converts, the asset may be pegged towards the INR. The absolute prohibition of cryptocurrency in India is the worst-case scenario. The overall consensus is that, despite rumors to the contrary, it may be challenging to completely outlaw cryptocurrency gaming given the expanding crypto market.

Why GameFi, a Cryptocurrency Gaming Platform, is Becoming a New Source of Income?

Since cryptocurrencies are still a worldwide phenomenon, businesses all over the world are looking for new ways to integrate this genuinely breakthrough technology into their essential goods and services. Particularly in this area, online gaming has emerged as a hotbed of innovative growth. Developers are coming up with innovative ways to use cryptocurrencies to pay for and trade goods, personal care products, unlock character types, and other things in video games. metaverse, the meeting point of the physical and virtual worlds, has never looked better.

Sony, Tencent, Nintendo, and Microsoft are some of the largest video game companies, with each generating more than $10 billion in revenues. With a huge revenue of around $25 billion, Sony is at the top of the rankings. The most renowned gaming studios in the globe include Electronic Arts, Sega Games, Konami Holdings Companies, and Gameloft. The Covid-19 global epidemic caused several economies to collapse in 2020, but the industry of video games was among the few industries to unexpectedly experience growth. People naturally turned to finding entertainment in their homes during the repeated cycles of restrictions as several countries imposed nationwide shut downs. Activision Blizzard, Epic Games, and Electronic Arts are just a few of the major game developers that forecast significant increases in total sales and user engagement in 2020. The rise in in-game purchases coincided with the surge in active users. The last few decades have seen a significant evolution in video games. The worldwide gaming market, that was estimated to be worth Dollars 173.70 billion in 2020, is expected to grow at a CAGR of 9.64% from 2021 to 2026 to reach USD 314.40 billion.

FINAL IMPRESSIONS

Finally, it is important to address the impact that its growing popularity of it will have on the future of gaming, both in terms of technology and business. This topic cannot be overlooked as this is where it will have a lasting effect on our society and the way that we play games. It has disrupted the traditional gaming industry by permitting gamers to purchase in-game items with it. This has provided gamers with a more convenient way to pay for in-game purchases, as well as allowed developers to receive payments quickly and without third-party mediation. However, there are several challenges that it presents in the gaming industry. These include fraud and hacks, regulatory uncertainty, and limited gamer adoption. To overcome these challenges, the gaming industry must work together with companies and regulators to create something secure. Users frequently encounter scams where victims are unable to withdraw money or where credit or debit card information is obtained through the cloning of personal information. Having a place to instruct their concerns would significantly raise users' trust in the industry.

ADDITIONAL READING

Assomull, V. (2022, June 19). Crypto Gaming In India: Here's Everything You Need to Know. *Inc 42*. https://inc42.com/

Beach, P. F. (2022, Sept. 20). Global Online Game Market Revenue for 2022 Expected To Exceed $196 Billion. *PRNewswire*. https://www.prnewswire.com/

Brown, C. (2023, January 16). How Crypto is revolutionizing the Online Gambling Industry. *Crypto news flash*. https://www.crypto-news-flash.com/

Bunjaku, F., & Olivera, G.-T. Emilija, MitevaKacarski. (2017). Cryptocurrencies – Advantages and Disadvantages. *Journal of Economics, 2*(1). https://www.doi.org/10.46763/JOE

Duggan, W., & Powell, F. (2022, September 5). What is Crypto Gaming. *Forbes Advisor*. https://www.forbes.com/

Griffiths, M. D. (2012). Internet gambling, player protection, and social responsibility. In *Routledge international handbook of Internet gambling* (pp. 247–269). Routledge.

Guest. (2021, September 9). How Crypto gaming (GameFi) is emerging as the new way to make money. *Financial Express*. https://www.financialexpress.com/

Guest, (2022, May 21). The impact of cryptocurrency on the gaming industry. *Invisible Fiction*. https://invisiblefiction.com/

Jani, S. (2018). The growth of cryptocurrency in India: Its challenges & potential impacts on legislation. *Research gate publication*.

Zoltan, T. (2022, January 24). How Cryptocurrency Will Impact The Gaming Industry. *European Gaming*. https://europeangaming.eu/

Chapter 11
Cryptocurrencies:
Issues and Challenges in Financial Reporting

Fathima Farzana J.
https://orcid.org/0000-0002-4597-0161
St. Joseph's University, India

ABSTRACT

With the advent of cryptocurrency during 2009, a new regime of exchange consideration, as well as an investment avenue without physical existence and centralized regulatory authority, started attracting the investors. These extremely volatile neo currencies created regulatory issues among apex monitoring authorities and also raised various challenges in the front of financial reporting. The main purpose of financial reporting is to present the true and fair view of the financial statement of a company. Any violation in this regard creates serious issue of corporate governance. On acceptance of cryptocurrencies as a legal tender, disclosure of such transactions will be mandatory on the part of the company trading and investing on it. At the same time, International Accounting Standard Board (IASB), has not yet issued any standards of IFRS as a guideline for accounting cryptocurrency. In this regard, a detail analysis has been presented in this chapter comprising various issues and challenges in recognizing cryptocurrency in financial statements under IFRS.

DOI: 10.4018/978-1-6684-5691-0.ch011

1. INTRODUCTION

The economic environment of the continent has been undergoing constant changes. This change has also affected the mode of transactions vibrantly. Originating from the barter system, the economy has witnessed coins, currencies, cheques, drafts, and many other modes of legal tenders including Unified Payments Interfaces (UPI). Of late investors ventured into investing on currencies of foreign nation in view of hedging or as an investment avenue. Until this time, all these modes of transactions were regulated and monitored by the Government and other regulatory authorities through regulatory guidelines, considering the utmost protection of investors' interest. With the advent of cryptocurrency during 2009, a new regime of exchange consideration as well as an investment avenue without physical existence and centralized regulatory authority, started attracting the investors. These neo currencies, being extremely volatile, not only created regulatory issues among apex monitoring authorities but also raised various challenges in the front of financial reporting.

The main purpose of financial reporting is to present the true and fair view of the performance and position of a company to its stakeholders. Any violation in this regard will create a serious issue pertaining to corporate governance of the organization. As an impact of globalization and global investment avenues of the companies, 166 countries adopted International Financial Reporting Standards (IFRS, n.d.) to have harmonization in preparation and understanding of financial statements. Hence, it is mandatory on the part of the company to disclose cryptocurrencies, if in case there are some transactions or investments made on it. As per IFRS, there are criteria to recognize, measure, present, disclose and de-recognize every element of the financial statement. Since countries started accepting cryptocurrencies as a legal tender, disclosure of such transactions will be mandatory on the side of the company trading and investing on it. At the same time, International Accounting Standard Board (IASB), have not yet issued any standards of IFRS as a guideline for accounting cryptocurrency. Moreover, guidelines as to which element of financial statement will it be categorized into, is yet another challenge in recognition.

Taking all these points into consideration, the present chapter will focus on a detail analysis of various issues and challenges in recognizing cryptocurrency in financial statements under IFRS.

According to RBI, Crypto currencies are digital currencies in decentralized systems that are authenticated by participants with consensus through outright bypass of financial systems and its controls, which cannot be traced or confiscated by Governments. They are anonymous and work over the internet without any restriction of borders (Sankar, 2022).

Over 9,999 types of cryptocurrencies are in existence as of June 2022 (Coin Market Cap, n.d.), with Bitcoins being the pioneer in this category. The entire lot of cryptocurrencies sparing Bitcoins were collectively called as altcoins, who claims that they are improved or modified version of Bitcoin but all of them possess a low level of security compared to Bitcoin networks. Cryptocurrencies are designated for payments across decentralized network of users using blockchain technology and may sometimes called as tokens. These tokens can be issued as a part of ICO (Initial Coin Offering), representing a stake in blockchain project. If the same tokens were linked to the value of a company or project, they are called as security tokens. Some other variants of these tokens were called as utility tokens, in which the tokens issued have a particular use case or function like share file across a decentralized network, DNS (Domain Name System) service for internet addresses and the like. Since all these types of tokens were traded on crypto exchanges without showing any bifurcation, it is the duty of the traders to check on the categories of the tokens before investing on them (Hayes, 2022).

2. ISSUES IN RECOGNIZING CRYPTO IN FINANCIAL STATEMENTS

Even though cryptocurrencies are considered as currencies, can they be recognized as currencies? Do they have an issuer like a sovereign entity to call them as currency? If not currency, then how cryptos need to be recognized in financial statements. Considering the requisite of financial reporting, an entity should faithfully represent its transactions and other events that it purports to represent. Moreover, the transactions should be accounted for and presented according to their substance and economic reality than their legal form, according to the principle of substance over form (Paper 7F Examining Team, 2008). Further emphasis should be given from the materiality aspect of the transaction as well. With this note, let us look into the conceptual issues in recognizing cryptocurrency in financial statements of an entity.

2.1. Elements of Financial Statements

To appropriately report the financial performance and position of an entity, the financial statements should contain five significant elements in it (International Accounting Standards Board, 2010), Figure 1 shows the elements in detail. These elements should be depicted in words and by monetary amount in the financial statements.

Figure 1. Elements of financial statements

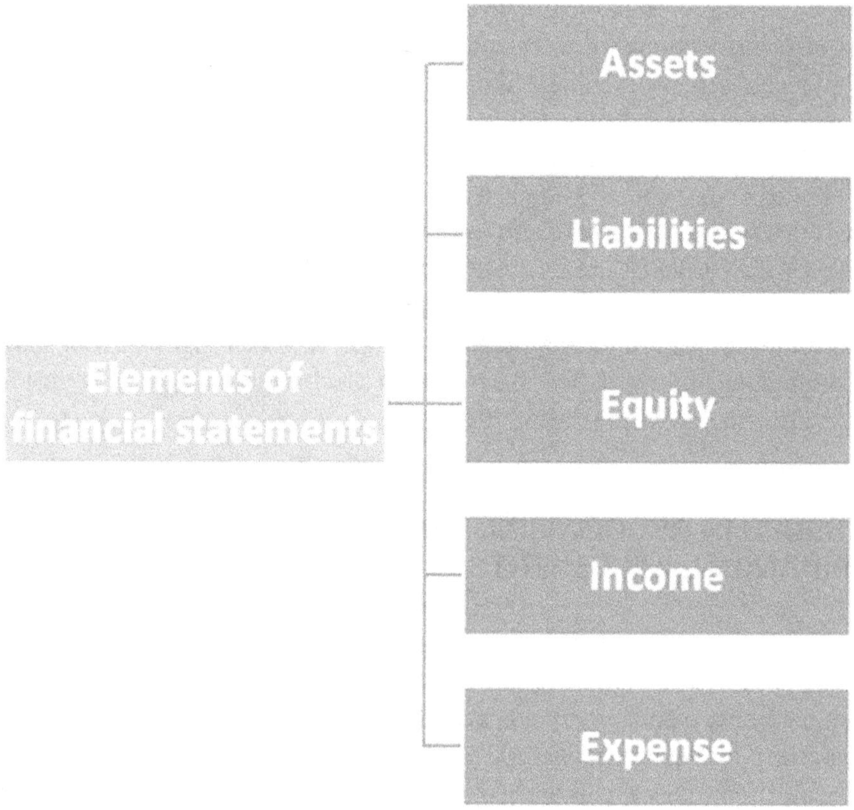

2.1.1. Asset

An asset is defined as a present economic resource controlled by the entity as a result of past events (IFRS conceptual framework Para 4.3). Wherein economic resource is a right that has the potential to produce economic benefits. An asset can only be recognized if it can be reliably measured and can be supported with sufficient evidence to prove its existence.

2.1.2. Liability

A liability is defined as a present obligation of the entity to transfer an economic resource as a result of past events (IFRS conceptual framework Para 4.26). Following three criteria must be satisfied to conclude a liability to be existing (IFRS conceptual framework Para 4.27):

(i) The entity has an obligation;
(ii) The obligation is to transfer an economic resource; and
(iii) The obligation is a present obligation that exists as a result of past events.

A liability can only be recognized if it can be reliably measured and is supported by sufficient evidence that there is an obligation to transfer economic benefits due to a past transactions or events.

2.1.3. Equity

Equity is defined as the residual interest in the assets of the entity after deducting all its liabilities (IFRS conceptual framework Para 4.63).

2.1.4. Income

Income is defined as increases in assets, or decreases in liabilities, that result in increases in equity, other than those relating to contributions from holders of equity claims (IFRS conceptual framework Para 4.68). Recognition of income in profit or loss is possible only if the increase can be measured reliably.

2.1.5. Expense

Expense is defined as decreases in assets, or increases in liabilities, that result in decreases in equity, other than those relating to distributions to holders of equity claims (IFRS conceptual framework Para 4.69). Recognition of expense in profit or loss is possible only if the increase can be measured reliably.

In practice financial position approach is used to recognize the elements in the financial statements. This implies that an income is recorded if an asset increases or a liability decreases. Similarly an expense is recorded if there is an increase in liability or decrease in an asset.

2.2 Cryptocurrency as an Element in Financial Statement

If cryptocurrency is traded by an entity, such investment must be faithfully represented in the financial report, to help the stakeholders in making economic decisions. But any such item to be reported should be recognized in the financial statements if they meet the definition of an element. Accordingly, a clear analysis about cryptocurrency regarding its classification category of an element of financial statement is presented below.

2.2.1. Is Cryptocurrency an Asset?

As per the definition of an asset, control is the ability to obtain the economic benefits and to restrict the access of others (ACCA Examining Team, n.d.). According to this definition it can be said that cryptocurrency is an asset since it can be used to trade or buy goods. Now comes a question that under which category of asset will it fall?

Figure 2. Classification of assets

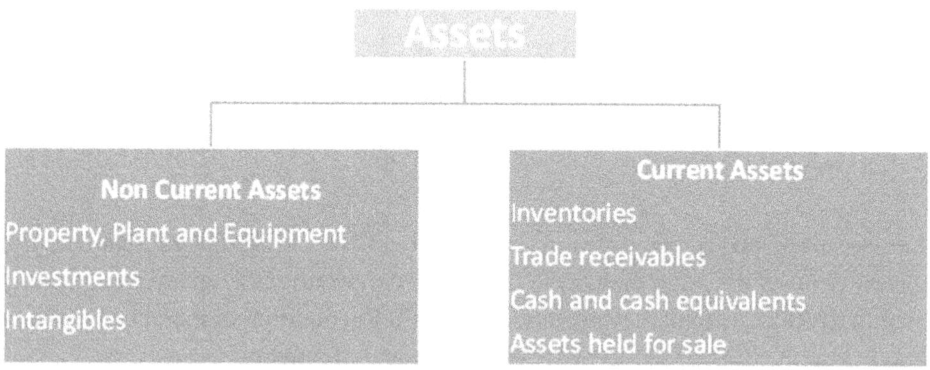

Figure 2 clearly portrays the types of assets as per IAS 1, accordingly any assets that forms the part of an entity's normal operating cycle will be classified as current and any assets held for more than a year will be classified into non-current. Considering the nature of cryptocurrency, having high volatility in its value wherein investors trade and benefit using the price fluctuations, it cannot be classified into non-current assets. If it is a current asset, then which category will be the suitable option? Can it be an inventory? No, because as per IAS 2 inventory should be valued on cost or Net Realizable Value whichever is lower. Due to price fluctuation, valuing the Net Realizable Value (NRV) is quite challenging. Can it be a cash and cash equivalent? No, it does not constitute cash as it cannot be immediately exchanged for goods and services. Further, it is subject to significant risk due to volatility hence it does not qualify as a cash equivalent as well. Can cryptocurrency be classified as Assets held for sale?

2.2.1.1. IFRS 5 Assets Held for Sale and Discontinued Operations

As per IFRS 5, para 6, "An entity shall classify a non-current asset as held for sale if it carrying amount will be recovered principally through a sale transaction rather than through continuing use".

To classify an item as held for sale, it must satisfy all the following conditions:

(i) According to IFRS 5, para 7, the asset must be available for immediate sale in its present condition.
(ii) As per IFRS 5, para 8, the sale of such asset must be highly probable, which means:
   - Management is 'committed to a plan to sell the asset,
   - An active programme to locate a buyer is in action, and
   - The asset is being actively marketed at a price that is reasonable.
(iii) The sale is anticipated to be executed within one year from the date of such classification as held for sale, according to IFRS 5, para 8.
(iv) As per IFRS 5, para 8, it is unlikely that significant changes to the plan will be made or that the plan will be withdrawn.

According to the mentioned criteria of IFRS 5, cryptocurrency is immediately available for sale, is highly probable of getting sold within a span of one year and no investor withdraw the plan of selling a cryptocurrency when it is profitable to execute. Since all the criteria are met by the cryptocurrency can it be classified into IFRS 5? No, because non-current assets that qualify as held for sale should be measured at the lower of their carrying amount and fair value less costs to sell. Since cryptocurrency is volatile in nature, determining NRV as well as fair value is difficult. Hence it is clear that cryptocurrency cannot be classified as non-current assets held for sale.

2.2.1.2. IAS 2 Inventories

Can cryptocurrency be classified as an inventory? It might be appropriate to consider cryptocurrencies in accordance with IAS 2 (ACCA Global, n.d.), Inventories, as IAS 2 applies to inventories of intangible assets. According to IAS 2 Inventories are defined as assets:

- Held for sale in the ordinary course of business
- In the process of production of such sale, or
- In the form of materials or supplies to be consumed in the production process or in the rendering of services.

As per the definition cryptocurrency can fits in the first line of classification namely held for sale in ordinary course of business, hence it could be treated as inventory. As per definition it can be said as an inventory. How about its measurement of initial recognition? The recognition measurement of inventory is lower of cost and NRV.

In case if the entity acts as a broker-trader[1] of cryptocurrency, according to IAS 2 it should be measured only at NRV. In both way of initial recognition assessment, NRV is a mandate. But, due to cryptocurrency's nature of high volatility, calculating NRV is a difficult task. Therefore, it cannot be regarded as an inventory.

2.2.1.3. Investments in Financial Instruments

Is cryptocurrency, a financial asset? It might appear that cryptocurrency should be reported as a financial asset, due to the various options for measurement choices given. Figure 3 describes the classification and measurement of financial assets.

Figure 3. Financial instruments

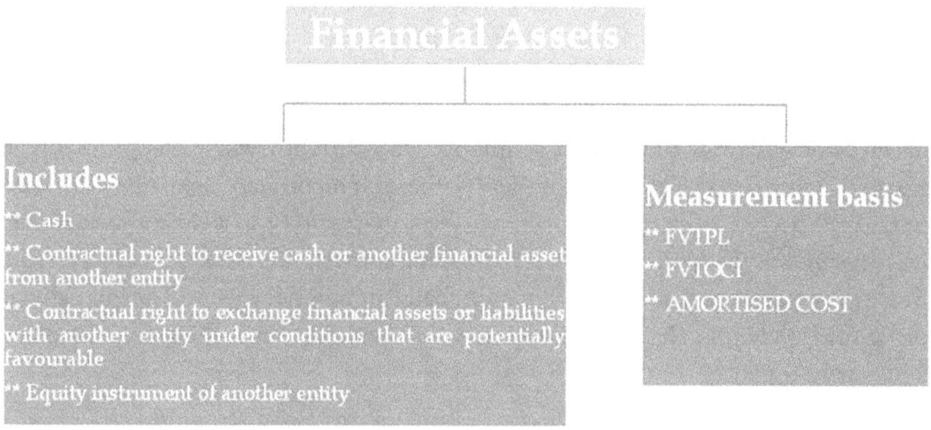

Financial instruments are reported using three standards of IFRS namely:

IAS 32: Financial instruments – Presentation
IFRS 7: Financial instruments – Disclosures
IFRS 9: Financial instruments – Recognition and Measurements

Accordingly, IAS 32 deals with the classification and presentation of financial instruments in the financial statements, IFRS 9 deals with recognition and measurement of financial instruments, and IFRS 7 deals with the disclosure requirements of financial instruments in financial statements. As per IAS 32, para 11, Financial asset is any asset that is "Cash; a contractual right to receive cash or another financial asset from another entity; a contractual right to exchange financial assets or liabilities with another entity under conditions that are potentially favorable; and an equity instrument of another entity". At initial recognition, all types of financial assets both equity and debt nature are measured using fair value. But when considering subsequent measurement of financial assets there are three methods, each classified based on the instrument passing two tests viz., Business model test and contractual cash flow characteristics tests.

- Business model test: Takes into consideration the purpose of the entity in holding the investment like holding period.
- Contractual cash flow characteristics test: Inflow of cash on holding the investment like certainty in receiving the return.

As mentioned in figure 3, financial instruments can be measured subsequently under Amortised cost method, or Fair Value Through profit or loss (FVTPL); or fair value through other comprehensive income (FVTOCI).

Equity instruments obtained through purchases of shares in other companies, can be measured only through FVTPL or FVTOCI. Whereas the default category of equity investment is to measure through FVTPL as they are held for short period of time according to business model test and unguaranteed cash flow considering contractual cash flow characteristics test. Hence if the measurement choice is FVTPL then any transaction costs incurred in the purchase of these instruments are expensed to profit or loss. At the end of each year any gain or loss due to revaluation to fair value will be presented in statement of profit or loss. Sometimes, equity instruments are classified to measure under FVTOCI. This designation can only be done if the investment is intended as a long-term investment. Hence, the transaction costs incurred will be capitalized and any gain or loss in revaluation will be presented in OCI and investment reserve in equity part of financial position statement. And on disposal, the investment reserve can be transferred to retained earnings or can remain the same.

Debt instruments by default are measured under FVTPL. Hence if an entity prefers to measure under any of the other two method, then it can do so, provided the instrument passes the business model test and contractual cash flow test. Accordingly, Instrument which are held until maturity that give rise to cash flows, indicates that it passes both the tests and will be subsequently measured using amortised cost. In this case the interest income will be presented in statement of profit or loss. If the entity intends to hold the investment to maturity but may also sell it if the yield is high, then the instrument should be measured using FVTOCI. In this case the interest income will be presented in statement of profit or loss and the revaluation gain if any will be shown in other comprehensive income.

Now taking into consideration of cryptocurrency, considering its trade frequency, it might appear that it should be accounted as a financial asset at FVTPL. But if critically examined, it is not a cash nor an equity interest in an entity. Can it be classified as a debt instrument? A debt instrument is a fixed income asset that allows the lender to earn a fixed interest along with principal repayment (Goel, 2017). Therefore, it cannot be classified as a debt instrument. Even though it appears suitable to measure at FVTPL, such type of measurement will not reflect a true performance or position of an entity. This is because the non-operating expense or income component may vary drastically due to the high volatility of cryptocurrencies price.

2.2.1.4 IAS 38 Intangible Assets

Is cryptocurrency an intangible asset? For an asset to be classified as IAS 38 Intangible assets, it must fall into one of the following categories:

- Separable
- Arises from legal/contractual rights

Apart from this it should also satisfy the definition of an asset, intangible asset and meet the below recognition criteria of the framework (IAS 38, para 18):

- Probable future economic benefits attributable to the asset will flow to the entity
- The cost of the asset can be reliably measured

If an intangible asset is purchased separately, it should be recognized at cost initially. Whereas subsequent measurement provides a choice between cost model and revaluation model. Under cost model, the carrying amount of intangible asset should be cost less amortization less impairment losses if any. Further, if the intangible asset is with a finite useful life, the amortization should be over the life and if it is with indefinite useful life, then there will be no amortization and instead impairment test should be carried out annually or more often if there is an indication. If any asset does not have an active market, then such assets should be measured using cost model. Taking cryptocurrencies into consideration, they are often traded on an exchange and therefore cost model cannot be applicable instead it may be possible to apply the revaluation model (ACCA Global, n.d.).

If any asset is measured using revaluation model, then as per IAS 38 the increase in revaluation should be recognized in other comprehensive income component of statement of profit or loss and as a revaluation surplus in equity. While recognizing revaluation increase in profit or loss, it should be recorded only up to the extent that it reverses a revaluation decrease of the same asset that was previously recognized in profit or loss. Meanwhile, revaluation loss should be recognized in profit or loss rather than other comprehensive income. However, the decrease due to revaluation loss can be recognized in other comprehensive income after adjusting with the credit balance in revaluation surplus if available in line with the same asset. In general, it is unusual for an intangible asset to have an active market. But in case cryptocurrency can be classified as an intangible asset, since it has an active market, it should be recognized using revaluation model. Again, there arise a question. If it is revaluation model, how to arrive at the fair value price? IFRS 13 defines fair value as "the price that would be received to sell an asset or paid to transfer a liability in an orderly transaction between market participants at the measurement date" (IFRS 13 Appendix A). Accordingly, IFRS 13 shows three level hierarchy of valuation techniques to measure fair value that is demonstrated in Figure 4.

Figure 4. Fair value hierarchy

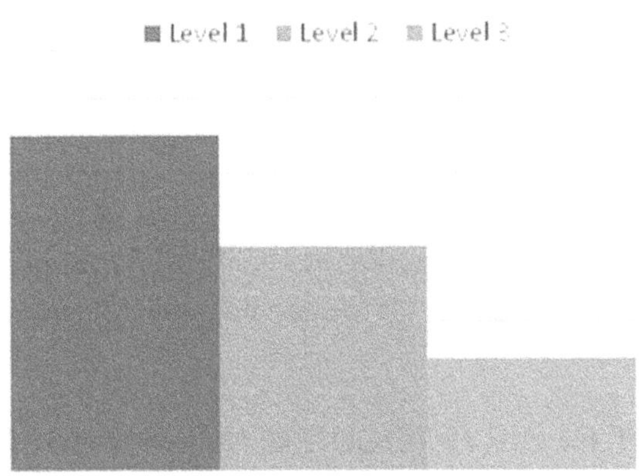

- **Level 1**

These inputs comprise of quoted prices (observable) that are available in active markets for identical assets and liabilities at the measurement date. These are considered as the most reliable evidence of fair value and hence it will be used without adjustment.

- **Level 2**

These inputs are observable inputs, apart from those included in level 1. These can be observable directly or indirectly and may include quoted prices of similar assets or liabilities that are not identical in active market or prices of identical or similar assets and liabilities that are in inactive markets. These require some degree of adjustment to arrive at a fair value measurement.

- **Level 3**

These are unobservable inputs for assets or liability, based upon the best available information that includes information that are reasonably available relating to market participants.

On analysing the levels of fair value measurement, cryptocurrencies should be valued using revaluation model using level 1 inputs. According to revaluation model, the carrying amount and the fair value will be compared and the difference, if gain should be shown in other comprehensive income and on the other hand if it is a loss, it should be shown in profit or loss. Therefore, fair value can be assessed from active market, whereas, to compute carrying amount it should be decided whether to amortise or not. Cryptocurrencies should be considered as having an indefinite useful life and hence it will not be amortised and instead annual impairment test will be conducted. As cryptocurrencies are traded due to the benefit attained in its price fluctuations, the unrealized gain or loss depicted in the profit or loss statement may not reflect the true financial performance and position of the company. Moreover, the reversal of revaluation gain from equity should need to be accounted frequently, questioning whether these can be classified into intangible assets or not.

3. TREATMENT OF CRYPTOCURRENCIES UNDER US GAAP

Though it is rare to find a solid example of IFRS-based companies using cryptocurrencies in their financial statements, US GAAP based companies like Tesla and MicroStrategy do account cryptocurrencies in their financial statements. US GAAP companies record impairment losses on indefinite-lived intangible assets when their value falls, but they cannot revalue them up outside of Mergers and Acquisition deals, whereas such kind of upward revaluation is allowed in IFRS-based companies. US GAAP companies record cryptocurrencies as a "Digital Asset" under intangible assets in their financial position statement. But revaluation gain will not be entered in the financial statements but will record impairment loss on digital assets in the performance statement. This will account for deferred tax asset impact since unrealized losses are not immediately deductible under tax purposes. Meanwhile, Financial service firms under US GAAP accounts cryptocurrencies as investments or financial assets. Therefore, it records both realized and unrealized gains and losses in its income statements.

3.1. Impact of Adoption of Cryptocurrencies

Since US GAAP companies adopt cryptocurrencies in their financial statements, there may be some negative impact on the effectiveness of net income and PE measurement. Net income will be skewed because of all the unrealized gains. On the other hand, value-based metrics such as EBITDA will gain more weightage due to the exclusion of such gains and losses. Since only few high-profile companies under US GAAP accounts for cryptocurrency, the accounting issues may not be relevant until considerable percentage of the S&P 500 companies account for it (DeChesare, 2020).

4. REQUIREMENT OF A STANDARD UNDER IFRS

After scrutinizing the above stated various aspects, it can be rightly said that accounting cryptocurrencies are not a simple task as the available standards do not accommodate it into any particular element of financial statements. Since usage of cryptocurrencies has abundantly increased in the last few years by big corporates like Microsoft, PayPal and the like, national accounting authorities have expressed the requirement for guidance and a proper standard to avoid inconsistency in accounting and to promote harmonization (Hyytia & Sundqvist, 2019). The general guideline is that if there are no existing standards to account any item of financial statements, the conceptual framework has to be referred or a new standard will be proposed by IASB. Sometimes the existing standards will be updated to accommodate a new item as an element of financial statements. On the other hand, an existing standard will be scratched and a new standard can be introduced. In this regard, let us have a detail understanding about IASB, IFRS, the standard issuing procedure and the like in the following paragraphs.

4.1. International Financial Reporting Standard

The London based group namely the International Accounting Standards Committee (IASC), responsible for developing International Accounting Standards, was established in June 1973. It comprises of the professional accountancy bodies of over 75 countries. IASC was established, in the public interest, to formulate and publish, International Accounting Standards to be followed in the presentation of financial statements. International Accounting Standards were issued to promote acceptance and observance of International Accounting Standards worldwide. The members of IASC have undertaken a responsibility to support the standards promulgated by IASC and to propagate those standards in their respective countries.

Between 1973 and 2001, the International Accounting Standards Committee (IASC) released International Accounting Standards (IAS). Between 1997 and 1999, the IASC restructured their organisation, which resulted in formation of International Accounting Standards Board (IASB). These changes came into effect on 1st April 2001. Subsequently, IASB issued statements about current and future standards; IASB publishes its Standards in a series of pronouncements called International Financial Reporting Standards (IFRS). However, IASB has not rejected the standards issued by the IASC. Those pronouncements continue to be designated as "International Accounting Standards" (IAS). Hence the term IFRS comprises of:

- IFRS issued by IASB;
- IAS issued by IASC;
- Interpretations issued by Standard Interpretations Committee (SIC); and
- Interpretations of International Financial Reporting Interpretations Committee (IFRIC) of the IASB.

International Financial Reporting Standards (IFRSs) are considered a "principles based" set of standards. In fact, they establish broad rules rather than dictating specific treatment.

4.2. Development of an IFRS Standard

The accounting standards are not developed over night. Based on the need and the requirement in recognizing and accounting a particular item which demands a standard, the following procedure will be followed by IASB while considering issuing a standard.

- The Board identifies a subject and appoints an advisory committee to advise on the issues.
- The Board may issue a discussion paper based on the recommendation of the advisory committee, to encourage comment from the members and the national accounting authorities .
- After considering the comments on the discussion paper, the Board publishes an exposure draft, being a draft version of the intended standard.
- Following the consideration of comments received on the draft, the Board publishes the final text of the IFRS Standard.
- The publication of an IFRS Standard, exposure draft or IFRIC Interpretation requires the votes of at least eight of the 15 Board members (ACCA Examining Team, n.d.).

5. CONCLUSION

Having hundreds of brokers, numerous intermediaries and exchanges trading with cryptocurrency, 29 different types of cryptocurrency frauds have been identified so far (Trozze et al., 2022). With absence of obligation to provide tax reports to market participants though a few may do so at their own discretion (Seth, 2022), there are notable number ethical fallouts. Adding to this, issues faced by accountants in accounting cryptocurrencies will surmount to lack of transparency and fair presentation of financial statements. Hence, it is highly recommended and expected that IASB will issue an exposure draft to give clarity in accounting and presenting cryptocurrencies in the financial statements to maintain harmonization in the application and reporting of the financial data.

REFERENCES

ACCA Examining Team. (n.d.). Financial reporting study text, Kaplan Publishing.

ACCA Global. (n.d.). Accounting for Cryptocurrencies: Home. ACCA. https://www.accaglobal.com/in/en/student/exam-support-resources/professional-exams-study-resources/strategic-business-reporting/technical-articles/cryptocurrencies.html

Coin Market Cap. (n.d.). *Today's Cryptocurrency Prices by Market Cap* [Data set]. Coin Market Cap. https://coinmarketcap.com/

DeChesare, B. (2020). Cryptocurrency accounting: Why Net Income and the P/E Multiple Have Become Even More Useless. Mergers & Inquisitions. https://mergersandinquisitions.com/cryptocurrency-accounting/

Goel, S. (2017). What is a debt instrument? The Economic Times. https://economictimes.indiatimes.com/markets/stocks/news/what-is-a-debt-instrument/articleshow/59530686.cms

Hayes, A. (2022). 10 Important Cryptocurrencies Other Than Bitcoin. Investopedia. https://www.investopedia.com/tech/most-important-cryptocurrencies-other-than-bitcoin/#citation-1

Hyytia, PSundqvist, E. (2019). Accounting for Cryptocurrencies- A Nightmare for Accountants. UMEA School of Business, Economics, and Statistics. http://www.diva-portal.org/smash/get/diva2:1331799/FULLTEXT01.pdf

IFRS. (n.d.). Who uses IFRS Accounting Standards? https://www.ifrs.org/use-around-the-world/use-of-ifrs-standards-by-jurisdiction/

International Accounting Standards Board. (2010). Conceptual Framework for Financial Reporting. International Accounting Standards Board. https://www.ifrs.org/content/dam/ifrs/publications/pdf-standards/english/2021/issued/part-a/conceptual-framework-for-financial-reporting.pdf

Paper 7F Examining Team. (2008). The need for and an understanding of a conceptual framework. ACCA. https://www.accaglobal.com/gb/en/student/exam-support-resources/fundamentals-exams-study-resources/f7/technical-articles/conceptual-framework-need.html

Sankar, S. (2022). Speeches and Interviews. Reserve Bank of India. https://rbi.org.in/Scripts/BS_SpeechesView.aspx?Id=1196

Seth, S. (2022). How to Prepare Your Bitcoin Tax Filing. Investopedia. https://www.investopedia.com/tech/how-prepare-bitcoin-tax-filing/#toc-bitcoin-record-keeping-is-your-responsibility

TrozzeA.KampsJ.AkartunaE. A.HetzelF. J.KleinbergB.DaviesT. JohnsonS. D. (2022). Cryptocurrencies and future financial crime. Crime Science. https://crimesciencejournal.biomedcentral.com/articles/10.1186/s40163-021-00163-8

Chapter 12
A Revolutionary Impact on Cryptocurrency

Elaiyaraja A.
St. Thomas College of Arts and Science, India

ABSTRACT

Cryptocurrency is the form of currency that resides digitally or virtually. The transaction can be secured by using cryptography. Since the decentralized system is applied to record the transactions the cryptocurrency does not have a central issuing or regulating authority. Besides, it explains the perception of blockchain technology. Among the several metrics in the market cap, cryptocurrency endures as the number one digital currency in the world. In the past decade, with novelty and a collective market capitalization the size of the cryptocurrency space has grown exponentially. Cryptocurrencies desire determined and secure mining methods. In this study, we survey and analysed the current mining. In this study, we survey and compare the current mining approach applied to the extensive Cryptocurrencies. We assess the strengths, deficiencies, and viable threats to each mining approach. On the whole, corresponding efficacy, assurance and the site show the exceptional threats and strengths are delineated.

INTRODUCTION

Any type of virtual or digital currency that uses cryptography to safeguard transactions is referred to as a crypto currency. Cryptocurrencies use a decentralised mechanism to track transactions and issue new units rather than a central authority to issue or regulate them (Goldwasser, 1990).

DOI: 10.4018/978-1-6684-5691-0.ch012

Despite the rise of new digital currencies that have revolutionised the market, one digital currency has continued to command the public's attention more than any other: A bit coin

BIT COIN

The phrase "the network timestamps transactions by hashing them into an on-going chain of hash-based proof-of-work, producing a record that cannot be modified without redoing the proof-of-work" is used for the first time in Bit Coin's description of the idea of block chain technology.

Without a doubt, bit coin has had a revolutionary impact on the world of digital currencies. By market cap and several other metrics, it continues to be the top digital currency in the world (Conti, *et.al.,* 2018).

A token currency that could be safely and privately transferred between people; once more, the parallels to contemporary crypto currencies are obvious.

A crypto currency is a type of digital tokens or "coins" that reside on a decentralised and distributed ledger known as a block chain (Schilling & Uhlig, 2019).

Bit coin continues to dominate the group of crypto currencies in terms of market capitalization, user base, and popularity.

Cryptocurrencies based on a decentralised peer-to-peer network.

Teams often create crypto currencies as code, adding in methods for issuance (often, but not always, through the mining process) and other regulations.

On cryptocurrency exchanges, cryptocurrencies are traded.

Ethereum (ETH)

The first alternative to Bit coins on our list is Ethereum (ETH), a decentralised software platform that makes it possible to create and run smart contracts and decentralised apps (dApps) free from third-party interference, fraud, or control (Tikhomirov, 2018).

Ethereum uses ether, a platform-specific cryptographic token, to power its apps. Developers that want to build and run applications on the Ethereum platform, as well as investors wishing to buy other digital currencies using ether, seek out ether (ETH), which functions as a mode of transportation on the Ethereum network (Casino, Dasaklis & Patsakis, 2019).

Although it trails the leading cryptocurrency by a wide margin, Ether, which was introduced in 2015, is currently the second-largest digital currency by market capitalization behind Bitcoin.

Blockchain-based crypto currencies enable people to conduct peer-to-peer financial transactions or sign contracts because they are decentralised platforms. No trustworthy third-party mediator, such as a bank, monetary authority, court, or judge, is required in any scenario. This might upend the current financial system and democratise finance. The size of the cryptocurrency market has increased dramatically over the past ten years thanks to new developments and a market valuation of more than $1.75 trillion.

Electronic Cash

David Chaum, an American cryptographer, experimented with a distinct kind of electronic money. He envisioned a token currency that could be securely and quietly exchanged between people; once more, the parallels to contemporary crypto currencies are startling (Chaum, Fiat & Naor, 2007).

Altcoins

Although this fundamental component of the sector has come under scrutiny as cryptocurrencies have gained more popularity, it is usually always the case that they are not intended to be subject to government manipulation or control. The term “altcoins” refers to all cryptocurrencies designed to be like Bitcoin (Cagli, 2019).

Digital Token

For instance, experts frequently place a high value on how coins are ranked against one another in terms of market capitalization. Although we have taken this into account, there are still additional factors that could lead to a digital token being included to the list.

While many crypto users today are aware of and appreciative of these variations, traders and non-technical investors might not be able to tell the difference because all token categories often trade on crypto exchanges in the same way (Benedetti & Nikbakht, 2021).

One of the top three cryptocurrencies in the world is the ether (ETH) blockchain token. After Bitcoin’s around $800 billion market value as of January 2022, it has the second-highest market value at around $380 billion, surpassing Binance Coin’s third-place market cap of about $75 billion.

Fiat Exchanges

The type of exchange is one of the most important factors to consider when selecting a bitcoin trading platform. Trading platforms for cryptocurrencies can either be fiat exchanges or coin to cryptocurrency exchanges (C2C). Investors can trade Ethereum, one of the two biggest cryptocurrencies in the world, with ease on exchanges that deal in fiat currency.

Some investors may want to pay closer attention to C2C exchanges if they wish to trade several currencies or have the option of quickly converting other currencies into Ethereum. Additionally, many investors have numerous accounts with both a fiat exchange and a C2C exchange (Kovenock & Vries, 2002).

Recall that cryptocurrencies are extremely unregulated and innovating quickly. This might open fantastic market opportunities but also raise the possibility of fraud, so it's crucial to be certain you have faith in the reliability of the trading platform exchange you select.

Wallet

ETH can be withdrawn into your bank account or a wallet that you control after being purchased through the exchange. It is simple to withdraw ETH from fiat exchanges by selling and depositing the proceeds to your bank account. Platforms for C2C transactions take longer. You would have to code transfer your ETH to a fiat exchange on a C2C marketplace, then sell to pay out. You may often send ETH to a wallet on all platforms as well (Shin, 2009).

The fact that proof of work requires a lot of computer power and is hence very energy-intensive is one of its main detractors. Proof of stake replaces mining with staking, which uses less energy, and validators instead of miners stake their cryptocurrency holdings to provide the capacity to create new blocks.

REVOLUTIONARY IMPACT

Under the alias Satoshi Nakamoto, a programmer (or perhaps a group of programmers) created bitcoin in 2009, ushering in a new era of decentralised digital currencies and blockchain technology. The concept of blockchain technology is first introduced in Satoshi's whitepaper that introduces bitcoin, which states that "the network timestamps transactions by hashing them into an ongoing chain of hash-based proof-of-work, forming a record that cannot be changed without redoing the proof-of-work." 1 Without a doubt, bitcoin has had a revolutionary impact on the cryptocurrency space. As of this writing, it has given rise to dozens of forks and imitators and continues to be the leading digital currency in the world by market cap and several other metrics. However, is it the original cryptocurrency?

One of the earliest attempts to create a cryptocurrency existed approximately 20 years before bitcoin, according to a story in Bitcoin Magazine. The Netherlands experienced nocturnal thefts at gas stations. A team of developers tried to connect money to recently developed smartcards rather than station guards and put their safety at danger. These cards would be carried by truck drivers who needed access to the stations rather than cash, and the stations would not have any extra paper money lying around. This may have been the first instance of electronic cash and it has connections to modern digital currencies.

Blinded Cash

American cryptographer David Chaum experimented with a distinct type of electronic money at around the same time, or possibly even earlier. He envisioned a token currency that could be securely and privately transferred between people; once more, the parallels to contemporary cryptocurrencies are startling. Chaum created a "blinding formula" that is used to encrypt data transmitted between people (Benedetti & Nikbakht, 2021). As a result, "blinded cash" which has the potential to be altered without leaving a trace could be safely transferred between people. A few years later, Chaum created DigiCash to put his idea into action. Despite going out of business in 1998, DigiCash's ideas, along with certain of its algorithms and encryption tools, were crucial to the development of following digital currencies.

Web-Based Money

Several businesses tried to further DigiCash's objectives in the 1990s. Of them, PayPal may have had the most significant long-term effects on the larger financial world (PYPL). Payments between individuals online have been transformed by PayPal. People were able to transfer money fast and securely using a web browser. By integrating with the eBay community, PayPal was able to gain a loyal user base that fuelled its expansion and success. It is still a significant payment service today. Additionally, PayPal served as an inspiration for businesses that tried to offer a way to trade gold using a web browser. E-gold was one of these businesses that was more successful, offering people internet credit in return for actual gold and other precious metals. However, this business encountered problems with several scams and was ultimately shut down by the federal government in 2005.

B-Money

B-money is an "anonymous, distributed electronic cash system" that was proposed in 1998 by developer Wei Dai. Dai proposed two distinct protocols, one of which required an unjammable and synchronous broadcast channel. In the end, B-money failed miserably and was in many respects very dissimilar from bitcoin. However, it was also an attempt at a private, secure, and anonymous electronic payment system. Digital pseudonyms would be used in the B-money system to transfer money via a decentralised network. The system even provided a way to enforce contracts directly within the network, without the use of a third party. Despite Wei Dai's whitepaper proposal for B-money, the project eventually fell short of attracting enough interest for a successful launch. However, the influence of B-money on the present digital currency mania cannot be denied as Satoshi made references to parts of B-money in his bitcoin whitepaper some ten years later (Tikhomirov, 2018).

Bit Gold

Bit Gold was another electronic currency system from the same era as B-money, not to be confused with the modern gold-based exchange of the same name. Bit Gold, which was proposed by Nick Szabo, has a proof-of-work mechanism of its own that, in some aspects, is like the bitcoin mining process currently in use. In a manner like a contemporary blockchain, solutions were synthesised cryptographically through this process and then made publicly available (Tikhomirov, 2018).

However, the Bit Gold concept's departure from centralised status may have been its most revolutionary feature. In order to reduce reliance on centralised currency providers and regulators, Bit Gold was created. Szabo wanted Bit Gold to replicate the characteristics of actual gold so that consumers could completely cut out the middlemen. Bit Gold, like B-money, failed in the end. But it also served as an example for a sizable number of digital currencies that would be on the market a decade or more after its debut.

Hashcash

According to The Merkle, one of the most popular pre-bitcoin digital currencies was Hashcash, which was created in the middle of the 1990s (Casino, Dasaklis, & Patsakis, 2019). Hashcash opened a vast range of possibilities that would not be realised for nearly two decades. Hashcash was created for several objectives, including reducing email spam and mitigating DDoS attacks. Like many modern cryptocurrencies, Hashcash employed a proof-of-work method to facilitate the creation and distribution of new coins. Indeed, Hashcash had many of the same issues as modern cryptocurrencies do today; in 1997, due to a growing demand for processing power, Hashcash gradually started to lose its effectiveness. Despite finally dying out, Hashcash attracted a lot of interest when it was at its peak. The creation of bitcoin also incorporated several aspects of the Hashcash system.

A new generation of digital currencies was introduced in 2009 with the creation of bitcoin. In contrast to many of its predecessors, Bitcoin is decentralised and has advanced blockchain technology. Without the earlier attempts at cryptocurrencies and electronic money in the decades before to the birth of bitcoin, it is difficult to envisage the establishment of bitcoin, let alone the hundreds of other digital currencies which have subsequently launched. In addition to setting trends and launching a wave of decentralised peer-to-peer based cryptocurrencies, Bitcoin has also established itself as the de facto industry standard and attracted a sizable following.

KEY TAKEAWAYS

A cryptocurrency is a type of digital tokens or "coins" that reside on a decentralised and distributed ledger known as a blockchain. In addition, since Bitcoin was introduced more than ten years ago, the area of cryptocurrencies has grown significantly, and the next big digital token could be introduced tomorrow.

In terms of market value, user base, and acceptance, Bitcoin remains the most well-known and widely used cryptocurrency.

Ethereum and other virtual currencies contribute to the development of decentralised financial (DeFi) systems.

Some alternative currencies (altcoins) have been promoted as having more advanced characteristics than Bitcoin, such the capacity to process more transactions per second or the use of alternative consensus techniques like proof of stake.

How Do Cryptocurrencies Work?

Let us take a step back and quickly define concepts like cryptocurrency and altcoin before we look more closely at some of these alternatives to Bitcoin (BTC). In a broad sense, a cryptocurrency is described as virtual or digital currency that appears as tokens or "coins." Even though some cryptocurrencies have made their way into the real world through credit cards or other initiatives, the vast majority are still only digital.

Altcoins

Other than Bitcoin, we will look at some of the most significant digital currencies below. But first, a disclaimer: It is impossible for a list like this to be completely exhaustive. One explanation for this is the availability of more than 18,000 cryptocurrencies as of March 2022 (Goldwasser, 1990). Although many of these cryptocurrencies have little to no followers or trading volume, some of them are quite well-liked among devoted investor and supporter communities.

In addition, the world of cryptocurrencies is constantly growing, therefore tomorrow might see the introduction of the next fantastic digital token. Even though Bitcoin is regarded as a pioneer in the realm of cryptocurrencies, analysts use a variety of techniques to assess tokens other than BTC. For instance, experts frequently place a high value on how coins are ranked against one another in terms of market capitalization. Although we have taken this into account, there are still additional factors that could lead to a digital token being included to the list.

Types of Altcoins

Cryptocurrencies

Cryptocurrencies are designed to be used for payments, sending value (like virtual currency) via a decentralised user network. Numerous altcoins those that are not Bitcoin or occasionally Ethereum are categorised in this fashion and are occasionally referred to as value tokens.

Tokens

Additionally, there are blockchain-based tokens created for purposes other than monetary exchange. A token that represents a stake in a blockchain or decentralised finance (DeFi) project and was released as part of an initial coin offering (ICO) is one illustration. Security tokens are those tokens that are connected to the project or company's worth (as in securities like stocks, not safety).

Some tokens are used for specific purposes. Examples include Namecoin, which offers decentralised Domain Name System (DNS) service for Internet addresses, or Storj tokens, which enable file sharing across a decentralised network. The term "utility tokens" refers to them (Chaum, Fiat & Naor, 2007).

While many crypto users today are aware of and appreciative of these variations, traders and non-technical investors might not be able to tell the difference because all token categories often trade on crypto exchanges in the same way.

1. Ethereum (ETH)

The first Bitcoin substitute on our list is Ethereum (ETH), a decentralised platform for building and executing smart contracts and decentralised applications (dApps) free from third-party interference, fraud, or control. Ethereum aims to build a decentralised ecosystem of financial services that anybody in the world can use freely, regardless of their country of origin, race, or religion. 4 Because people in some nations who lack governmental infrastructure and official identification can access bank accounts, loans, insurance, and a wide range of other financial products, this factor makes the implications for such people more compelling.

2. Litecoin (LTC)

One of the first cryptocurrencies to imitate Bitcoin was Litecoin (LTC), which was introduced in 2011. It is frequently referred to as the "silver to Bitcoin's gold." Charlie Lee, an MIT graduate and former Google developer, developed it.

Litecoin is based on an open-source, decentralised global payment network that use scrypt as a proof-of-work (PoW) algorithm that can be cracked with consumer-grade CPUs (CPUs). Litecoin is like Bitcoin in many aspects, but it also offers faster transaction confirmation times since it generates blocks at a faster rate.

3. Cardano (ADA)

A cryptocurrency called Cardano (ADA) was developed using a research-based methodology by engineers, mathematicians, and cryptography professionals. It uses the "Ouroboros proof-of-stake" algorithm. Charles Hoskinson, one of the original five founding members of Ethereum, co-founded the project. He left Ethereum after having some problems with the course that it was following, subsequently participating in the creation of Cardano.

Cardano's development team built its blockchain through thorough testing and peer-reviewed research. The project's researchers have authored more than 120 publications on blockchain technology covering a variety of subjects. 14 The core of Cardano is built on this study.

4. Polkadot (DOT)

A distinct PoS coin called Polkadot (DOT) aims to foster interoperability between different blockchains. Its protocol is made to link oracles, permissioned and permissionless blockchains, and other systems to enable collaboration between them. The relay chain, which enables network interoperability, is the fundamental part of Polkadot. Parachains, or parallel blockchains, with their own native tokens for certain use cases are also permitted.

Polkadot differs from Ethereum in that developers can create their own blockchains while utilising the security that Polkadot's chain already provides, as opposed to only developing dApps on Polkadot. Because the larger a blockchain is, the more security it has, developers using Ethereum can establish new blockchains, but they must also create their own security mechanisms. This leaves new and smaller projects vulnerable to attack. In Polkadot, this idea is referred to as shared security.

5. Bitcoin Cash (BCH)

Because it was one of the first and most successful hard forks of the original Bitcoin, Bitcoin Cash BCH has a significant role in the history of alternative currencies. A split occurs in the bitcoin realm as a result of discussions and disagreements between developers and miners. Due to the decentralised nature of digital currencies, major modifications to the source code underpinning the token or coin in question must be approved by the majority; the specific cryptocurrency determines the mechanism for this process.

When competing factions cannot come to an agreement, the digital currency may occasionally split, with the previous chain maintaining its original code and the new chain starting as a new iteration of the prior coin with updated code.

One of these splits gave birth to BCH in August 2017. BCH was created as a result of a discussion over the scalability of the Bitcoin network, which has a 1-megabyte block size restriction (MB). Block sizes in BCH are increased from 1MB to 8MBs, with the rationale being that larger

6. Stellar (XLM)

Stellar (XLM) is an open blockchain network created to connect financial institutions for the purpose of massive transactions, hence providing corporate solutions. Huge transactions between banks and investment firms, which used to take days, require a lot of intermediaries, and are expensive, can now be completed almost instantly and with little to no expense to the parties involved.

Stellar is still an open blockchain that anybody may use, even though it has positioned itself as an enterprise blockchain for institutional transactions. The mechanism enables international exchanges between any currencies. Lumens are the native currency of Stellar (XLM). 20 Users must possess Lumens in order to conduct transactions on the network.

7. Dogecoin (DOGE)

Some consider Dogecoin (DOGE) to be the first "memecoin," and the coin's skyrocketing value created a stir in 2021. The Dallas Mavericks, Kronos, and—possibly most significantly—SpaceX, an American aerospace business controlled by Elon Musk, all accept the token as a means of payment. The coin features a Shiba Inu image as its avatar.

Billy Markus and Jackson Palmer, two software programmers, developed Dogecoin in 2013. According to reports, Markus and Palmer invented the coin as a joke in response to the irrational speculation in the cryptocurrency market.

8. Binance Coin (BNB)

A utility cryptocurrency called Binance Coin (BNB) is used to pay the commissions for trading on the Binance Exchange. It ranks third in terms of market capitalization among all cryptocurrencies. Trades can be made at a discount for those who pay for the exchange using the token.

The blockchain that powers Binance Coin also serves as the foundation for Binance's decentralised exchange. Based on trade volumes, Changpeng Zhao launched the Binance Exchange, which is among the most popular exchanges worldwide.

Initially, Binance Coin was an Ethereum blockchain-based ERC-20 coin. It eventually had a main net launch of its own. The system employs a PoS.

9. Tether (USDT)

One of the first and most well-known stablecoins cryptocurrencies that attempt to tether their market value to a currency or other external reference point in order to lessen volatility was Tether (USDT). Most digital currencies, including popular ones like Bitcoin, have frequently experienced periods of extremely high volatility. Tether and other stablecoins aim to reduce this volatility in order to draw in consumers who may otherwise be wary. The cost of Tether is directly correlated with the value of the US dollar. Instead of truly converting to fiat money, the system enables users to transfer funds more quickly and easily from other cryptocurrencies back to dollars.

Tether, which was introduced in 2014, identifies as "a blockchain-enabled platform...to facilitate the use of fiat currency digitally." Effectively, this coin reduces the volatility and complexity frequently associated with digital currencies by enabling people to use a blockchain network and related technology to transact in traditional currencies.

10. Monero (XMR)

A safe, private, and undetectable currency is Monero XMR. When this open-source cryptocurrency first appeared in April 2014, the cryptography community and its supporters quickly became quite interested in it. This coin is entirely community- and donation-driven in its development.

With a heavy emphasis on decentralisation and scalability from the beginning, Monero provides total privacy using a unique method known as "ring signatures."

With this method, a collection of cryptographic signatures with at least one real participant appears, but it is impossible to identify the real one because they all seem to be legitimate.

Why Is It Important to Use Cryptocurrencies?

Blockchain-based cryptocurrencies enable people to conduct peer-to-peer financial transactions or sign contracts because they are decentralised platforms. No trustworthy third-party mediator, such as a bank, monetary authority, court, or judge, is required in any scenario. This might upend the current financial system and democratise finance. The size of the cryptocurrency market has increased dramatically over the last ten years, thanks to new developments and a market valuation of more than $1.75 trillion.

Why Do Cryptocurrencies Exist in Such Abundance?

Most cryptocurrencies in use today have some connection to Bitcoin, which has a censorship-resistant architecture and open-source code. This implies that anyone can duplicate the code, make changes, and produce their own unique coin. Additionally, it implies that anyone is free to join its network and conduct business there.

What Other Significant Cryptocurrencies Exist?

Numerous cryptocurrencies have grown in significance or have the potential to do so. For instance, Elon Musk, the CEO of Tesla, popularised the meme-based joke coin Dogecoin on social media. In addition to Dogecoin and the other cryptocurrencies mentioned above, there are several other Bitcoin forks, including Bitcoin Gold and Bitcoin SV. Ripple (XRP), Solana, USD Coin, and Tezos are some further significant coins.

Why Is Bitcoin the Most Valuable Cryptocurrency Today?

Despite the proliferation of hundreds of rivals, Bitcoin, the first cryptocurrency, continues to dominate in terms of usage and economic worth. As of February 2022, each coin (BTC) had a value of about $44,000 and a market capitalization of more than $830 billion.

1. Identify a Platform for Trading

The ideal trading platform for your needs should be chosen as the foundation for all trades. When it comes to cryptocurrencies, there are a few possibilities, and some of the best platforms include Coinbase, Kraken, Bitstamp, Gemini, Binance, and Bitfinex. These exchanges all provide Ethereum.

The type of exchange is one of the most important factors to consider when selecting a bitcoin trading platform. Trading platforms for cryptocurrencies can either be fiat exchanges or coin to cryptocurrency exchanges (C2C). Investors can trade Ethereum, one of the two biggest cryptocurrencies in the world, with ease on exchanges that deal in fiat currency.

Recall that cryptocurrencies are extremely unregulated and innovating quickly. This might open fantastic market opportunities but also raise the possibility of fraud, so it's crucial to be certain you have faith in the reliability of the trading platform exchange you select. When thinking about an exchange, you should consider the following questions: • Where are the headquarters?

- Is a licence present?
- Is their website secure?
- How safe are your funds, exactly?
- Who are the top management officials?

2. Create an Account

The next step is to open an account once you have chosen a trading platform that meets your needs. Like opening an account with a brokerage platform, this procedure. Your name, address, social security number, as well as other information, will be required. Once you feel comfortable using a website, creating an account may typically be done fast.

The last stage in the account opening procedure is often account verification. You must validate your account in one or more ways on almost all exchanges. You will probably need to upload documents to prove your identification and make sure your account complies with regulatory requirements at this point.

3. Deposit Currency

The next step is to add money to your account. After your payment information has been verified for platforms using fiat cash, this may be rather simple. Simply add money using the debit card or bank account that is already set up. You can deposit as little as $5 or as much as $1,000 or more on cryptocurrency exchanges because their minimum investment requirements are often low. It may be advisable to trade large quantities all at once because most exchanges charge per deal fees (Cagli, 2019).

Currency deposits in C2C exchanges can occasionally be a little more challenging. These exchanges demand that you transmit cryptocurrency between locations using a code. Having a lot of Ethereum on hand can be advantageous because it is a common depositing currency for many C2C services. Code transfers normally take up to an hour to complete, taking a little longer (Schilling & Uhlig, 2019).

4. Begin Trading

You can start using the exchange to buy Ethereum and other cryptocurrencies after you have a confirmed account and funds deposited into it. Although the interfaces of each exchange vary slightly, you should be ready to confirm transactions and allow time for processing, which may also be influenced by the total number of transactions you request.

5. Withdraw ETH into a Wallet

ETH can be withdrawn into your bank account or a wallet that you control after being purchased through the exchange. It is simple to withdraw ETH from fiat exchanges by selling and depositing the proceeds to your bank account. Platforms for C2C transactions take longer. You would have to code transfer your ETH to a fiat exchange on a C2C marketplace, then sell to pay out. You may often send ETH to a wallet on all platforms as well.

CONCLUSION

This section aims to demonstrate how Web security can be implemented using cryptography. It begins with a list of obstacles to data protection, from a technical perspective, cryptography provides a solution to many of the security issues that the Internet faces today. Most algorithms cannot be demonstrated to be secure. For this reason, many cryptographic algorithms are viewed with scepticism. The way society is going right now suggests that cryptography is becoming more significant. In the future, cryptography may be utilised extensively on the Internet, including for electronic correspondence and the transmission of documents used for online sales. Cryptography is expected to be used and discussed extensively for many more years.

REFERENCES

Benedetti, H., & Nikbakht, E. (2021). Returns and network growth of digital tokens after cross-listings. *Journal of Corporate Finance*, *66*(101853). doi:10.1016/j.jcorpfin.2020.101853

Cagli, E. C. (2019). Explosive behavior in the prices of Bitcoin and altcoins. *Finance Research Letters*, *29*, 398–403. doi:10.1016/j.frl.2018.09.007

Casino, F., Dasaklis, T. K., & Patsakis, C. (2019). A systematic literature review of blockchain-based applications: Current status, classification and open issues. *Telematics and Informatics*, *36*, 55–81. doi:10.1016/j.tele.2018.11.006

Chaum, D., Fiat, A., & Naor, M. (2007). Untraceable Electronic Cash. In *Advances in Cryptology — CRYPTO' 88* (pp. 319–327). Springer New York.

Conti, M., Sandeep Kumar, E., Lal, C., & Ruj, S. (2018). A Survey on Security and Privacy Issues of Bitcoin. IEEE Communications Surveys & Tutorials, 20(4), 3416-3452. doi:10.1109/COMST.2018.2842460

Goldwasser, S. (Ed.). (1990). *Advances in Cryptology — CRYPTO' 88: Proceedings*. Springer New York. doi:10.1007/0-387-34799-2

Kovenock, D., & Vries, C. G. (2002). Fiat exchange in finite economies. *Economic Inquiry*, *40*(2), 147–157. doi:10.1093/ei/40.2.147

Schilling, L., & Uhlig, H. (2019). Some simple bitcoin economics. *Journal of Monetary Economics*, *106*, 16–26. doi:10.1016/j.jmoneco.2019.07.002

Shin, D.-H. (2009). Towards an understanding of the consumer acceptance of mobile wallet. *Computers in Human Behavior*, *25*(6), 1343–1354. doi:10.1016/j.chb.2009.06.001

Tikhomirov, S. (2018). Ethereum: State of knowledge and research perspectives. In *Foundations and Practice of Security* (pp. 206–221). Springer International Publishing. doi:10.1007/978-3-319-75650-9_14

Compilation of References

ACCA Examining Team. (n.d.). Financial reporting study text, Kaplan Publishing.

ACCA Global. (n.d.). Accounting for Cryptocurrencies: Home. ACCA. https://www.accaglobal.com/in/en/student/exam-support-resources/professional-exams-study-resources/strategic-business-reporting/technical-articles/cryptocurrencies.html

Acharya, S., Thomas, A., & Pani, B. (2018). Volatility of Bitcoin and Its Implication to be a Currency. *International Journal of Engineering Technology Science and Research*, *5*(1), 1017–1024.

Acharya, V. V., & Pedersen, L. H. (2005). Asset pricing with liquidity risk. *Journal of Financial Economics*, *77*(2), 375–410. https://doi.org/10.1016/j.jfineco.2004.06.007

Adhami, S., Giudici, G., & Martinazzi, S. (2018). Why Do Businesses Go Crypto? An Empirical Analysis of Initial Coin Offerings. *Journal of Economics and Business*, *100*, 64–75. doi:10.1016/j.jeconbus.2018.04.001

Afzal, A., & Asif, A. (2019). Cryptocurrencies, Blockchain and Regulation: A Review. *The Lahore Journal of Economics*, *24*(1), 103–130. doi:10.35536/lje.2019.v24.i1.a5

Akbas, F., Armstrong, W. J., & Petkova, R. (2011). *Idiosyncratic volatility of liquidity and expected stock returns.* Semantic Scholar.

Akhtaruzzaman, M., Sensoy, A., & Corbet, S. (2020). The influence of bitcoin on portfolio *diversification and design. Finance Research Letters*, *37*, 101344. https://doi.org/10.1016/j.frl.2019.101344

Ali, H. Abdullah, R. Zaini, Z. 2019. Fintech and Its Potential Impact on Islamic Banking and Finance, Industry: A Case Study of Brunei Darussalam and Malaysia.

Álvez, M., Lluberas, R., & Ponce, J. (2020). The Cost of Using Cash and Checks in Uruguay. *Journal of Central Banking Theory and Practice*, *9*(2), 109–129. doi:10.2478/jcbtp-2020-0016

Assomull, V. (2022, June 19). Crypto Gaming In India: Here's Everything You Need to Know. *Inc 42*. https://inc42.com/

Auer, R. & Böhme, R. (2020). The technology of retail central bank digital currency. *BIS Quarterly Review*.

Babkin, A. V., Burkaltseva, D., Pshenichnikov, W., & Tyulin, A. (2017). Cryptocurrency and Blockchain-Technology in Digital Economy: *Development Genesis. St. Petersburg State Polytechnical University Journal. Economics*, *67*(5), 9–22.

Babu, S., & Abraham, K. M. (2021). Central bank digital currencies: policy and operational perspectives for India. *CSI transactions on ICT*, *9*, 85-94. doi:10.1007/s40012-021-00327-6

Baldwin, J. (2018). In Digital We Trust: Bitcoin Discourse, Digital Currencies, and Decentralized Network Fetishism. *Palgrave Communications*, *4*(1), 1–10. doi:10.105741599-018-0065-0

Banka, H. (2018). *Initial findings from the implementation of the Practical Guide for Measuring Retail Payment Costs*. World Bank Private Sector Development Blog. https:// blogs.worldbank.org/psd/initial-findings-implementation-practical-guide-measuringretail-%0Apayment-costs

Baumöhl, E. (2019). Are cryptocurrencies connected to forex? A quantile cross-spectral approach. *Finance Research Letters*, *29*, 363–372. doi:10.1016/j.frl.2018.09.002

Baur, D. G., Hong, K., & Lee, A. D. (2015). *Bitcoin: Medium of Exchange or Speculative Assets?* SSRN. https://dx.doi.org/10.2139/ssrn.2561183

Baur, D., Lee, A., & Hong, K. (2020). *(PDF) Bitcoin: Medium Of Exchange Or Speculative Assets?* ResearchGate. https://www.researchgate.net/publication/321988034_Bitcoin_Medium_of_Exchange_or_Speculative_Assets

Baur, D. G., Dimpfl, T., & Kuck, K. (2018). Bitcoin, gold and the US dollar – a replication and extension. *Finance Research Letters*, *25*, 103–110. doi:10.1016/j.frl.2017.10.012

Bauwens, L., Laurent, S., & Rombouts, J. V. (2006). Multivariate Garch Models: A survey. *Journal of Applied Econometrics*, *21*(1), 79–109. doi:10.1002/jae.842

Beach, P. F. (2022, Sept. 20). Global Online Game Market Revenue for 2022 Expected To Exceed $196 Billion. *PRNewswire*. https://www.prnewswire.com/

Benedetti, H., & Nikbakht, E. (2021). Returns and network growth of digital tokens after cross-listings. *Journal of Corporate Finance*, *66*(101853). doi:10.1016/j.jcorpfin.2020.101853

Berg, C., Davidson, S., & Potts, J. (2019). Blockchain Technology as Economic Infrastructure: *Revisiting the Electronic Markets Hypothesis. Frontiers in Blockchain*, *2*, 22. doi:10.3389/fbloc.2019.00022

BIS Committee. (2021). Central Bank Digital Currencies for cross-border payments. *Report to the G20*.

Bitcoinblockhalf.com. (2020). *Bitcoin Block Reward Halving Countdown*. Bitcoin BlockHalf. https://www.bitcoinblockhalf.com/

Blockgeeks. (2020). *What Is Cryptocurrency: [Everything You Need To Know!]*. Block Geeks. https://blockgeeks.com/guides/what-is-cryptocurrency/

Boffelli, S., & Urga, G. (2016). *Financial econometrics using stata*. Stata Press.

Böhmecke-Schwafert, M., Wehinger, M., & Teigland, R. (2022). Blockchain for the circular economy: Theorizing blockchain's role in the transition to a circular economy through an empirical investigation. *Business Strategy and the Environment*, *31*(8), 3786–3801. doi:10.1002/bse.3032

Bollerslev, T. (1986). Generalized Autoregressive Conditional Heteroscedasticity. *Journal of Econometrics*, *31*(3), 307–327. https://doi.org/10.1016/0304-4076(86)90063-1

Bollerslev, T., Engle, R. F., & Wooldridge, J. M. (1988). A capital asset pricing model with time-varying covariances. *Journal of Political Economy*, *96*(1), 116–131. doi:10.1086/261527

Bondrako, O., Kichuk, O., & Antonov, A. (2019). The possibilities of using investment tools based on cryptocurrency in the development of the national economy.

Bouri, E., Das, M., Gupta, R., & Roubaud, D. (2018). Spillovers between Bitcoin and other assets during bear and bull markets. *Applied Economics*, *50*(55), 5935–5949. https://doi.org/10.1080/00036846.2018.1488075

Bouri, E., Gupta, R., Lau, C. K. M., Roubaud, D., & Wang, S. (2018). Bitcoin and global financial stress: A copula-based approach to dependence and causality in the quantiles. *The Quarterly Review of Economics and Finance*, *69*, 297–307. doi:10.1016/j.qref.2018.04.003

Bouri, E., Gupta, R., Tiwari, A. K., & Roubaud, D. (2017). Does Bitcoin hedge global uncertainty? Evidence from wavelet-based quantile-in-quantile regressions. *Finance Research Letters*, *23*, 87–95. https://doi.org/10.1016/j.frl.2017.02.009

Brauneis, A., & Mestel, R. (2018). Price discovery of cryptocurrencies: Bitcoin and beyond. *Economics Letters*, *165*, 58–61. https://doi.org/10.1016/j.econlet.2018.02.001

Brauneis, A., Mestel, R., Riordan, R., & Theissen, E. (2021a). How to measure the liquidity of cryptocurrency markets? *Journal of Banking & Finance*, *124*, 106041. https://doi.org/10.1016/j.jbankfin.2020.106041

Brauneis, A., Mestel, R., & Theissen, E. (2021b). What drives the liquidity of cryptocurrencies? A long-term analysis. *Finance Research Letters*, *39*, 101537. https://doi.org/10.1016/j.frl.2020.101537

Briere, M., Oosterlinck, K., & Szafarz, A. (2013). Virtual currency, tangible return: Portfolio diversification with bitcoins ULB–Universite Libre de Bruxelles. *Working Papers CEB*, 13-031.

BritoJ.ShadabH. B.Castillo O'SullivanA. (2015). Bitcoin Financial Regulation: Securities, Derivatives, Prediction Markets, and Gambling. SSRN.

Brown, C. (2023, January 16). How Crypto is revolutionizing the Online Gambling Industry. *Crypto news flash*. https://www.crypto-news-flash.com/

Buisness Today. (2017). RBI, commercial banks spend Rs 21,000 crore on currency management. *Business Today.* https://www.businesstoday.in/current/economy-politics/rbi-banks-spend-currency-management-cash/ story/ 251299.html

Bulut, A. (2018). Cryptocurrencies in the new economy. Journal of International Trade. *Logistics and Law*, *4*(2), 45–52.

Bunjaku, F., & Olivera, G.-T. Emilija, MitevaKacarski. (2017). Cryptocurrencies – Advantages and Disadvantages. *Journal of Economics, 2*(1). https://www.doi.org/10.46763/JOE

Burniske, C., & White, A. (2017). *Bitcoin: Ringing the bell for a new asset class.* Ark Invest. https://Research.Ark-Invest.Com/Hubfs/1_Download_Files_ARK- Invest/White_Papers/Bitcoin-Ringing-The-Bell-For-A-New-Asset-Class. Pdf.

Button, S. (2018). Cryptocurrency and Blockchains in Emerging Economies. *Software Quality Professional, 20*(3).

Cagli, E. C. (2019). Explosive behavior in the prices of Bitcoin and altcoins. *Finance Research Letters*, *29*, 398–403. doi:10.1016/j.frl.2018.09.007

Calcaterra, C., Kaal, W. A., & Rao, V. (2020). Stable Cryptocurrencies. *Washington University Journal of Law and Policy*, *61*, 193–228.

Cambridge English Dictionary.. (2020). *Awareness.* Google.com https://www.google.com/amp/s/dictionary.cambridge.org/amp/en glish/awareness

Carstens, A. (2021). *Digital currencies and the future of the monetary system.* Bank for International Settlements, Hoover Institution policy seminar.

Casino, F., Dasaklis, T. K., & Patsakis, C. (2019). A systematic literature review of blockchain-based applications: Current status, classification and open issues. *Telematics and Informatics*, *36*, 55–81. doi:10.1016/j.tele.2018.11.006

CCI. (2021). *Cryptocurrency Crime and Anti-Money Laundering Report.* Ciphertrace Cryptocurrency Intelligence.

Ccoingossip.com. 2018. *Advantages And Disadvantages Of Cryptocurrency.* C-Coin Gossip. https://ccoingossip.com/advantages-and-disadvantages-of-cryptocurrency/

Cennamo, C., Marchesi, C., & Meyer, T. (2020). Two Sides of The Same Coin? Decentralized Versus Proprietary Blockchains and The Performance of Digital Currencies. *Academy of Management Discoveries*, *6*(3), amd.2019.0044. doi:10.5465/amd.2019.0044

Çetin, S., Gruis, V., & Straub, A. (2022). Digitalization for a circular economy in the building industry: Multiple-case study of Dutch social housing organizations. *Resources. Conservation & Recycling Advances*, *15*, 200110. doi:10.1016/j.rcradv.2022.200110

Chauhan, A., Jakhar, S. K., & Chauhan, C. (2021). The interplay of circular economy with industry 4.0 enabled smart city drivers of healthcare waste disposal. *Journal of Cleaner Production, 279*, 123854. doi:10.1016/j.jclepro.2020.123854 PMID:32863607

Chaum, D., Fiat, A., & Naor, M. (2007). Untraceable Electronic Cash. In *Advances in Cryptology — CRYPTO' 88* (pp. 319–327). Springer New York.

Cheah, C. G., Chia, W. Y., Lai, S. F., Chew, K. W., Chia, S. R., & Show, P. L. (2022). Innovation designs of industry 4.0 based solid waste management: Machinery and digital circular economy. *Environmental Research, 213*, 113619. doi:10.1016/j.envres.2022.113619 PMID:35700763

Chemkha, R., BenSaïda, A., & Ghorbel, A. (2021). Connectedness between cryptocurrencies and foreign exchange markets: Implication for Risk Management. *Journal of Multinational Financial Management, 59*, 100666. doi:10.1016/j.mulfin.2020.100666

Chen, Q., Feng, H., & de Soto, B. G. (2021). Revamping construction supply chain processes with circular economy strategies: A systematic literature review. *Journal of Cleaner Production, 335*, 130240. doi:10.1016/j.jclepro.2021.130240

Chiaroni, D., Fraccascia, L., Giannoccaro, I., & Urbinati, A. (2022). Enabling factors for the diffusion of circular economy and their impacts on sustainability. *Resources. Conservation & Recycling Advances, 15*, 200101. doi:10.1016/j.rcradv.2022.200101

Chillieh, V. (2020). *What Is Public Perception?* Powers That Beat. https://powersthatbeat.wordpress.com/2012/08/24/what-is-publ ic-perception/

Chohan, U. W. (2017). The Double Spending Problem and Cryptocurrencies. Scholarly Paper ID 3090174.

Chordia, T., Roll, R., & Subrahmanyam, A. (2002). Market liquidity and trading activity. *The Journal of Finance, 56*(2), 501–530. https://doi.org/10.1111/0022-1082.00335

Ciaian, P., Rajcaniova, M., & Kancs, D. A. (2016). The economics of Bitcoin price formation. *Applied Economics, 48*(19), 1799–1815. https://doi.org/10.1080/00036846.2015.1109038

Clark, B., & Burstall, R. (2018). Blockchain, IP and The Pharma Industry-How Distributed Ledger Technologies Can Help Secure the Pharma Supply Chain. *Journal of Intellectual Property Law & Practice, 13*(7), 531–533. doi:10.1093/jiplp/jpy069

Coin Market Cap. (n.d.). *Today's Cryptocurrency Prices by Market Cap* [Data set]. Coin Market Cap. https://coinmarketcap.com/

Coinbase. (2018). *The Rise Of Crypto In Higher Education*. Coinbase. https://blog.coinbase.com/the-rise-of-crypto-in-higher-educa tion-81b648c2466f

Coinbase. (2022). *What is volatility?* Coinbase. https://www.coinbase.com/learn/crypto-basics/what-is-volatility

Committee on Payments and Market Infrastructure. (2018). Markets Committee Papers. Bank for International Settlements.

Committee on Payments and Market Infrastructures. (2016). *Fast payments – Enhancing the speed and availability of retail payments*. Bank for International Settlements.

Conklin, A. 2020. *What Are The Benefits Of Cryptocurrency?* Fox Business. https://www.foxbusiness.com/money/what-are-the-benefits-of-cryptocurrency

Consumer Information. 2018. *What To Know About Cryptocurrency*. Consumer Information. https://www.consumer.ftc.gov/articles/what-know-about-cryptocurrency

Conti, M., Sandeep Kumar, E., Lal, C., & Ruj, S. (2018). A Survey on Security and Privacy Issues of Bitcoin. IEEE Communications Surveys & Tutorials, 20(4), 3416-3452. doi:10.1109/COMST.2018.2842460

Corbet, S., Lucey, B., Urquhart, A., & Yarovaya, L. (2019). Cryptocurrencies as a Financial Asset: A Systematic Analysis. *International Review of Financial Analysis*, *62*, 182–199. doi:10.1016/j.irfa.2018.09.003

Corbet, S., Meegan, A., Larkin, C., Lucey, B., & Yarovaya, L. (2018). Exploring the dynamic relationships between cryptocurrencies and other financial assets. *Economics Letters*, *165*, 28–34. https://doi.org/10.1016/j.econlet.2018.01.004

CRSIL. (2017). *Bitcoin: Currency of the future or money laundering vehicle*. Lead Analyst, Financial Crime and Compliance Analytics.

Danielsson, J (2018a). *Cryptocurrencies don't make sense*. VoxEU.org.

Danielsson, J (2018b). *Cryptocurrencies are lousy investments*. VoxEU.org.

Danielsson, J, Shin, H. S., & Zigrand, J.-P. (2009). *Modelling financial turmoil through endogenous risk*. VoxEU.org.

Danielsson, J. (2018c). Cryptocurrencies: Policy, economics and fairness. *LSE Systemic Risk Centre Discussion Paper 86*.

Dantas, T. E. T., de-Souza, E. D., Destro, I. R., Hammes, G., Rodriguez, C. M. T., & Soares, S. R. (2021). How the combination of Circular Economy and Industry 4.0 can contribute towards achieving the Sustainable Development Goals. *Sustainable Production and Consumption*, *26*, 213–227. doi:10.1016/j.spc.2020.10.005

Dashkevich, N., Counsell, S., & Destefanis, G. (2020). Blockchain Application for Central Banks: A Systematic Mapping Study. *IEEE Access: Practical Innovations, Open Solutions*, *8*, 139918–139952. doi:10.1109/ACCESS.2020.3012295

DeChesare, B. (2020). Cryptocurrency accounting: Why Net Income and the P/E Multiple Have Become Even More Useless. Mergers & Inquisitions. https://mergersandinquisitions.com/cryptocurrency-accounting /

Degiannakis, S., Duffy, D., & Filis, G. (2014). Business Cycle Synchronization in EU: A Time-varying approach. *Scottish Journal of Political Economy*, *61*(4), 348–370. doi:10.1111jpe.12049

Demestichas, K., & Daskalakis, E. (2020). Information and communication technology solutions for the circular economy. *Sustainability*, *12*(18), 1–19. doi:10.3390u12187272

Demidenko, D. S., Malevskaia-Malevich, E. D., & Dubolazova, Y. A. (2018). ISO as a Real Source of Funding Pricing issues. 2018 International Conference on Information Networking (ICOIN), (pp. 622– 625). IEEE. 10.1109/ICOIN.2018.8343193

Den Haan, W., Ellison, M., Ilzetzki, E., McMahon, M., & Reis, R. (2017). *Economists relaxed about bitcoin: New CFM-CEPR expert survey on cryptocurrencies, the ðnancial system, and economic policy.* VoxEU.org.

Dimitrova, V., Fernández-Martínez, M., Sánchez-Granero, M. A., & Segovia, J. E. T. (2019). Some Comments on Bitcoin Market (In)Efficiency. *PLoS One*, *14*(7), e0219243. doi:10.1371/journal.pone.0219243 PMID:31283773

Dodd, N. (2018). The Social Life of Bitcoin. *Theory, Culture & Society*, *35*(3), 35–56. doi:10.1177/0263276417746464

Dorfleitner, G., & Lung, C. (2018). Cryptocurrencies from The Perspective of Euro Investors: A Re- examination of Diversification Benefits and a New Day-of-The-Week Effect. *Journal of Asset Management*, *19*(7), 472–494. doi:10.105741260-018-0093-8

Dostov, V., & Shust, P. (2014). Cryptocurrencies: An unconventional Challenge to the AML/CFT Regulators? *Journal of Financial Crime*, *21*(3), 249–263. doi:10.1108/JFC-06-2013-0043

Duggan, W., & Powell, F. (2022, September 5). What is Crypto Gaming. *Forbes Advisor*. https://www.forbes.com/

Duque, J. J. (2020). State Involvement in Cryptocurrencies. A Potential World Money? *Journal of Political Economy*, *46*(1), 65–82. doi:10.1080/2329194X.2020.1763185

Dutta, P., Chavhan, R., Gowtham, P., & Singh, A. (2022). The individual and integrated impact of Blockchain and IoT on sustainable supply chains: A systematic review. In *Supply Chain Forum: An International Journal* (pp. 1-24). 10.1080/16258312.2022.2082851

Dwyer, G. P. (2015). The economics of Bitcoin and similar private digital currencies. *Journal of Financial Stability*, *17*, 81–91. https://doi.org/10.1016/j.jfs.2014.11.006

Dyhrberg, A. H. (2016). Hedging capabilities of bitcoin. Is it the virtual gold? *Finance Research Letters, 16*, 139–144. https://doi.org/10.1016/j.frl.2015.10.025

Elsayed, A. H., Gozgor, G., & Lau, C. K. (2020). Causality and dynamic spillovers among cryptocurrencies and currency markets. *International Journal of Finance & Economics, 27*(2), 2026–2040. doi:10.1002/ijfe.2257

Engle, R. F. (1982). Autoregressive Conditional Heteroscedasticity with Estimates of the Variance of the United Kingdom Inflation. *Econometrica, 50*(4), 987–1007. https://doi.org/10.2307/1912773

Engle, R. F., & Kroner, K. F. (1995). Multivariate simultaneous generalized arch. *Econometric Theory, 11*(1), 122–150. doi:10.1017/S0266466600009063

Eraky, M., Elsayed, M., Qyyum, M. A., Ai, P., & Tawfik, A. (2022). A new cutting-edge review on the bioremediation of anaerobic digestate for environmental applications and cleaner bioenergy. *Environmental Research, 213*, 113708. doi:10.1016/j.envres.2022.113708 PMID:35724728

Expert Commentator. (2019). *Why are cryptocurrencies so volatile?* Smart Insights. https://www.smartinsights.com/digital-marketing-strategy/volatile-cryptocurrencies/

Fadeyi, O., Krejcar, O., Maresova, P., Kuca, K., Brida, P., & Selamat, A. (2020). Opinions on Sustainability of Smart Cities in the Context of Energy Challenges Posed by Cryptocurrency Mining. *Sustainability, 12*(1), 169. doi:10.3390u12010169

Fantacci, L. (2019). Cryptocurrencies and the Denationalization of Money. *International Journal of Political Economy, 48*(2), 105–126. doi:10.1080/08911916.2019.1624319

Federal Reserve System. (2022). Money and Payments: The U.S. Dollar in the Age of Digital Transformation. Board of Governors of the Federal Reserve System.

Fernando, Y., Rozuar, N. H. M., & Mergeresa, F. (2021). The blockchain-enabled technology and carbon performance: Insights from early adopters. *Technology in Society, 64*, 101507. doi:10.1016/j.techsoc.2020.101507

Fiedler, S. (2019). The Future of Money. Study for the Committee on Economic and Monetary Affairs, Policy Department for Economic, Scientific and Quality of Life Policies, European Parliament, Luxembourg.

Figueiredo, K., Hammad, A. W., Haddad, A., & Tam, V. W. (2022). Assessing the usability of blockchain for sustainability: Extending key themes to the construction industry. *Journal of Cleaner Production, 343*, 131047. doi:10.1016/j.jclepro.2022.131047

Financial Stability Board. (2018). Crypto asset markets. *Potential channels for future ðnancial stability implications, technical report.* www.fsb.org/wp-content/uploads/P101018.pdf

Flori, A. (2019). Cryptocurrencies In Finance: Review and Applications. *International Journal of Theoretical and Applied Finance, 22*(5), 1–22. doi:10.1142/S0219024919500201

Foley, S., Karlsen, J. R., & Putniņš, T. J. (2019). Sex, Drugs, and Bitcoin: How Much Illegal Activity Is Financed through Cryptocurrencies? *Review of Financial Studies*, *32*(5), 1798–1853. doi:10.1093/rfs/hhz015

Fry, J., & Cheah, E. T. (2016). Negative bubbles and shocks in cryptocurrency markets. *International Review of Financial Analysis*, *47*, 343–352. https://doi.org/10.1016/j.irfa.2016.02.008

García-Medina, A., & Hernández, J. B. (2020). Network Analysis of Multivariate Transfer Entropy of Cryptocurrencies in Times of Turbulence. *Entropy (Basel, Switzerland)*, *22*(7), 760–762. doi:10.3390/e22070760 PMID:33286532

Geetha, R.S., & Girisha, M. C. (2018). A conceptual study on the impact of Bitcoins on the Indian economy. *International journal of Business and Management Invention (IJBMI).*

Giudici, P., & Polinesi, G. (2021). Crypto price discovery through correlation networks. *Annals of Operations Research*, *299*(1), 443–457. https://doi.org/10.1007/s10479-019-03282-3

Glaser, F., & Bezzenberger, L. (2015). Beyond Cryptocurrencies-A Taxonomy of Decentralized Consensus Systems. Scholarly Paper ID 2605803.

Goel, S. (2017). What is a debt instrument? The Economic Times. https://economictimes.indiatimes.com/markets/stocks/news/wha t-is-a-debt-instrument/articleshow/59530686.cms

Goldwasser, S. (Ed.). (1990). *Advances in Cryptology — CRYPTO' 88: Proceedings.* Springer New York. doi:10.1007/0-387-34799-2

Gott, M., Ward, S., Gardiner, C., Cobb, M., & Ingleton, C. (2011). A Narrative Literature Review of The Evidence Regarding the Economic Impact of Avoidable hospitalizations Amongst Palliative Care Patients in the UK. *Progress in Palliative Care*, *19*(6), 291–298. doi:10.1179/1 743291X11Y.0000000014

Griffiths, M. D. (2012). Internet gambling, player protection, and social responsibility. In *Routledge international handbook of Internet gambling* (pp. 247–269). Routledge.

Guest, (2022, May 21). The impact of cryptocurrency on the gaming industry. *Invisible Fiction.* https://invisiblefiction.com/

Guest. (2021, September 9). How Crypto gaming (GameFi) is emerging as the new way to make money. *Financial Express.* https://www.financialexpress.com/

Guizani, S., & Nafti, I. K. (2019). The determinants of bitcoin price volatility: An investigation with ARDL model. *Procedia Computer Science*, *164*, 233–238. https://doi.org/10.1016/j.procs.2019.12.177

Gupta, S. (2020). *Cryptocurrency Volatility – a Friend or a Foe.* AITHORITY (AI Technological Insights). https://aithority.com/guest-authors/cryptocurrency-volatilit y-a-friend-or-a-foe/

Hao, K. (2018). The First Rule Of Being A Woman In Crypto. [online] *Quartz*. https://qz.com/1262167/the-first-rule-of-being-a-woman-in-crypto-is-you-do-not-talk-about-being-a-woman-in-crypto/

Harvey, J., & Branco-Illodo, I. (2020). Why Cryptocurrencies Want Privacy: A Review of Political Motivations and Branding Expressed in "Privacy Coin" Whitepapers. *Journal of Political Marketing*, *19*(1–2), 107–136. doi:10.1080/15377857.2019.1652223

Hashemi Joo, M., Nishikawa, Y., & Dandapani, K. (2019). Cryptocurrency, a Successful Application of Blockchain Technology. *Managerial Finance*, *46*(6), 715–733. doi:10.1108/MF-09-2018-0451

Hayes, A. (2015). A Cost of Production Model for Bitcoin. *Working Papers No. 1505*. New School for Social Research, Department of Economics.

Hayes, A. (2022). 10 Important Cryptocurrencies Other Than Bitcoin. Investopedia. https://www.investopedia.com/tech/most-important-cryptocurrencies-other-than-bitcoin/#citation-1

Hennemann Hilario da Silva, T., & Sehnem, S. (2022). The circular economy and Industry 4.0: Synergies and challenges. *Revista de Gestão*, *29*(3), 300–313. doi:10.1108/REGE-07-2021-0121

Honest Pros and Cons. (2019). Advantages And Disadvantages Of Cryptocurrency - Honest Pros And Cons. *Honest Pros and Cons*. https://honestproscons.com/advantages-and-disadvantages-of-cryptocurrency/

How blockchain and cryptocurrency can create a greener future . (n.d.). World Economic Forum. https://www.weforum.org/agenda/2021/06/how-blockchain-and-cryptocurrencies-can-help-build-a-greener-future/

How to make cryptocurrency sustainable. (n.d.). World Economic Forum. https://www.weforum.org/agenda/2021/11/how-to-make-bitcoin-and-cryptocurrency-sustainable-renewable-energy-blockchain-crypto-mining/

Hsu, S., Sheu, C., & Yoon, J. (2021). Risk spillovers between cryptocurrencies and traditional currencies and gold under different global economic conditions. *The North American Journal of Economics and Finance*, *57*, 101443. doi:10.1016/j.najef.2021.101443

Hu, A., Parlour, C. A., & Rajan, U. (2018). Cryptocurrencies: Stylized Facts on a New Investible Instrument. Scholarly Paper ID 3182113. doi:10.2139/ssrn.3182113

Hudson, R., & Urquhart, A. (2019). Technical Trading and Cryptocurrencies. *Annals of Operations Research*, *297*(1-2), 191–220. doi:10.100710479-019-03357-1

Hulliet, M. (2019). 1 In 5 European Crypto Holders Are Women, New Report Reveals. *Cointelegraph*. https://cointelegraph.com/news/1-in-5-european-crypto-holders-are-women-new-report-reveals

Hyytia, PSundqvist, E. (2019). Accounting for Cryptocurrencies- A Nightmare for Accountants. UMEA School of Business, Economics, and Statistics. http://www.diva-portal.org/smash/get/diva2:1331799/FULLTEXT0 1.pdf

IFRS. (n.d.). Who uses IFRS Accounting Standards? https:// www.ifrs.org/use-around-the-world/use-of-ifrs-standa rds-by-jurisdiction/

Igalavithana, A. D., Yuan, X., Attanayake, C. P., Wang, S., You, S., Tsang, D. C., Nzihou, A., & Ok, Y. S. (2022). Sustainable management of plastic wastes in COVID-19 pandemic: The biochar solution. *Environmental Research*, *212*, 113495. doi:10.1016/j.envres.2022.113495 PMID:35660402

Imoniana, J. O., Silva, W. L., Reginato, L., Slomski, V., & Slomski, V. G. (2020). Sustainable technologies for the transition of auditing towards a circular economy. *Sustainability*, *13*(1), 1–24. doi:10.3390u13010218

Ingham, L. (2019). Cryptocurrency May Replace Cash Within A Decade, Says Deutsche Bank. *Verdict*. https://www.verdict.co.uk/cryptocurrency-replace-cash/

International Accounting Standards Board. (2010). Conceptual Framework for Financial Reporting. International Accounting Standards Board. https://www.ifrs.org/content/dam/ifrs/publications/pdf-stand ards/english/2021/issued/part-a/conceptual-framework-for-fin ancial-reporting.pdf

Jani, S. (2018). The growth of cryptocurrency in India: Its challenges & potential impacts on legislation. *Research gate publication.*

Javaid, A. (n.d.). *CBDC in India: What is Central Bank Digital Currency (CBDC)?* Jahran Josh. https://www.jagranjosh.com/general-knowledge/central-bank-digital-currency-cbdc-1612241965-1 5.

Jin, S., & Chang, H. (2022). The trends of blockchain in environmental management research: A bibliometric analysis. *Environmental Science and Pollution Research International*, 1–18. doi:10.100711356-022-19856-x PMID:35349072

Joshi, C. M. (2021, March 18). Crypto Currency Financial Crime Risk. *Indiaforensic*. https://indiaforensic.com/certifications/crypto-currency-fin ancial-crime-risk/

Jovic, Z. Kunjadic, G. (2018) *Economic, Security and Information aspects of the application of cryptocurrency and their impact on the South East European countries.* Research Gate.

Karoles, R. (2018). *Cryptocurrencies and the economy: a review of literature*. University Honor Capstone.

Katsiampa, P. (2017). Volatility estimation for Bitcoin: A comparison of GARCH models. *Economics Letters*, *158*, 3–6. https://doi.org/10.1016/j.econlet.2017.06.023

Ken State University. (2020). Spss Tutorials: Chi-Square Test of Independence. *Libguides*. https://libguides.library.kent.edu/SPSS/ChiSquare

Keogh, J. G., Dube, L., Rejeb, A., Hand, K. J., Khan, N., & Dean, K. (2020). The Future Food Chain: Digitization as an Enabler of Society 5.0. In D. Detwiler (Ed.), *Building the Future of Food Safety Technology*. Elsevier. doi:10.1016/B978-0-12-818956-6.00002-6

Keogh, J. G., Rejeb, A., Khan, N., Dean, K., & Hand, K. J. (2020). Blockchain and GS1 Standards in the Food Chain: A Review of the Possibilities and Challenges. In D. Detwiler (Ed.), *Building the Future of Food Safety Technology*. Elsevier.

Kerr, J. (2018). How Can Legislators Protect Sport from the Integrity Threat Posed by Cryptocurrencies? *The International Sports Law Journal*, *18*(1), 79–97. doi:10.100740318-018-0132-0

Khan, S. A. R., Shah, A. S. A., Yu, Z., & Tanveer, M. (2022). A systematic literature review on circular economy practices: Challenges, opportunities and future trends. *Journal of Entrepreneurship in Emerging Economies*, *14*(5), 754–795. doi:10.1108/JEEE-09-2021-0349

Khan, S. A. R., Zia-ul-haq, H. M., Umar, M., & Yu, Z. (2021). Digital technology and circular economy practices: An strategy to improve organizational performance. *Business Strategy & Development*, *4*(4), 482–490. doi:10.1002/bsd2.176

Khare, R. (2006). *What Is Decentralization?* Isr.uci.edu. https://isr.uci.edu/projects/pace/decentralization.html

Klein, T., Thu, H. P., & Walther, T. (2018). Bitcoin is not the New Gold–A comparison of volatility, correlation, and portfolio performance. *International Review of Financial Analysis*, *59*, 105–116. https://doi.org/10.1016/j.irfa.2018.07.010

Klumov, G. (2020). From Cash to Crypto: Covid-19 is changing the way the world sees money. *Coin Telegraph*. https://cointelegraph.com/news/from-cash-to-crypto-covid-19-is-changing-the-way-the-world-sees-money

Koirala, B. (2021) 16 advantages and disadvantages of cryptocurrency. *Honest Pros and Cons*. https://honestproscons.com/advantages-and-disadvantages-of-c ryptocurrency/.

Koning, JP. (2016). Fedcoin: A Central Bank-issued Cryptocurrency. *R3 reports*.

Kosse, A., Chen, H., Felt, M.-H., Jiongo, V., Nield, K., & Welte, A. (2017). *The Costs of Point-of-Sale Payments in Canada*. Discussion Papers.

Kostika, E., & Laopodis, N. T. (2019). Dynamic linkages among cryptocurrencies, exchange rates and global equity markets. *Studies in Economics and Finance*, *37*(2), 243–265. doi:10.1108/SEF-01-2019-0032

Kovenock, D., & Vries, C. G. (2002). Fiat exchange in finite economies. *Economic Inquiry, 40*(2), 147–157. doi:10.1093/ei/40.2.147

Kristjanpoller, W., & Bouri, E. (2019). Asymmetric multifractal cross-correlations between the main world currencies and the main cryptocurrencies. *Physica A, 523*, 1057–1071. doi:10.1016/j.physa.2019.04.115

Kristoffersen, E., Blomsma, F., Mikalef, P., & Li, J. (2020). The smart circular economy: A digital-enabled circular strategies framework for manufacturing companies. *Journal of Business Research, 120*, 241–261. doi:10.1016/j.jbusres.2020.07.044

Kuchler, H. (2020). *Bitcoin: Why Is It So Male-Dominated?* Ft.com. https://www.ft.com/content/259734ca-0b95-11e8-839d-41ca06376bf2

Kumar, H. (2021). *Here Is Why Cryptocurrencies Are So Volatile.* Outlook. https://www.outlookindia.com/website/story/business-news-here-is-why-are-cryptocurrencies-so-volatile/398988

Kushwah, S., Dhir, A., Sagar, M., & Gupta, B. (2019). Determinants of organic food consumption. A systematic literature review on motives and barriers. *Appetite, 143*, 104402. Advance online publication. doi:10.1016/j.appet.2019.104402 PMID:31421197

Lapin, N. (2021). Explaining Crypto's Volatility. *Forbes*. https://www.forbes.com/sites/nicolelapin/2021/12/23/explaining-cryptos-volatility/?sh=1e66d2d27b54

Larios-Hernández, G. J. (2017). Blockchain Entrepreneurship Opportunity in The Practices of The Unbanked. *Business Horizons, 60*(6), 865–874. doi:10.1016/j.bushor.2017.07.012

Leirvik, T. (2022). Cryptocurrency returns and the volatility of liquidity. *Finance Research Letters, 44*, 102031. https://doi.org/10.1016/j.frl.2021.102031

Lind, C. H., Kang, O., Ljung, A., & Rosenbaum, P. (2022). Involvement of multinational corporations in social innovation: Exploring an emerging phenomenon. *Journal of Business Research, 151*, 207–221. doi:10.1016/j.jbusres.2022.07.003

Liu, Y., & Tsyvinski, A. (2021). Risks and returns of cryptocurrency. *Review of Financial Studies, 34*(6), 2689–2727. doi:10.1093/rfs/hhaa113

Lu, Q., Xu, X., Liu, Y., Weber, I., Zhu, L., & Zhang, W. (2019). uBaaS: A Unified Blockchain as a Service Platform. *Future Generation Computer Systems, 101*, 564–575. doi:10.1016/j.future.2019.05.051

Macroanalyst.blogspot.com. (2020). *Economic Assets Vs Speculative Assets.* Blogspot. https://macroanalyst.blogspot.com/2011/04/economic-assets-vs-speculative-assets.html

Mancini-Griffoli, T., Martinez Peria, M. S., Agur, I., Ari, A., Kiff, J., Popescu, A., & Rochon, C. (2018). Casting Light on Central Bank Digital Currencies. IMF Staff Discussion Note, International Monetary Fund.

Mangion, D. (2021). Cryptocurrency Money Laundering Risks. Cryptocurrency Money Laundering Risks. *Skillcast.* https://www.skillcast.com/blog/cryptocurrency-money-launderi ng-risks

Marian, O. (2013). Are Cryptocurrencies Super Tax Havens? *Michigan Law Review First Impressions, 112*(1), 38–48. https://repository.law.umich.edu/mlr_fi/vol112/iss1/2

Martinez-Marquez, D., Florin, N., Hall, W., Majewski, P., Wang, H., & Stewart, R. A. (2022). State-of-the-art review of product stewardship strategies for large composite wind turbine blades. *Resources. Conservation & Recycling Advances, 15*, 200109. doi:10.1016/j.rcradv.2022.200109

McAleer, M., Chan, F., Hoti, S., & Lieberman, O. (2008). Generalized autoregressive conditional correlation. *Econometric Theory, 24*(6), 1554–1583. doi:10.1017/S0266466608080614

McLeod, A. I., & Li, W. K. (1983). Diagnostic checking ARMA time series models using squared-residual autocorrelations. *Journal of Time Series Analysis, 4*(4), 269–273. doi:10.1111/j.1467-9892.1983.tb00373.x

Mendoza-Tello, J. C., Mora, H., Pujol-López, F. A., & Lytras, M. D. (2018). Social Commerce as a Driver to Enhance Trust and Intention to Use Cryptocurrencies for Electronic Payments. *IEEE Access: Practical Innovations, Open Solutions, 6*, 50737–50751. doi:10.1109/ACCESS.2018.2869359

Mendoza-Tello, J. C., Mora, H., Pujol-López, F. A., & Lytras, M. D. (2019). Disruptive Innovation of Cryptocurrencies in Consumer Acceptance and Trust. *Information Systems and e-Business Management, 17*(2), 195–222. doi:10.100710257-019-00415-w

Merriam-Webster. (2020). *Adaptation.* Merriam-Webster. https://www.merriam-webster.com/dictionary/adaptation

Michelman, P. (2017). Seeing Beyond the Blockchain Hype. *MIT Sloan Management Review, 58*(4), 17–20.

Miller, P. (2016). The Cryptocurrency Enigma. In J. Sammons (Ed.), *Digital Forensics* (pp. 1–25). Syngress. doi:10.1016/B978-0-12-804526-8.00001-0

Milne, A. (2018). Cryptocurrencies from an Austrian Perspective. In A. Godart-van der Kroon & P. Vonlanthen (Eds.), *Banking and Monetary Policy from the Perspective of Austrian Economics* (pp. 223–257). Springer International Publishing. doi:10.1007/978-3-319-75817-6_12

Momtaz, P. P. (2019). The Pricing and Performance of Cryptocurrency. *European Journal of Finance*, 1–14. doi:10.1080/1351847X.2019.1647259

Money Laundering via Cryptocurrencies: All You Need to Know. (2020). Tookitaki. https://www.tookitaki.com/blog/news-views/moneylaundering-via-cryptocurrencies

N. D. T. V. (2021). *Volatility in the Cryptocurrency Industry: What Determines Heightened Price Fluctuation?* NDTV. https://www.ndtv.com/business/why-is-bitcoin-or-any-other-cryptocurrency-so-volatile-2546933

Naboulsi, N., & Neubrt, M. (2018). *Impact of digital currencies on economic development in Kenya.* ACBSP Region 8 Annual Conference, Paris, France.

Nag, K. A. (2021). A Proposed Architecture for a Central Bank Digital Currency for India. *ORF Occasional Paper No. 340*, Observer Research Foundation.

Nandi, S., Sarkis, J., Hervani, A., & Helms, M. (2021). Do blockchain and circular economy practices improve post COVID-19 supply chains? A resource-based and resource dependence perspective. *Industrial Management & Data Systems, 121*(2), 333–363. doi:10.1108/IMDS-09-2020-0560

Narayan, R., & Tidström, A. (2020). Tokenizing coopetition in a blockchain for a transition to circular economy. *Journal of Cleaner Production, 263*, 121437. doi:10.1016/j.jclepro.2020.121437

Nibley, B. (2021). *Bitcoin Price History: 2009-2022.* SoFi Learn. https://www.sofi.com/learn/content/bitcoin-price-history/

Nica, O., Piotrowska, K., & Reiner, K. 2017. Economic benefits and risks. *Fintech Working paper no 2.* University of Manchester.

Nicholls, Jack & Kuppa, Aditya & Le-Khac, Nhien-An. (2021). *Financial Cybercrime: A Comprehensive Survey of Deep Learning Approaches to Tackle the Evolving Financial Crime Landscape.* IEEE Access. . doi:10.1109/ACCESS.2021.3134076

Omane-Adjepong, M., & Alagidede, I. P. (2020). High- and Low-Level Chaos in The Time and Frequency Market Returns of Leading Cryptocurrencies and Emerging Assets. *Chaos, Solitons, and Fractals, 132*, 109563. doi:10.1016/j.chaos.2019.109563

Omane-Adjepong, M., Alagidede, P., & Akosah, N. K. (2019). Wavelet Time-Scale Persistence Analysis of Cryptocurrency Market Returns and Volatility. *Physica A, 514*, 105–120. doi:10.1016/j.physa.2018.09.013

Online, F. E. (2022). Cryptocurrency markets project high price volatility. *Financial Express.* https://www.financialexpress.com/digital-currency/cryptocurrency-markets-project-high-price-volatility-report/2502562/

Palazzi, R. B., Júnior, G. D., & Klotzle, M. C. (2021). The dynamic relationship between Bitcoin and the foreign exchange market: A nonlinear approach to test causality between Bitcoin and currencies. *Finance Research Letters, 42*, 101893. doi:10.1016/j.frl.2020.101893

Panetta, F. (2022). *Central bank digital currencies: defining the problems, designing the solutions.* Speech by Fabio Panetta to a panel discussion on central bank digital currencies at the US Monetary Policy Forum. https://www.ecb.europa.eu/press/key/date/2022/html/ecb.sp220218_1~938e881b13.en.html

Paper 7F Examining Team. (2008). The need for and an understanding of a conceptual framework. ACCA. https://www.accaglobal.com/gb/en/student/exam-support-resources/fundamentals-exams-study-resources/f7/technical-articles/conceptual-framework-need.html

Pereira, J. P., & Zhang, H. H. (2010). Stock returns and the volatility of liquidity. *Journal of Financial and Quantitative Analysis*, *45*(4), 1077–1110. https://doi.org/10.1017/S0022109010000323

Platanakis, E., & Urquhart, A. (2020). Should investors include bitcoin in their portfolios? A portfolio theory approach. *The British Accounting Review*, *52*(4), 100837. https://doi.org/10.1016/j.bar.2019.100837

Polasik, M., Piotrowska, A. I., Wisniewski, T. P., Kotkowski, R., & Lightfoot, G. (2015). Price Fluctuations and the Use of Bitcoin: An Empirical Inquiry. *International Journal of Electronic Commerce*, *20*(1), 9–49. doi:10.1080/10864415.2016.1061413

Popper, N. (2016). *Digital Gold: Bitcoin and the inside story of the misfits and millionaires trying to reinvent money*. Harper.

Pournader, M., Shi, Y., Seuring, S., & Koh, S. C. L. (2020). Blockchain Applications in Supply Chains, Transport and Logistics: A Systematic Review of the Literature. *International Journal of Production Research*, *58*(7), 2063–2081. doi:10.1080/00207543.2019.1650976

Priyadarshini, D., & Kar, S. (2021). Central Bank Digital Currency (CBDC): Critical Issues and the Indian Perspective. *IRG working paper no.444*.

PwC (2021), Central Bank Digital Currency in the Indian context. PwC.

Radar, C. (2019). *Largest Bitcoin Ownership Survey Reveals 6.2% Of Americans Own Bitcoin, While 7.3% Are Planning To Buy Some*. Prnewswire.com. https://www.prnewswire.com/news-releases/largest-bitcoin-ownership-survey-reveals-6-2-of-americans-own-bitcoin-while-7-3-are-planning-to-buy-some-300928651.html

Rajagopal, K. (2019). Draft banning of cryptocurrency & regulation of official digital currency bill. *The Hindu.* https://prsindia.org/billtrack/draft-banning-of-cryptocurrencyregulation-of-official-digital-currency-bill

Raymaekers, W. (2015). Cryptocurrency Bitcoin: Disruption, Challenges and Opportunities. *Journal of Payments Strategy & Systems*, *9*(1), 30–46.

Raza, S. A., Ahmed, M., & Aloui, C. (2022). On the asymmetrical connectedness between cryptocurrencies and foreign exchange markets: Evidence from the nonparametric quantile on quantile approach. *Research in International Business and Finance*, *61*, 101627. doi:10.1016/j.ribaf.2022.101627

Rehman Khan, S. A., Yu, Z., Sarwat, S., Godil, D. I., Amin, S., & Shujaat, S. (2022). The role of block chain technology in circular economy practices to improve organisational performance. *International Journal of Logistics Research and Applications*, *25*(4-5), 605–622. doi:10.1080/13675567.2021.1872512

Reiff, N. (2022). *Why Is Bitcoin Volatile?* Investopedia. https://www.investopedia.com/articles/investing/052014/why-b itcoins-value-so-volatile.asp

Rejeb, A., & Bell, L. (2019). Potentials of Blockchain for Healthcare: Case of Tunisia. *World Scientific News*, *136*, 173–193. doi:10.2139srn.3475246

Rejeb, A., Keogh, J. G., & Treiblmaier, H. (2019a). Leveraging the Internet of Things and Blockchain Technology in Supply Chain Management. *Future Internet*, *11*(7), 161. doi:10.3390/fi11070161

Rejeb, A., Sűle, E., & Keogh, J. G. (2018). Exploring new technologies in procurement. *Transport & Logistics: The International Journal*, *18*(45), 76–86.

Research, H. (2022, December 12). Global Crypto Industry Overview and Trends[2022–2023 Annual Report]. *Medium*. https://medium.com/huobi-research/global-crypto-industry-ove rview-and-trends-2022-2023-annual-report-first-part-e15372f2 9c

Sackheim, M. S., & Howell, A. N. (2018). *The Virtual Currency Regulation Review*. Law Business Research Ltd.

Said, A. (2019). The economic impact of Digital Fiat Currency (DFC): Opportunities and Challenges. *Econstar.*

Sankar, R.T. (2021). Central Bank Digital Currency – Is This the Future of Money. Keynote address delivered by Shri T Rabi Sankar. *Vidhi Centre for Legal Policy*, New Delhi.

Sankar, S. (2022). Speeches and Interviews. Reserve Bank of India. https://rbi.org.in/Scripts/BS_SpeechesView.aspx?Id=1196

Scharding, T. (2019). National Currency, World Currency, Cryptocurrency: A Fichtean Approach to the Ethics of Bitcoin. *Business and Society Review*, *124*(2), 219–238. doi:10.1111/basr.12169

Scharnowski, S. (2021). Understanding bitcoin liquidity. *Finance Research Letters*, *38*, 101477. https://doi.org/10.1016/j.frl.2020.101477

Schilling, L., & Uhlig, H. (2019). Some simple bitcoin economics. *Journal of Monetary Economics*, *106*, 16–26. doi:10.1016/j.jmoneco.2019.07.002

Searing, J. M., & MacLeod, D. (2019). Cryptocurrency Gift Strategies for Not-for-Profits: Here's What Organizations Should Consider as They Ponder Whether and How to Accept Donations of Virtual Currency. *Journal of Accountancy*, *227*(2), 34–36.

Seetharaman, A. Saravanan, A.S. Patwa, N. Mehta, J. (2017). Impact of Bitcoin as world currency. *SciEdu.*

Selgin, G. (2015). Synthetic Commodity Money. *Journal of Financial Stability*, *17*, 92–99. doi:10.1016/j.jfs.2014.07.002

Seth, S. (2022). How to Prepare Your Bitcoin Tax Filing. Investopedia. https://www.investopedia.com/tech/how-prepare-bitcoin-tax-fi ling/#toc-bitcoin-record-keeping-is-your-responsibility

Shahzad, F., Xiu, G., Wang, J., & Shahbaz, M. (2018). An Empirical Investigation on the Adoption of Cryptocurrencies Among the People of Mainland China. *Technology in Society*, *55*, 33–40. doi:10.1016/j.techsoc.2018.05.006

Sharma, A. K., & Kumar, S. (2010). Economic Value Added (EVA)-Literature Review and Relevant Issues. *International Journal of Economics and Finance*, *2*(2), 200–220. doi:10.5539/ijef.v2n2p200

Shin, D.-H. (2009). Towards an understanding of the consumer acceptance of mobile wallet. *Computers in Human Behavior*, *25*(6), 1343–1354. doi:10.1016/j.chb.2009.06.001

Shukla, V & Misra, M., & Chaturvedi, A. (2022). *Journey of Cryptocurrency in India in View of Financial Budget 2022-23.* Research Gate.

Sigalos, M. (2021). *Bitcoin's wild price moves stem from its design - you'll need strong nerves to trade it.* CNBC. https://www.cnbc.com/2021/05/19/why-is-bitcoin-so-volatile.h tml

Singh, A. K., & Raj, M. (2022).A study of Analytics and Exploration of Bitcoin Challenges and Blockchain. *2022 International Conference on Electronics and Renewable Systems (ICEARS)*, Tuticorin, India. 10.1109/ICEARS53579.2022.9751821

Stancel, D. (2015). *Economic Consequences of Cryptocurrencies and Associated Decentralized Systems.* Research Gate.

Statistics How To. (2020). *Chi-Square Statistic: How To Calculate It / Distribution – Statistics How To.* Statistics. https://www.statisticshowto.com/probability-and-statistics/c hi-square/

Sudzina, F. (2018). Distribution of Foreign Aid in Cryptocurrencies: Initial Considerations. *International Advances in Economic Research*, *24*(4), 387–388. doi:10.100711294-018-9715-7

Symitsi, E., & Chalvatzis, K. J. (2018). Return, Volatility and Shock Spillovers of Bitcoin with Energy and Technology Companies. *Economics Letters*, *170*, 127–130. doi:10.1016/j.econlet.2018.06.012

Tama, B. A., Kweka, B. J., Park, Y., & Rhee, K.-H. (2017). A Critical Review of Blockchain and Its Current Applications. *2017 International Conference on Electrical Engineering and Computer Science (ICECOS)*, (pp. 109–113). IEEE. 10.1109/ICECOS.2017.8167115

Tastan, H. (2006). Estimating time-varying conditional correlations between stock and foreign exchange markets. *Physica A*, *360*(2), 445–458. doi:10.1016/j.physa.2005.06.062

Technology, V. (2020). Top 5 Disadvantages Of Cryptocurrency. *Medium*. https://medium.com/the-capital/top-5-disadvantages-of-crypto currency-925d6679195d

Tikhomirov, S. (2018). Ethereum: State of knowledge and research perspectives. In *Foundations and Practice of Security* (pp. 206–221). Springer International Publishing. doi:10.1007/978-3-319-75650-9_14

Till, B. M., Peters, A. W., Afshar, S., & Meara, J. G. (2017). From Blockchain Technology to Global Health Equity: Can Cryptocurrencies Finance Universal Health Coverage? *BMJ Global Health*, *2*(4), e000570. doi:10.1136/bmjgh-2017-000570 PMID:29177101

Todd, R. & Rogers, M. (2020). *A Global Look at Central Bank Digital Currencies*. The Block Research.

Torre, C., Rocha, J. G., Falcão, M. I., Taniar, D., Apduhan, B. O., & Gervasi, O. (2014). *Computational Science and Its Applications*, 720–732. Berlin: Springer International Publishing.

Trautman, L. J. (2014). Virtual Currencies; Bitcoin & What Now After Liberty Reserve, Silk Road, and Mt. Gox? *Richmond Journal of Law and Technology*, *20*(4), 1–108.

Treiblmaier, H. (2018). The Impact of The Blockchain on The Supply Chain: A Theory-Based Research Framework and a Call for Action. *Supply Chain Management*, *23*(6), 545–559. doi:10.1108/SCM-01-2018-0029

TrozzeA.KampsJ.AkartunaE. A.HetzelF. J.KleinbergB.DaviesT. JohnsonS. D. (2022). Cryptocurrencies and future financial crime. Crime Science. https://crimesciencejournal.biomedcentral.com/articles/10.11 86/s40163-021-00163-8

Trozze, A., Kamps, J., Akartuna, E., Hetzel, F., Kleinberg, B., Davies, T., & Johnson, S. (2022). Cryptocurrencies and future financial crime. *Crime Science*, *11*(1), 1. doi:10.118640163-021-00163-8 PMID:35013699

Tucker, T. (2013). Bitcoin's Volatility Problem: Why Today's Selloff Won't Be the Last. *Bloomberg.Com*. https://www.bloomberg.com/news/articles/2013-12-05/bitcoins-volatility-problem- why-todays-selloff-wont-be-the-last

Uddin, M. A., Stranieri, A., Gondal, I., & Balasubramanian, V. (2019). A Lightweight Blockchain Based Framework for Underwater IoT. *Electronics (Basel)*, *8*(12), 1552. doi:10.3390/electronics8121552

Umar, Z., & Gubareva, M. (2020). A Time–frequency analysis of the impact of the COVID-19 induced panic on the volatility of currency and cryptocurrency markets. *Journal of Behavioral and Experimental Finance*, *28*, 100404. doi:10.1016/j.jbef.2020.100404 PMID:32983899

United Nation Development Program. (2020). *Covid-19 Socio-economic impact.* UN. https://www.undp.org/content/undp/en/home/coronavirus/socio-economic-impact-of-covid-19.html

Urquhart, A., & Zhang, H. (2019). Is bitcoin a hedge or safe haven for currencies? an intraday analysis. *International Review of Financial Analysis*, *63*, 49–57. doi:10.1016/j.irfa.2019.02.009

Vandezande, N. (2017). Virtual Currencies Under EU Anti-money Laundering Law. *Computer Law & Security Review*, *33*(3), 341–353. doi:10.1016/j.clsr.2017.03.011

Vaz, J., & Brown, K. (2020). Sustainable Development and Cryptocurrencies as Private Money. *Economia e Politica Industriale*, *47*(1), 163–184. doi:10.100740812-019-00139-5

Vidal-Tomás, D., Ibáñez, A. M., & Farinós, J. E. (2019). Weak efficiency of the cryptocurrency market: A market portfolio approach. *Applied Economics Letters*, *26*(19), 1627–1633. doi:10.1080/13504851.2019.1591583

Vincent, O., & Evans, O. (2019). Can Cryptocurrency, Mobile Phones, and Internet Herald Sustainable Financial Sector Development in Emerging Markets? *Journal of Transnational Management*, *24*(3), 259–279. doi:10.1080/15475778.2019.1633170

Volosovych, S., & Baraniuk, Y. (2018). Tax control of cryptocurrency transactions in Ukraine. *Banks and Bank Systems*, *13*(2), 89–106. https://www.ceeol.com/search/article-detail?id=696926

Walther, T., Klein, T., & Bouri, E. (2019). Exogenous drivers of Bitcoin and cryptocurrency volatility – a mixed data sampling approach to forecasting. *Journal of International Financial Markets, Institutions and Money*, *63*, 101133. doi:10.1016/j.intfin.2019.101133

Wang, G. (2019). Marx's Monetary Theory and Its Practical Value. *China Political Economy*, *2*(2), 182–200. doi:10.1108/CPE-10-2019-0026

Ward, O., & Rochemont, S. (2019). *An addendum to "A Cashless Society-Benefits, Risks and Issues (Interim paper)" Understanding Central Bank Digital Currencies (CBDC) By Orla Ward Sabrina Rochemont.* Actuaries.org. https:// www.actuaries.org.uk/system/files/field/document/Understanding CBDCs Final - disc.pdf

Why the crypto industry needs to be AML and KYC compliant. (2022). World Economic Forum. https://www.weforum.org/agenda/2022/09/why-crypto-businesses-need-anti-money-laundering-regulations/

Woebbeking, F. (2021). Cryptocurrency volatility markets. *Digital finance, 3*(3-4), 273–298. doi:10.1007/s42521-021-00037-3

Yermack, D. (2015). Is bitcoin a real currency? an economic appraisal. Handbook of Digital Currency, 31-43. doi:10.1016/B978-0-12-802117-0.00002-3

Yi, S., Xu, Z., & Wang, G. (2018). Volatility connectedness in the cryptocurrency market: Is bitcoin a dominant cryptocurrency? *International Review of Financial Analysis*, *60*, 98–114. doi:10.1016/j.irfa.2018.08.012

Yue, W., Zhang, S., & Zhang, Q. (2021). Asymmetric news effects on cryptocurrency liquidity: An Event study perspective. *Finance Research Letters*, *41*, 101799. https://doi.org/10.1016/j.frl.2020.101799

Zoltan, T. (2022, January 24). How Cryptocurrency Will Impact The Gaming Industry. *European Gaming*. https://europeangaming.eu/

Related References

To continue our tradition of advancing information science and technology research, we have compiled a list of recommended IGI Global readings. These references will provide additional information and guidance to further enrich your knowledge and assist you with your own research and future publications.

Abdul Razak, R., & Mansor, N. A. (2021). Instagram Influencers in Social Media-Induced Tourism: Rethinking Tourist Trust Towards Tourism Destination. In M. Dinis, L. Bonixe, S. Lamy, & Z. Breda (Eds.), *Impact of New Media in Tourism* (pp. 135-144). IGI Global. https://doi.org/10.4018/978-1-7998-7095-1.ch009

Abir, T., & Khan, M. Y. (2022). Importance of ICT Advancement and Culture of Adaptation in the Tourism and Hospitality Industry for Developing Countries. In C. Ramos, S. Quinteiro, & A. Gonçalves (Eds.), *ICT as Innovator Between Tourism and Culture* (pp. 30–41). IGI Global. https://doi.org/10.4018/978-1-7998-8165-0.ch003

Abtahi, M. S., Behboudi, L., & Hasanabad, H. M. (2017). Factors Affecting Internet Advertising Adoption in Ad Agencies. *International Journal of Innovation in the Digital Economy*, *8*(4), 18–29. doi:10.4018/IJIDE.2017100102

Afenyo-Agbe, E., & Mensah, I. (2022). Principles, Benefits, and Barriers to Community-Based Tourism: Implications for Management. In I. Mensah & E. Afenyo-Agbe (Eds.), *Prospects and Challenges of Community-Based Tourism and Changing Demographics* (pp. 1–29). IGI Global. doi:10.4018/978-1-7998-7335-8.ch001

Agbo, V. M. (2022). Distributive Justice Issues in Community-Based Tourism. In I. Mensah & E. Afenyo-Agbe (Eds.), *Prospects and Challenges of Community-Based Tourism and Changing Demographics* (pp. 107–129). IGI Global. https://doi.org/10.4018/978-1-7998-7335-8.ch005

Agrawal, S. (2017). The Impact of Emerging Technologies and Social Media on Different Business(es): Marketing and Management. In O. Rishi & A. Sharma (Eds.), *Maximizing Business Performance and Efficiency Through Intelligent Systems* (pp. 37–49). Hershey, PA: IGI Global. doi:10.4018/978-1-5225-2234-8.ch002

Ahmad, A., & Johari, S. (2022). Georgetown as a Gastronomy Tourism Destination: Visitor Awareness Towards Revisit Intention of Nasi Kandar Restaurant. In M. Valeri (Ed.), *New Governance and Management in Touristic Destinations* (pp. 71–83). IGI Global. https://doi.org/10.4018/978-1-6684-3889-3.ch005

Alkhatib, G., & Bayouq, S. T. (2021). A TAM-Based Model of Technological Factors Affecting Use of E-Tourism. *International Journal of Tourism and Hospitality Management in the Digital Age*, *5*(2), 50–67. https://doi.org/10.4018/IJTHMDA.20210701.oa1

Altinay Ozdemir, M. (2021). Virtual Reality (VR) and Augmented Reality (AR) Technologies for Accessibility and Marketing in the Tourism Industry. In C. Eusébio, L. Teixeira, & M. Carneiro (Eds.), *ICT Tools and Applications for Accessible Tourism* (pp. 277-301). IGI Global. https://doi.org/10.4018/978-1-7998-6428-8.ch013

Anantharaman, R. N., Rajeswari, K. S., Angusamy, A., & Kuppusamy, J. (2017). Role of Self-Efficacy and Collective Efficacy as Moderators of Occupational Stress Among Software Development Professionals. *International Journal of Human Capital and Information Technology Professionals*, *8*(2), 45–58. doi:10.4018/IJHCITP.2017040103

Aninze, F., El-Gohary, H., & Hussain, J. (2018). The Role of Microfinance to Empower Women: The Case of Developing Countries. *International Journal of Customer Relationship Marketing and Management*, *9*(1), 54–78. doi:10.4018/IJCRMM.2018010104

Antosova, G., Sabogal-Salamanca, M., & Krizova, E. (2021). Human Capital in Tourism: A Practical Model of Endogenous and Exogenous Territorial Tourism Planning in Bahía Solano, Colombia. In V. Costa, A. Moura, & M. Mira (Eds.), *Handbook of Research on Human Capital and People Management in the Tourism Industry* (pp. 282–302). IGI Global. https://doi.org/10.4018/978-1-7998-4318-4.ch014

Arsenijević, O. M., Orčić, D., & Kastratović, E. (2017). Development of an Optimization Tool for Intangibles in SMEs: A Case Study from Serbia with a Pilot Research in the Prestige by Milka Company. In M. Vemić (Ed.), *Optimal Management Strategies in Small and Medium Enterprises* (pp. 320–347). Hershey, PA: IGI Global. doi:10.4018/978-1-5225-1949-2.ch015

Aryanto, V. D., Wismantoro, Y., & Widyatmoko, K. (2018). Implementing Eco-Innovation by Utilizing the Internet to Enhance Firm's Marketing Performance: Study of Green Batik Small and Medium Enterprises in Indonesia. *International Journal of E-Business Research, 14*(1), 21–36. doi:10.4018/IJEBR.2018010102

Asero, V., & Billi, S. (2022). New Perspective of Networking in the DMO Model. In M. Valeri (Ed.), *New Governance and Management in Touristic Destinations* (pp. 105–118). IGI Global. https://doi.org/10.4018/978-1-6684-3889-3.ch007

Atiku, S. O., & Fields, Z. (2017). Multicultural Orientations for 21st Century Global Leadership. In N. Baporikar (Ed.), *Management Education for Global Leadership* (pp. 28–51). Hershey, PA: IGI Global. doi:10.4018/978-1-5225-1013-0.ch002

Atiku, S. O., & Fields, Z. (2018). Organisational Learning Dimensions and Talent Retention Strategies for the Service Industries. In N. Baporikar (Ed.), *Global Practices in Knowledge Management for Societal and Organizational Development* (pp. 358–381). Hershey, PA: IGI Global. doi:10.4018/978-1-5225-3009-1.ch017

Atsa'am, D. D., & Kuset Bodur, E. (2021). Pattern Mining on How Organizational Tenure Affects the Psychological Capital of Employees Within the Hospitality and Tourism Industry: Linking Employees' Organizational Tenure With PsyCap. *International Journal of Tourism and Hospitality Management in the Digital Age, 5*(2), 17–28. https://doi.org/10.4018/IJTHMDA.2021070102

Ávila, L., & Teixeira, L. (2018). The Main Concepts Behind the Dematerialization of Business Processes. In M. Khosrow-Pour, D.B.A. (Ed.), Encyclopedia of Information Science and Technology, Fourth Edition (pp. 888-898). Hershey, PA: IGI Global. https://doi.org/ doi:10.4018/978-1-5225-2255-3.ch076

Ayorekire, J., Mugizi, F., Obua, J., & Ampaire, G. (2022). Community-Based Tourism and Local People's Perceptions Towards Conservation: The Case of Queen Elizabeth Conservation Area, Uganda. In I. Mensah & E. Afenyo-Agbe (Eds.), *Prospects and Challenges of Community-Based Tourism and Changing Demographics* (pp. 56–82). IGI Global. https://doi.org/10.4018/978-1-7998-7335-8.ch003

Baleiro, R. (2022). Tourist Literature and the Architecture of Travel in Olga Tokarczuk and Patti Smith. In R. Baleiro & R. Pereira (Eds.), *Global Perspectives on Literary Tourism and Film-Induced Tourism* (pp. 202-216). IGI Global. https://doi.org/10.4018/978-1-7998-8262-6.ch011

Barat, S. (2021). Looking at the Future of Medical Tourism in Asia. *International Journal of Tourism and Hospitality Management in the Digital Age, 5*(1), 19–33. https://doi.org/10.4018/IJTHMDA.2021010102

Barbosa, C. A., Magalhães, M., & Nunes, M. R. (2021). Travel Instagramability: A Way of Choosing a Destination? In M. Dinis, L. Bonixe, S. Lamy, & Z. Breda (Eds.), *Impact of New Media in Tourism* (pp. 173-190). IGI Global. https://doi.org/10.4018/978-1-7998-7095-1.ch011

Bari, M. W., & Khan, Q. (2021). Pakistan as a Destination of Religious Tourism. In E. Alaverdov & M. Bari (Eds.), *Global Development of Religious Tourism* (pp. 1-10). IGI Global. https://doi.org/10.4018/978-1-7998-5792-1.ch001

Bartens, Y., Chunpir, H. I., Schulte, F., & Voß, S. (2017). Business/IT Alignment in Two-Sided Markets: A COBIT 5 Analysis for Media Streaming Business Models. In S. De Haes & W. Van Grembergen (Eds.), *Strategic IT Governance and Alignment in Business Settings* (pp. 82–111). Hershey, PA: IGI Global. doi:10.4018/978-1-5225-0861-8.ch004

Bashayreh, A. M. (2018). Organizational Culture and Organizational Performance. In W. Lee & F. Sabetzadeh (Eds.), *Contemporary Knowledge and Systems Science* (pp. 50–69). Hershey, PA: IGI Global. doi:10.4018/978-1-5225-5655-8.ch003

Bechthold, L., Lude, M., & Prügl, R. (2021). Crisis Favors the Prepared Firm: How Organizational Ambidexterity Relates to Perceptions of Organizational Resilience. In A. Zehrer, G. Glowka, K. Schwaiger, & V. Ranacher-Lackner (Eds.), *Resiliency Models and Addressing Future Risks for Family Firms in the Tourism Industry* (pp. 178–205). IGI Global. https://doi.org/10.4018/978-1-7998-7352-5.ch008

Bedford, D. A. (2018). Sustainable Knowledge Management Strategies: Aligning Business Capabilities and Knowledge Management Goals. In N. Baporikar (Ed.), *Global Practices in Knowledge Management for Societal and Organizational Development* (pp. 46–73). Hershey, PA: IGI Global. doi:10.4018/978-1-5225-3009-1.ch003

Bekjanov, D., & Matyusupov, B. (2021). Influence of Innovative Processes in the Competitiveness of Tourist Destination. In J. Soares (Ed.), *Innovation and Entrepreneurial Opportunities in Community Tourism* (pp. 243–263). IGI Global. https://doi.org/10.4018/978-1-7998-4855-4.ch014

Bharwani, S., & Musunuri, D. (2018). Reflection as a Process From Theory to Practice. In M. Khosrow-Pour, D.B.A. (Ed.), Encyclopedia of Information Science and Technology, Fourth Edition (pp. 1529-1539). Hershey, PA: IGI Global. doi:10.4018/978-1-5225-2255-3.ch132

Bhatt, G. D., Wang, Z., & Rodger, J. A. (2017). Information Systems Capabilities and Their Effects on Competitive Advantages: A Study of Chinese Companies. *Information Resources Management Journal, 30*(3), 41–57. doi:10.4018/IRMJ.2017070103

Bhushan, M., & Yadav, A. (2017). Concept of Cloud Computing in ESB. In R. Bhadoria, N. Chaudhari, G. Tomar, & S. Singh (Eds.), *Exploring Enterprise Service Bus in the Service-Oriented Architecture Paradigm* (pp. 116–127). Hershey, PA: IGI Global. doi:10.4018/978-1-5225-2157-0.ch008

Bhushan, S. (2017). System Dynamics Base-Model of Humanitarian Supply Chain (HSCM) in Disaster Prone Eco-Communities of India: A Discussion on Simulation and Scenario Results. *International Journal of System Dynamics Applications*, *6*(3), 20–37. doi:10.4018/IJSDA.2017070102

Binder, D., & Miller, J. W. (2021). A Generations' Perspective on Employer Branding in Tourism. In V. Costa, A. Moura, & M. Mira (Eds.), *Handbook of Research on Human Capital and People Management in the Tourism Industry* (pp. 152–174). IGI Global. https://doi.org/10.4018/978-1-7998-4318-4.ch008

Birch Freeman, A. A., Mensah, I., & Antwi, K. B. (2022). Smiling vs. Frowning Faces: Community Participation for Sustainable Tourism in Ghanaian Communities. In I. Mensah & E. Afenyo-Agbe (Eds.), *Prospects and Challenges of Community-Based Tourism and Changing Demographics* (pp. 83–106). IGI Global. https://doi.org/10.4018/978-1-7998-7335-8.ch004

Biswas, A., & De, A. K. (2017). On Development of a Fuzzy Stochastic Programming Model with Its Application to Business Management. In S. Trivedi, S. Dey, A. Kumar, & T. Panda (Eds.), *Handbook of Research on Advanced Data Mining Techniques and Applications for Business Intelligence* (pp. 353–378). Hershey, PA: IGI Global. doi:10.4018/978-1-5225-2031-3.ch021

Boragnio, A., & Faracce Macia, C. (2021). "Taking Care of Yourself at Home": Use of E-Commerce About Food and Care During the COVID-19 Pandemic in the City of Buenos Aires. In M. Korstanje (Ed.), *Socio-Economic Effects and Recovery Efforts for the Rental Industry: Post-COVID-19 Strategies* (pp. 45–71). IGI Global. https://doi.org/10.4018/978-1-7998-7287-0.ch003

Borges, V. D. (2021). Happiness: The Basis for Public Policy in Tourism. In A. Perinotto, V. Mayer, & J. Soares (Eds.), *Rebuilding and Restructuring the Tourism Industry: Infusion of Happiness and Quality of Life* (pp. 1–25). IGI Global. https://doi.org/10.4018/978-1-7998-7239-9.ch001

Bücker, J., & Ernste, K. (2018). Use of Brand Heroes in Strategic Reputation Management: The Case of Bacardi, Adidas, and Daimler. In A. Erdemir (Ed.), *Reputation Management Techniques in Public Relations* (pp. 126–150). Hershey, PA: IGI Global. doi:10.4018/978-1-5225-3619-2.ch007

Buluk Eşitti, B. (2021). COVID-19 and Alternative Tourism: New Destinations and New Tourism Products. In M. Demir, A. Dalgıç, & F. Ergen (Eds.), *Handbook of Research on the Impacts and Implications of COVID-19 on the Tourism Industry* (pp. 786–805). IGI Global. https://doi.org/10.4018/978-1-7998-8231-2.ch038

Bureš, V. (2018). Industry 4.0 From the Systems Engineering Perspective: Alternative Holistic Framework Development. In R. Brunet-Thornton & F. Martinez (Eds.), *Analyzing the Impacts of Industry 4.0 in Modern Business Environments* (pp. 199–223). Hershey, PA: IGI Global. doi:10.4018/978-1-5225-3468-6.ch011

Buzady, Z. (2017). Resolving the Magic Cube of Effective Case Teaching: Benchmarking Case Teaching Practices in Emerging Markets – Insights from the Central European University Business School, Hungary. In D. Latusek (Ed.), *Case Studies as a Teaching Tool in Management Education* (pp. 79–103). Hershey, PA: IGI Global. doi:10.4018/978-1-5225-0770-3.ch005

Camillo, A. (2021). *Legal Matters, Risk Management, and Risk Prevention: From Forming a Business to Legal Representation.* IGI Global. doi:10.4018/978-1-7998-4342-9.ch004

Căpusneanu, S., & Topor, D. I. (2018). Business Ethics and Cost Management in SMEs: Theories of Business Ethics and Cost Management Ethos. In I. Oncioiu (Ed.), *Ethics and Decision-Making for Sustainable Business Practices* (pp. 109–127). Hershey, PA: IGI Global. doi:10.4018/978-1-5225-3773-1.ch007

Chan, R. L., Mo, P. L., & Moon, K. K. (2018). Strategic and Tactical Measures in Managing Enterprise Risks: A Study of the Textile and Apparel Industry. In K. Strang, M. Korstanje, & N. Vajjhala (Eds.), *Research, Practices, and Innovations in Global Risk and Contingency Management* (pp. 1–19). Hershey, PA: IGI Global. doi:10.4018/978-1-5225-4754-9.ch001

Charlier, S. D., Burke-Smalley, L. A., & Fisher, S. L. (2018). Undergraduate Programs in the U.S: A Contextual and Content-Based Analysis. In J. Mendy (Ed.), *Teaching Human Resources and Organizational Behavior at the College Level* (pp. 26–57). Hershey, PA: IGI Global. doi:10.4018/978-1-5225-2820-3.ch002

Chumillas, J., Güell, M., & Quer, P. (2022). The Use of ICT in Tourist and Educational Literary Routes: The Role of the Guide. In C. Ramos, S. Quinteiro, & A. Gonçalves (Eds.), *ICT as Innovator Between Tourism and Culture* (pp. 15–29). IGI Global. https://doi.org/10.4018/978-1-7998-8165-0.ch002

Dahlberg, T., Kivijärvi, H., & Saarinen, T. (2017). IT Investment Consistency and Other Factors Influencing the Success of IT Performance. In S. De Haes & W. Van Grembergen (Eds.), *Strategic IT Governance and Alignment in Business Settings* (pp. 176–208). Hershey, PA: IGI Global. doi:10.4018/978-1-5225-0861-8.ch007

Damnjanović, A. M. (2017). Knowledge Management Optimization through IT and E-Business Utilization: A Qualitative Study on Serbian SMEs. In M. Vemić (Ed.), *Optimal Management Strategies in Small and Medium Enterprises* (pp. 249–267). Hershey, PA: IGI Global. doi:10.4018/978-1-5225-1949-2.ch012

Daneshpour, H. (2017). Integrating Sustainable Development into Project Portfolio Management through Application of Open Innovation. In M. Vemić (Ed.), *Optimal Management Strategies in Small and Medium Enterprises* (pp. 370–387). Hershey, PA: IGI Global. doi:10.4018/978-1-5225-1949-2.ch017

Daniel, A. D., & Reis de Castro, V. (2018). Entrepreneurship Education: How to Measure the Impact on Nascent Entrepreneurs. In A. Carrizo Moreira, J. Guilherme Leitão Dantas, & F. Manuel Valente (Eds.), *Nascent Entrepreneurship and Successful New Venture Creation* (pp. 85–110). Hershey, PA: IGI Global. doi:10.4018/978-1-5225-2936-1.ch004

David, R., Swami, B. N., & Tangirala, S. (2018). Ethics Impact on Knowledge Management in Organizational Development: A Case Study. In N. Baporikar (Ed.), *Global Practices in Knowledge Management for Societal and Organizational Development* (pp. 19–45). Hershey, PA: IGI Global. doi:10.4018/978-1-5225-3009-1.ch002

De Uña-Álvarez, E., & Villarino-Pérez, M. (2022). Fostering Ecocultural Resources, Identity, and Tourism in Inland Territories (Galicia, NW Spain). In G. Fernandes (Ed.), *Challenges and New Opportunities for Tourism in Inland Territories: Ecocultural Resources and Sustainable Initiatives* (pp. 1-16). IGI Global. https://doi.org/10.4018/978-1-7998-7339-6.ch001

Delias, P., & Lakiotaki, K. (2018). Discovering Process Horizontal Boundaries to Facilitate Process Comprehension. *International Journal of Operations Research and Information Systems*, *9*(2), 1–31. doi:10.4018/IJORIS.2018040101

Denholm, J., & Lee-Davies, L. (2018). Success Factors for Games in Business and Project Management. In *Enhancing Education and Training Initiatives Through Serious Games* (pp. 34–68). Hershey, PA: IGI Global. doi:10.4018/978-1-5225-3689-5.ch002

Deshpande, M. (2017). Best Practices in Management Institutions for Global Leadership: Policy Aspects. In N. Baporikar (Ed.), *Management Education for Global Leadership* (pp. 1–27). Hershey, PA: IGI Global. doi:10.4018/978-1-5225-1013-0.ch001

Deshpande, M. (2018). Policy Perspectives for SMEs Knowledge Management. In N. Baporikar (Ed.), *Knowledge Integration Strategies for Entrepreneurship and Sustainability* (pp. 23–46). Hershey, PA: IGI Global. doi:10.4018/978-1-5225-5115-7.ch002

Dezdar, S. (2017). ERP Implementation Projects in Asian Countries: A Comparative Study on Iran and China. *International Journal of Information Technology Project Management*, *8*(3), 52–68. doi:10.4018/IJITPM.2017070104

Domingos, D., Respício, A., & Martinho, R. (2017). Reliability of IoT-Aware BPMN Healthcare Processes. In C. Reis & M. Maximiano (Eds.), *Internet of Things and Advanced Application in Healthcare* (pp. 214–248). Hershey, PA: IGI Global. doi:10.4018/978-1-5225-1820-4.ch008

Dosumu, O., Hussain, J., & El-Gohary, H. (2017). An Exploratory Study of the Impact of Government Policies on the Development of Small and Medium Enterprises in Developing Countries: The Case of Nigeria. *International Journal of Customer Relationship Marketing and Management*, *8*(4), 51–62. doi:10.4018/IJCRMM.2017100104

Durst, S., Bruns, G., & Edvardsson, I. R. (2017). Retaining Knowledge in Smaller Building and Construction Firms. *International Journal of Knowledge and Systems Science*, *8*(3), 1–12. doi:10.4018/IJKSS.2017070101

Edvardsson, I. R., & Durst, S. (2017). Outsourcing, Knowledge, and Learning: A Critical Review. *International Journal of Knowledge-Based Organizations*, *7*(2), 13–26. doi:10.4018/IJKBO.2017040102

Edwards, J. S. (2018). Integrating Knowledge Management and Business Processes. In M. Khosrow-Pour, D.B.A. (Ed.), Encyclopedia of Information Science and Technology, Fourth Edition (pp. 5046-5055). Hershey, PA: IGI Global. doi:10.4018/978-1-5225-2255-3.ch437

Eichelberger, S., & Peters, M. (2021). Family Firm Management in Turbulent Times: Opportunities for Responsible Tourism. In A. Zehrer, G. Glowka, K. Schwaiger, & V. Ranacher-Lackner (Eds.), *Resiliency Models and Addressing Future Risks for Family Firms in the Tourism Industry* (pp. 103–124). IGI Global. https://doi.org/10.4018/978-1-7998-7352-5.ch005

Eide, D., Hjalager, A., & Hansen, M. (2022). Innovative Certifications in Adventure Tourism: Attributes and Diffusion. In R. Augusto Costa, F. Brandão, Z. Breda, & C. Costa (Eds.), *Planning and Managing the Experience Economy in Tourism* (pp. 161-175). IGI Global. https://doi.org/10.4018/978-1-7998-8775-1.ch009

Ejiogu, A. O. (2018). Economics of Farm Management. In *Agricultural Finance and Opportunities for Investment and Expansion* (pp. 56–72). Hershey, PA: IGI Global. doi:10.4018/978-1-5225-3059-6.ch003

Ekanem, I., & Abiade, G. E. (2018). Factors Influencing the Use of E-Commerce by Small Enterprises in Nigeria. *International Journal of ICT Research in Africa and the Middle East, 7*(1), 37–53. doi:10.4018/IJICTRAME.2018010103

Ekanem, I., & Alrossais, L. A. (2017). Succession Challenges Facing Family Businesses in Saudi Arabia. In P. Zgheib (Ed.), *Entrepreneurship and Business Innovation in the Middle East* (pp. 122–146). Hershey, PA: IGI Global. doi:10.4018/978-1-5225-2066-5.ch007

El Faquih, L., & Fredj, M. (2017). Ontology-Based Framework for Quality in Configurable Process Models. *Journal of Electronic Commerce in Organizations, 15*(2), 48–60. doi:10.4018/JECO.2017040104

Faisal, M. N., & Talib, F. (2017). Building Ambidextrous Supply Chains in SMEs: How to Tackle the Barriers? *International Journal of Information Systems and Supply Chain Management, 10*(4), 80–100. doi:10.4018/IJISSCM.2017100105

Fernandes, T. M., Gomes, J., & Romão, M. (2017). Investments in E-Government: A Benefit Management Case Study. *International Journal of Electronic Government Research, 13*(3), 1–17. doi:10.4018/IJEGR.2017070101

Figueira, L. M., Honrado, G. R., & Dionísio, M. S. (2021). Human Capital Management in the Tourism Industry in Portugal. In V. Costa, A. Moura, & M. Mira (Eds.), *Handbook of Research on Human Capital and People Management in the Tourism Industry* (pp. 1–19). IGI Global. doi:10.4018/978-1-7998-4318-4.ch001

Gao, S. S., Oreal, S., & Zhang, J. (2018). Contemporary Financial Risk Management Perceptions and Practices of Small-Sized Chinese Businesses. In I. Management Association (Ed.), Global Business Expansion: Concepts, Methodologies, Tools, and Applications (pp. 917-931). Hershey, PA: IGI Global. doi:10.4018/978-1-5225-5481-3.ch041

Garg, R., & Berning, S. C. (2017). Indigenous Chinese Management Philosophies: Key Concepts and Relevance for Modern Chinese Firms. In B. Christiansen & G. Koc (Eds.), *Transcontinental Strategies for Industrial Development and Economic Growth* (pp. 43–57). Hershey, PA: IGI Global. doi:10.4018/978-1-5225-2160-0.ch003

Gencer, Y. G. (2017). Supply Chain Management in Retailing Business. In U. Akkucuk (Ed.), *Ethics and Sustainability in Global Supply Chain Management* (pp. 197–210). Hershey, PA: IGI Global. doi:10.4018/978-1-5225-2036-8.ch011

Gera, R., Arora, S., & Malik, S. (2021). Emotional Labor in the Tourism Industry: Strategies, Antecedents, and Outcomes. In V. Costa, A. Moura, & M. Mira (Eds.), *Handbook of Research on Human Capital and People Management in the Tourism Industry* (pp. 73–91). IGI Global. https://doi.org/10.4018/978-1-7998-4318-4.ch004

Giacosa, E. (2018). The Increasing of the Regional Development Thanks to the Luxury Business Innovation. In L. Carvalho (Ed.), *Handbook of Research on Entrepreneurial Ecosystems and Social Dynamics in a Globalized World* (pp. 260–273). Hershey, PA: IGI Global. doi:10.4018/978-1-5225-3525-6.ch011

Glowka, G., Tusch, M., & Zehrer, A. (2021). The Risk Perception of Family Business Owner-Manager in the Tourism Industry: A Qualitative Comparison of the Intra-Firm Senior and Junior Generation. In A. Zehrer, G. Glowka, K. Schwaiger, & V. Ranacher-Lackner (Eds.), *Resiliency Models and Addressing Future Risks for Family Firms in the Tourism Industry* (pp. 126–153). IGI Global. https://doi.org/10.4018/978-1-7998-7352-5.ch006

Glykas, M., & George, J. (2017). Quality and Process Management Systems in the UAE Maritime Industry. *International Journal of Productivity Management and Assessment Technologies*, *5*(1), 20–39. doi:10.4018/IJPMAT.2017010102

Glykas, M., Valiris, G., Kokkinaki, A., & Koutsoukou, Z. (2018). Banking Business Process Management Implementation. *International Journal of Productivity Management and Assessment Technologies*, *6*(1), 50–69. doi:10.4018/IJPMAT.2018010104

Gomes, J., & Romão, M. (2017). The Balanced Scorecard: Keeping Updated and Aligned with Today's Business Trends. *International Journal of Productivity Management and Assessment Technologies*, *5*(2), 1–15. doi:10.4018/IJPMAT.2017070101

Gomes, J., & Romão, M. (2017). Aligning Information Systems and Technology with Benefit Management and Balanced Scorecard. In S. De Haes & W. Van Grembergen (Eds.), *Strategic IT Governance and Alignment in Business Settings* (pp. 112–131). Hershey, PA: IGI Global. doi:10.4018/978-1-5225-0861-8.ch005

Goyal, A. (2021). Communicating and Building Destination Brands With New Media. In M. Dinis, L. Bonixe, S. Lamy, & Z. Breda (Eds.), *Impact of New Media in Tourism* (pp. 1-20). IGI Global. https://doi.org/10.4018/978-1-7998-7095-1.ch001

Grefen, P., & Turetken, O. (2017). Advanced Business Process Management in Networked E-Business Scenarios. *International Journal of E-Business Research, 13*(4), 70–104. doi:10.4018/IJEBR.2017100105

Guasca, M., Van Broeck, A. M., & Vanneste, D. (2021). Tourism and the Social Reintegration of Colombian Ex-Combatants. In J. da Silva, Z. Breda, & F. Carbone (Eds.), *Role and Impact of Tourism in Peacebuilding and Conflict Transformation* (pp. 66-86). IGI Global. https://doi.org/10.4018/978-1-7998-5053-3.ch005

Haider, A., & Saetang, S. (2017). Strategic IT Alignment in Service Sector. In S. Rozenes & Y. Cohen (Eds.), *Handbook of Research on Strategic Alliances and Value Co-Creation in the Service Industry* (pp. 231–258). Hershey, PA: IGI Global. doi:10.4018/978-1-5225-2084-9.ch012

Hajilari, A. B., Ghadaksaz, M., & Fasghandis, G. S. (2017). Assessing Organizational Readiness for Implementing ERP System Using Fuzzy Expert System Approach. *International Journal of Enterprise Information Systems, 13*(1), 67–85. doi:10.4018/IJEIS.2017010105

Haldorai, A., Ramu, A., & Murugan, S. (2018). Social Aware Cognitive Radio Networks: Effectiveness of Social Networks as a Strategic Tool for Organizational Business Management. In H. Bansal, G. Shrivastava, G. Nguyen, & L. Stanciu (Eds.), *Social Network Analytics for Contemporary Business Organizations* (pp. 188–202). Hershey, PA: IGI Global. doi:10.4018/978-1-5225-5097-6.ch010

Hall, O. P. Jr. (2017). Social Media Driven Management Education. *International Journal of Knowledge-Based Organizations, 7*(2), 43–59. doi:10.4018/IJKBO.2017040104

Hanifah, H., Halim, H. A., Ahmad, N. H., & Vafaei-Zadeh, A. (2017). Innovation Culture as a Mediator Between Specific Human Capital and Innovation Performance Among Bumiputera SMEs in Malaysia. In N. Ahmad, T. Ramayah, H. Halim, & S. Rahman (Eds.), *Handbook of Research on Small and Medium Enterprises in Developing Countries* (pp. 261–279). Hershey, PA: IGI Global. doi:10.4018/978-1-5225-2165-5.ch012

Hartlieb, S., & Silvius, G. (2017). Handling Uncertainty in Project Management and Business Development: Similarities and Differences. In Y. Raydugin (Ed.), *Handbook of Research on Leveraging Risk and Uncertainties for Effective Project Management* (pp. 337–362). Hershey, PA: IGI Global. doi:10.4018/978-1-5225-1790-0.ch016

Hass, K. B. (2017). Living on the Edge: Managing Project Complexity. In Y. Raydugin (Ed.), *Handbook of Research on Leveraging Risk and Uncertainties for Effective Project Management* (pp. 177–201). Hershey, PA: IGI Global. doi:10.4018/978-1-5225-1790-0.ch009

Hawking, P., & Carmine Sellitto, C. (2017). Developing an Effective Strategy for Organizational Business Intelligence. In M. Tavana (Ed.), *Enterprise Information Systems and the Digitalization of Business Functions* (pp. 222–237). Hershey, PA: IGI Global. doi:10.4018/978-1-5225-2382-6.ch010

Hawking, P., & Sellitto, C. (2017). A Fast-Moving Consumer Goods Company and Business Intelligence Strategy Development. *International Journal of Enterprise Information Systems, 13*(2), 22–33. doi:10.4018/IJEIS.2017040102

Hawking, P., & Sellitto, C. (2017). Business Intelligence Strategy: Two Case Studies. *International Journal of Business Intelligence Research, 8*(2), 17–30. doi:10.4018/IJBIR.2017070102

Hee, W. J., Jalleh, G., Lai, H., & Lin, C. (2017). E-Commerce and IT Projects: Evaluation and Management Issues in Australian and Taiwanese Hospitals. *International Journal of Public Health Management and Ethics, 2*(1), 69–90. doi:10.4018/IJPHME.2017010104

Hernandez, A. A. (2018). Exploring the Factors to Green IT Adoption of SMEs in the Philippines. *Journal of Cases on Information Technology, 20*(2), 49–66. doi:10.4018/JCIT.2018040104

Hollman, A., Bickford, S., & Hollman, T. (2017). Cyber InSecurity: A Post-Mortem Attempt to Assess Cyber Problems from IT and Business Management Perspectives. *Journal of Cases on Information Technology, 19*(3), 42–70. doi:10.4018/JCIT.2017070104

Ibrahim, F., & Zainin, N. M. (2021). Exploring the Technological Impacts: The Case of Museums in Brunei Darussalam. *International Journal of Tourism and Hospitality Management in the Digital Age, 5*(1), 1–18. https://doi.org/10.4018/IJTHMDA.2021010101

Igbinakhase, I. (2017). Responsible and Sustainable Management Practices in Developing and Developed Business Environments. In Z. Fields (Ed.), *Collective Creativity for Responsible and Sustainable Business Practice* (pp. 180–207). Hershey, PA: IGI Global. doi:10.4018/978-1-5225-1823-5.ch010

Iwata, J. J., & Hoskins, R. G. (2017). Managing Indigenous Knowledge in Tanzania: A Business Perspective. In P. Jain & N. Mnjama (Eds.), *Managing Knowledge Resources and Records in Modern Organizations* (pp. 198–214). Hershey, PA: IGI Global. doi:10.4018/978-1-5225-1965-2.ch012

Jain, P. (2017). Ethical and Legal Issues in Knowledge Management Life-Cycle in Business. In P. Jain & N. Mnjama (Eds.), *Managing Knowledge Resources and Records in Modern Organizations* (pp. 82–101). Hershey, PA: IGI Global. doi:10.4018/978-1-5225-1965-2.ch006

James, S., & Hauli, E. (2017). Holistic Management Education at Tanzanian Rural Development Planning Institute. In N. Baporikar (Ed.), *Management Education for Global Leadership* (pp. 112–136). Hershey, PA: IGI Global. doi:10.4018/978-1-5225-1013-0.ch006

Janošková, M., Csikósová, A., & Čulková, K. (2018). Measurement of Company Performance as Part of Its Strategic Management. In R. Leon (Ed.), *Managerial Strategies for Business Sustainability During Turbulent Times* (pp. 309–335). Hershey, PA: IGI Global. doi:10.4018/978-1-5225-2716-9.ch017

Jean-Vasile, A., & Alecu, A. (2017). Theoretical and Practical Approaches in Understanding the Influences of Cost-Productivity-Profit Trinomial in Contemporary Enterprises. In A. Jean Vasile & D. Nicolò (Eds.), *Sustainable Entrepreneurship and Investments in the Green Economy* (pp. 28–62). Hershey, PA: IGI Global. doi:10.4018/978-1-5225-2075-7.ch002

Joia, L. A., & Correia, J. C. (2018). CIO Competencies From the IT Professional Perspective: Insights From Brazil. *Journal of Global Information Management, 26*(2), 74–103. doi:10.4018/JGIM.2018040104

Juma, A., & Mzera, N. (2017). Knowledge Management and Records Management and Competitive Advantage in Business. In P. Jain & N. Mnjama (Eds.), *Managing Knowledge Resources and Records in Modern Organizations* (pp. 15–28). Hershey, PA: IGI Global. doi:10.4018/978-1-5225-1965-2.ch002

K., I., & A, V. (2018). Monitoring and Auditing in the Cloud. In K. Munir (Ed.), *Cloud Computing Technologies for Green Enterprises* (pp. 318-350). Hershey, PA: IGI Global. https://doi.org/ doi:10.4018/978-1-5225-3038-1.ch013

Kabra, G., Ghosh, V., & Ramesh, A. (2018). Enterprise Integrated Business Process Management and Business Intelligence Framework for Business Process Sustainability. In A. Paul, D. Bhattacharyya, & S. Anand (Eds.), *Green Initiatives for Business Sustainability and Value Creation* (pp. 228–238). Hershey, PA: IGI Global. doi:10.4018/978-1-5225-2662-9.ch010

Kaoud, M. (2017). Investigation of Customer Knowledge Management: A Case Study Research. *International Journal of Service Science, Management, Engineering, and Technology*, *8*(2), 12–22. doi:10.4018/IJSSMET.2017040102

Katuu, S. (2018). A Comparative Assessment of Enterprise Content Management Maturity Models. In N. Gwangwava & M. Mutingi (Eds.), *E-Manufacturing and E-Service Strategies in Contemporary Organizations* (pp. 93–118). Hershey, PA: IGI Global. doi:10.4018/978-1-5225-3628-4.ch005

Khan, M. Y., & Abir, T. (2022). The Role of Social Media Marketing in the Tourism and Hospitality Industry: A Conceptual Study on Bangladesh. In C. Ramos, S. Quinteiro, & A. Gonçalves (Eds.), *ICT as Innovator Between Tourism and Culture* (pp. 213–229). IGI Global. https://doi.org/10.4018/978-1-7998-8165-0.ch013

Kinnunen, S., Ylä-Kujala, A., Marttonen-Arola, S., Kärri, T., & Baglee, D. (2018). Internet of Things in Asset Management: Insights from Industrial Professionals and Academia. *International Journal of Service Science, Management, Engineering, and Technology*, *9*(2), 104–119. doi:10.4018/IJSSMET.2018040105

Klein, A. Z., Sabino de Freitas, A., Machado, L., Freitas, J. C. Jr, Graziola, P. G. Jr, & Schlemmer, E. (2017). Virtual Worlds Applications for Management Education. In L. Tomei (Ed.), *Exploring the New Era of Technology-Infused Education* (pp. 279–299). Hershey, PA: IGI Global. doi:10.4018/978-1-5225-1709-2.ch017

Kővári, E., Saleh, M., & Steinbachné Hajmásy, G. (2022). The Impact of Corporate Digital Responsibility (CDR) on Internal Stakeholders' Satisfaction in Hungarian Upscale Hotels. In M. Valeri (Ed.), *New Governance and Management in Touristic Destinations* (pp. 35–51). IGI Global. https://doi.org/10.4018/978-1-6684-3889-3.ch003

Kożuch, B., & Jabłoński, A. (2017). Adopting the Concept of Business Models in Public Management. In M. Lewandowski & B. Kożuch (Eds.), *Public Sector Entrepreneurship and the Integration of Innovative Business Models* (pp. 10–46). Hershey, PA: IGI Global. doi:10.4018/978-1-5225-2215-7.ch002

Kumar, J., Adhikary, A., & Jha, A. (2017). Small Active Investors' Perceptions and Preferences Towards Tax Saving Mutual Fund Schemes in Eastern India: An Empirical Note. *International Journal of Asian Business and Information Management*, *8*(2), 35–45. doi:10.4018/IJABIM.2017040103

Latusi, S., & Fissore, M. (2021). Pilgrimage Routes to Happiness: Comparing the Camino de Santiago and Via Francigena. In A. Perinotto, V. Mayer, & J. Soares (Eds.), *Rebuilding and Restructuring the Tourism Industry: Infusion of Happiness and Quality of Life* (pp. 157–182). IGI Global. https://doi.org/10.4018/978-1-7998-7239-9.ch008

Lavassani, K. M., & Movahedi, B. (2017). Applications Driven Information Systems: Beyond Networks toward Business Ecosystems. *International Journal of Innovation in the Digital Economy*, *8*(1), 61–75. doi:10.4018/IJIDE.2017010104

Lazzareschi, V. H., & Brito, M. S. (2017). Strategic Information Management: Proposal of Business Project Model. In G. Jamil, A. Soares, & C. Pessoa (Eds.), *Handbook of Research on Information Management for Effective Logistics and Supply Chains* (pp. 59–88). Hershey, PA: IGI Global. doi:10.4018/978-1-5225-0973-8.ch004

Lechuga Sancho, M. P., & Martín Navarro, A. (2022). Evolution of the Literature on Social Responsibility in the Tourism Sector: A Systematic Literature Review. In G. Fernandes (Ed.), *Challenges and New Opportunities for Tourism in Inland Territories: Ecocultural Resources and Sustainable Initiatives* (pp. 169–186). IGI Global. https://doi.org/10.4018/978-1-7998-7339-6.ch010

Lederer, M., Kurz, M., & Lazarov, P. (2017). Usage and Suitability of Methods for Strategic Business Process Initiatives: A Multi Case Study Research. *International Journal of Productivity Management and Assessment Technologies*, *5*(1), 40–51. doi:10.4018/IJPMAT.2017010103

Lee, I. (2017). A Social Enterprise Business Model and a Case Study of Pacific Community Ventures (PCV). In V. Potocan, M. Üngan, & Z. Nedelko (Eds.), *Handbook of Research on Managerial Solutions in Non-Profit Organizations* (pp. 182–204). Hershey, PA: IGI Global. doi:10.4018/978-1-5225-0731-4.ch009

Leon, L. A., Seal, K. C., Przasnyski, Z. H., & Wiedenman, I. (2017). Skills and Competencies Required for Jobs in Business Analytics: A Content Analysis of Job Advertisements Using Text Mining. *International Journal of Business Intelligence Research*, *8*(1), 1–25. doi:10.4018/IJBIR.2017010101

Levy, C. L., & Elias, N. I. (2017). SOHO Users' Perceptions of Reliability and Continuity of Cloud-Based Services. In M. Moore (Ed.), *Cybersecurity Breaches and Issues Surrounding Online Threat Protection* (pp. 248–287). Hershey, PA: IGI Global. doi:10.4018/978-1-5225-1941-6.ch011

Levy, M. (2018). Change Management Serving Knowledge Management and Organizational Development: Reflections and Review. In N. Baporikar (Ed.), *Global Practices in Knowledge Management for Societal and Organizational Development* (pp. 256–270). Hershey, PA: IGI Global. doi:10.4018/978-1-5225-3009-1.ch012

Lewandowski, M. (2017). Public Organizations and Business Model Innovation: The Role of Public Service Design. In M. Lewandowski & B. Kożuch (Eds.), *Public Sector Entrepreneurship and the Integration of Innovative Business Models* (pp. 47–72). Hershey, PA: IGI Global. doi:10.4018/978-1-5225-2215-7.ch003

Lhannaoui, H., Kabbaj, M. I., & Bakkoury, Z. (2017). A Survey of Risk-Aware Business Process Modelling. *International Journal of Risk and Contingency Management, 6*(3), 14–26. doi:10.4018/IJRCM.2017070102

Li, J., Sun, W., Jiang, W., Yang, H., & Zhang, L. (2017). How the Nature of Exogenous Shocks and Crises Impact Company Performance?: The Effects of Industry Characteristics. *International Journal of Risk and Contingency Management, 6*(4), 40–55. doi:10.4018/IJRCM.2017100103

Lopez-Fernandez, M., Perez-Perez, M., Serrano-Bedia, A., & Cobo-Gonzalez, A. (2021). Small and Medium Tourism Enterprise Survival in Times of Crisis: "El Capricho de Gaudí. In D. Toubes & N. Araújo-Vila (Eds.), *Risk, Crisis, and Disaster Management in Small and Medium-Sized Tourism Enterprises* (pp. 103–129). IGI Global. doi:10.4018/978-1-7998-6996-2.ch005

Mahajan, A., Maidullah, S., & Hossain, M. R. (2022). Experience Toward Smart Tour Guide Apps in Travelling: An Analysis of Users' Reviews on Audio Odigos and Trip My Way. In R. Augusto Costa, F. Brandão, Z. Breda, & C. Costa (Eds.), *Planning and Managing the Experience Economy in Tourism* (pp. 255-273). IGI Global. https://doi.org/10.4018/978-1-7998-8775-1.ch014

Malega, P. (2017). Small and Medium Enterprises in the Slovak Republic: Status and Competitiveness of SMEs in the Global Markets and Possibilities of Optimization. In M. Vemić (Ed.), *Optimal Management Strategies in Small and Medium Enterprises* (pp. 102–124). Hershey, PA: IGI Global. doi:10.4018/978-1-5225-1949-2.ch006

Malewska, K. M. (2017). Intuition in Decision-Making on the Example of a Non-Profit Organization. In V. Potocan, M. Üngan, & Z. Nedelko (Eds.), *Handbook of Research on Managerial Solutions in Non-Profit Organizations* (pp. 378–399). Hershey, PA: IGI Global. doi:10.4018/978-1-5225-0731-4.ch018

Maroofi, F. (2017). Entrepreneurial Orientation and Organizational Learning Ability Analysis for Innovation and Firm Performance. In N. Baporikar (Ed.), *Innovation and Shifting Perspectives in Management Education* (pp. 144–165). Hershey, PA: IGI Global. doi:10.4018/978-1-5225-1019-2.ch007

Marques, M., Moleiro, D., Brito, T. M., & Marques, T. (2021). Customer Relationship Management as an Important Relationship Marketing Tool: The Case of the Hospitality Industry in Estoril Coast. In M. Dinis, L. Bonixe, S. Lamy, & Z. Breda (Eds.), Impact of New Media in Tourism (pp. 39-56). IGI Global. https://doi.org/doi:10.4018/978-1-7998-7095-1.ch003

Martins, P. V., & Zacarias, M. (2017). A Web-based Tool for Business Process Improvement. *International Journal of Web Portals*, *9*(2), 68–84. doi:10.4018/IJWP.2017070104

Matthies, B., & Coners, A. (2017). Exploring the Conceptual Nature of e-Business Projects. *Journal of Electronic Commerce in Organizations*, *15*(3), 33–63. doi:10.4018/JECO.2017070103

Mayer, V. F., Fraga, C. C., & Silva, L. C. (2021). Contributions of Neurosciences to Studies of Well-Being in Tourism. In A. Perinotto, V. Mayer, & J. Soares (Eds.), *Rebuilding and Restructuring the Tourism Industry: Infusion of Happiness and Quality of Life* (pp. 108–128). IGI Global. https://doi.org/10.4018/978-1-7998-7239-9.ch006

McKee, J. (2018). Architecture as a Tool to Solve Business Planning Problems. In M. Khosrow-Pour, D.B.A. (Ed.), Encyclopedia of Information Science and Technology, Fourth Edition (pp. 573-586). Hershey, PA: IGI Global. doi:10.4018/978-1-5225-2255-3.ch050

McMurray, A. J., Cross, J., & Caponecchia, C. (2018). The Risk Management Profession in Australia: Business Continuity Plan Practices. In N. Bajgoric (Ed.), *Always-On Enterprise Information Systems for Modern Organizations* (pp. 112–129). Hershey, PA: IGI Global. doi:10.4018/978-1-5225-3704-5.ch006

Meddah, I. H., & Belkadi, K. (2018). Mining Patterns Using Business Process Management. In R. Hamou (Ed.), *Handbook of Research on Biomimicry in Information Retrieval and Knowledge Management* (pp. 78–89). Hershey, PA: IGI Global. doi:10.4018/978-1-5225-3004-6.ch005

Melian, A. G., & Camprubí, R. (2021). The Accessibility of Museum Websites: The Case of Barcelona. In C. Eusébio, L. Teixeira, & M. Carneiro (Eds.), *ICT Tools and Applications for Accessible Tourism* (pp. 234–255). IGI Global. https://doi.org/10.4018/978-1-7998-6428-8.ch011

Mendes, L. (2017). TQM and Knowledge Management: An Integrated Approach Towards Tacit Knowledge Management. In D. Jaziri-Bouagina & G. Jamil (Eds.), *Handbook of Research on Tacit Knowledge Management for Organizational Success* (pp. 236–263). Hershey, PA: IGI Global. doi:10.4018/978-1-5225-2394-9.ch009

Menezes, V. D., & Cavagnaro, E. (2021). Communicating Sustainable Initiatives in the Hotel Industry: The Case of the Hotel Jakarta Amsterdam. In F. Brandão, Z. Breda, R. Costa, & C. Costa (Eds.), *Handbook of Research on the Role of Tourism in Achieving Sustainable Development Goals* (pp. 224-234). IGI Global. https://doi.org/10.4018/978-1-7998-5691-7.ch013

Menezes, V. D., & Cavagnaro, E. (2021). Communicating Sustainable Initiatives in the Hotel Industry: The Case of the Hotel Jakarta Amsterdam. In F. Brandão, Z. Breda, R. Costa, & C. Costa (Eds.), *Handbook of Research on the Role of Tourism in Achieving Sustainable Development Goals* (pp. 224-234). IGI Global. https://doi.org/10.4018/978-1-7998-5691-7.ch013

Mitas, O., Bastiaansen, M., & Boode, W. (2022). If You're Happy, I'm Happy: Emotion Contagion at a Tourist Information Center. In R. Augusto Costa, F. Brandão, Z. Breda, & C. Costa (Eds.), *Planning and Managing the Experience Economy in Tourism* (pp. 122-140). IGI Global. https://doi.org/10.4018/978-1-7998-8775-1.ch007

Mnjama, N. M. (2017). Preservation of Recorded Information in Public and Private Sector Organizations. In P. Jain & N. Mnjama (Eds.), *Managing Knowledge Resources and Records in Modern Organizations* (pp. 149–167). Hershey, PA: IGI Global. doi:10.4018/978-1-5225-1965-2.ch009

Mokoqama, M., & Fields, Z. (2017). Principles of Responsible Management Education (PRME): Call for Responsible Management Education. In Z. Fields (Ed.), *Collective Creativity for Responsible and Sustainable Business Practice* (pp. 229–241). Hershey, PA: IGI Global. doi:10.4018/978-1-5225-1823-5.ch012

Monteiro, A., Lopes, S., & Carbone, F. (2021). Academic Mobility: Bridging Tourism and Peace Education. In J. da Silva, Z. Breda, & F. Carbone (Eds.), *Role and Impact of Tourism in Peacebuilding and Conflict Transformation* (pp. 275-301). IGI Global. https://doi.org/10.4018/978-1-7998-5053-3.ch016

Muniapan, B. (2017). Philosophy and Management: The Relevance of Vedanta in Management. In P. Ordóñez de Pablos (Ed.), *Managerial Strategies and Solutions for Business Success in Asia* (pp. 124–139). Hershey, PA: IGI Global. doi:10.4018/978-1-5225-1886-0.ch007

Murad, S. E., & Dowaji, S. (2017). Using Value-Based Approach for Managing Cloud-Based Services. In A. Turuk, B. Sahoo, & S. Addya (Eds.), *Resource Management and Efficiency in Cloud Computing Environments* (pp. 33–60). Hershey, PA: IGI Global. doi:10.4018/978-1-5225-1721-4.ch002

Mutahar, A. M., Daud, N. M., Thurasamy, R., Isaac, O., & Abdulsalam, R. (2018). The Mediating of Perceived Usefulness and Perceived Ease of Use: The Case of Mobile Banking in Yemen. *International Journal of Technology Diffusion*, *9*(2), 21–40. doi:10.4018/IJTD.2018040102

Naidoo, V. (2017). E-Learning and Management Education at African Universities. In N. Baporikar (Ed.), *Management Education for Global Leadership* (pp. 181–201). Hershey, PA: IGI Global. doi:10.4018/978-1-5225-1013-0.ch009

Naidoo, V., & Igbinakhase, I. (2018). Opportunities and Challenges of Knowledge Retention in SMEs. In N. Baporikar (Ed.), *Knowledge Integration Strategies for Entrepreneurship and Sustainability* (pp. 70–94). Hershey, PA: IGI Global. doi:10.4018/978-1-5225-5115-7.ch004

Naumov, N., & Costandachi, G. (2021). Creativity and Entrepreneurship: Gastronomic Tourism in Mexico. In J. Soares (Ed.), *Innovation and Entrepreneurial Opportunities in Community Tourism* (pp. 90–108). IGI Global. https://doi.org/10.4018/978-1-7998-4855-4.ch006

Nayak, S., & Prabhu, N. (2017). Paradigm Shift in Management Education: Need for a Cross Functional Perspective. In N. Baporikar (Ed.), *Management Education for Global Leadership* (pp. 241–255). Hershey, PA: IGI Global. doi:10.4018/978-1-5225-1013-0.ch012

Nedelko, Z., & Potocan, V. (2017). Management Solutions in Non-Profit Organizations: Case of Slovenia. In V. Potocan, M. Üngan, & Z. Nedelko (Eds.), *Handbook of Research on Managerial Solutions in Non-Profit Organizations* (pp. 1–22). Hershey, PA: IGI Global. doi:10.4018/978-1-5225-0731-4.ch001

Nedelko, Z., & Potocan, V. (2017). Priority of Management Tools Utilization among Managers: International Comparison. In V. Wang (Ed.), *Encyclopedia of Strategic Leadership and Management* (pp. 1083–1094). Hershey, PA: IGI Global. doi:10.4018/978-1-5225-1049-9.ch075

Nedelko, Z., Raudeliūnienė, J., & Črešnar, R. (2018). Knowledge Dynamics in Supply Chain Management. In N. Baporikar (Ed.), *Knowledge Integration Strategies for Entrepreneurship and Sustainability* (pp. 150–166). Hershey, PA: IGI Global. doi:10.4018/978-1-5225-5115-7.ch008

Nguyen, H. T., & Hipsher, S. A. (2018). Innovation and Creativity Used by Private Sector Firms in a Resources-Constrained Environment. In S. Hipsher (Ed.), *Examining the Private Sector's Role in Wealth Creation and Poverty Reduction* (pp. 219–238). Hershey, PA: IGI Global. doi:10.4018/978-1-5225-3117-3.ch010

Obicci, P. A. (2017). Risk Sharing in a Partnership. In *Risk Management Strategies in Public-Private Partnerships* (pp. 115–152). Hershey, PA: IGI Global. doi:10.4018/978-1-5225-2503-5.ch004

Obidallah, W. J., & Raahemi, B. (2017). Managing Changes in Service Oriented Virtual Organizations: A Structural and Procedural Framework to Facilitate the Process of Change. *Journal of Electronic Commerce in Organizations, 15*(1), 59–83. doi:10.4018/JECO.2017010104

Ojo, O. (2017). Impact of Innovation on the Entrepreneurial Success in Selected Business Enterprises in South-West Nigeria. *International Journal of Innovation in the Digital Economy, 8*(2), 29–38. doi:10.4018/IJIDE.2017040103

Okdinawati, L., Simatupang, T. M., & Sunitiyoso, Y. (2017). Multi-Agent Reinforcement Learning for Value Co-Creation of Collaborative Transportation Management (CTM). *International Journal of Information Systems and Supply Chain Management, 10*(3), 84–95. doi:10.4018/IJISSCM.2017070105

Olivera, V. A., & Carrillo, I. M. (2021). Organizational Culture: A Key Element for the Development of Mexican Micro and Small Tourist Companies. In J. Soares (Ed.), *Innovation and Entrepreneurial Opportunities in Community Tourism* (pp. 227–242). IGI Global. doi:10.4018/978-1-7998-4855-4.ch013

Ossorio, M. (2022). Corporate Museum Experiences in Enogastronomic Tourism. In R. Augusto Costa, F. Brandão, Z. Breda, & C. Costa (Eds.), Planning and Managing the Experience Economy in Tourism (pp. 107-121). IGI Global. https://doi.org/doi:10.4018/978-1-7998-8775-1.ch006

Ossorio, M. (2022). Enogastronomic Tourism in Times of Pandemic. In G. Fernandes (Ed.), *Challenges and New Opportunities for Tourism in Inland Territories: Ecocultural Resources and Sustainable Initiatives* (pp. 241–255). IGI Global. https://doi.org/10.4018/978-1-7998-7339-6.ch014

Özekici, Y. K. (2022). ICT as an Acculturative Agent and Its Role in the Tourism Context: Introduction, Acculturation Theory, Progress of the Acculturation Theory in Extant Literature. In C. Ramos, S. Quinteiro, & A. Gonçalves (Eds.), *ICT as Innovator Between Tourism and Culture* (pp. 42–66). IGI Global. https://doi.org/10.4018/978-1-7998-8165-0.ch004

Pal, K. (2018). Building High Quality Big Data-Based Applications in Supply Chains. In A. Kumar & S. Saurav (Eds.), *Supply Chain Management Strategies and Risk Assessment in Retail Environments* (pp. 1–24). Hershey, PA: IGI Global. doi:10.4018/978-1-5225-3056-5.ch001

Palos-Sanchez, P. R., & Correia, M. B. (2018). Perspectives of the Adoption of Cloud Computing in the Tourism Sector. In J. Rodrigues, C. Ramos, P. Cardoso, & C. Henriques (Eds.), *Handbook of Research on Technological Developments for Cultural Heritage and eTourism Applications* (pp. 377–400). Hershey, PA: IGI Global. doi:10.4018/978-1-5225-2927-9.ch018

Papadopoulou, G. (2021). Promoting Gender Equality and Women Empowerment in the Tourism Sector. In F. Brandão, Z. Breda, R. Costa, & C. Costa (Eds.), Handbook of Research on the Role of Tourism in Achieving Sustainable Development Goals (pp. 152-174). IGI Global. https://doi.org/ doi:10.4018/978-1-7998-5691-7.ch009

Papp-Váry, Á. F., & Tóth, T. Z. (2022). Analysis of Budapest as a Film Tourism Destination. In R. Baleiro & R. Pereira (Eds.), *Global Perspectives on Literary Tourism and Film-Induced Tourism* (pp. 257-279). IGI Global. https://doi.org/10.4018/978-1-7998-8262-6.ch014

Patiño, B. E. (2017). New Generation Management by Convergence and Individual Identity: A Systemic and Human-Oriented Approach. In N. Baporikar (Ed.), *Innovation and Shifting Perspectives in Management Education* (pp. 119–143). Hershey, PA: IGI Global. doi:10.4018/978-1-5225-1019-2.ch006

Patro, C. S. (2021). Digital Tourism: Influence of E-Marketing Technology. In M. Dinis, L. Bonixe, S. Lamy, & Z. Breda (Eds.), *Impact of New Media in Tourism* (pp. 234-254). IGI Global. https://doi.org/10.4018/978-1-7998-7095-1.ch014

Pawliczek, A., & Rössler, M. (2017). Knowledge of Management Tools and Systems in SMEs: Knowledge Transfer in Management. In A. Bencsik (Ed.), *Knowledge Management Initiatives and Strategies in Small and Medium Enterprises* (pp. 180–203). Hershey, PA: IGI Global. doi:10.4018/978-1-5225-1642-2.ch009

Pejic-Bach, M., Omazic, M. A., Aleksic, A., & Zoroja, J. (2018). Knowledge-Based Decision Making: A Multi-Case Analysis. In R. Leon (Ed.), *Managerial Strategies for Business Sustainability During Turbulent Times* (pp. 160–184). Hershey, PA: IGI Global. doi:10.4018/978-1-5225-2716-9.ch009

Perano, M., Hysa, X., & Calabrese, M. (2018). Strategic Planning, Cultural Context, and Business Continuity Management: Business Cases in the City of Shkoder. In A. Presenza & L. Sheehan (Eds.), *Geopolitics and Strategic Management in the Global Economy* (pp. 57–77). Hershey, PA: IGI Global. doi:10.4018/978-1-5225-2673-5.ch004

Pereira, R., Mira da Silva, M., & Lapão, L. V. (2017). IT Governance Maturity Patterns in Portuguese Healthcare. In S. De Haes & W. Van Grembergen (Eds.), *Strategic IT Governance and Alignment in Business Settings* (pp. 24–52). Hershey, PA: IGI Global. doi:10.4018/978-1-5225-0861-8.ch002

Pérez-Uribe, R. I., Torres, D. A., Jurado, S. P., & Prada, D. M. (2018). Cloud Tools for the Development of Project Management in SMEs. In R. Perez-Uribe, C. Salcedo-Perez, & D. Ocampo-Guzman (Eds.), *Handbook of Research on Intrapreneurship and Organizational Sustainability in SMEs* (pp. 95–120). Hershey, PA: IGI Global. doi:10.4018/978-1-5225-3543-0.ch005

Petrisor, I., & Cozmiuc, D. (2017). Global Supply Chain Management Organization at Siemens in the Advent of Industry 4.0. In L. Saglietto & C. Cezanne (Eds.), *Global Intermediation and Logistics Service Providers* (pp. 123–142). Hershey, PA: IGI Global. doi:10.4018/978-1-5225-2133-4.ch007

Pierce, J. M., Velliaris, D. M., & Edwards, J. (2017). A Living Case Study: A Journey Not a Destination. In N. Silton (Ed.), *Exploring the Benefits of Creativity in Education, Media, and the Arts* (pp. 158–178). Hershey, PA: IGI Global. doi:10.4018/978-1-5225-0504-4.ch008

Pipia, S., & Pipia, S. (2021). Challenges of Religious Tourism in the Conflict Region: An Example of Jerusalem. In E. Alaverdov & M. Bari (Eds.), *Global Development of Religious Tourism* (pp. 135-148). IGI Global. https://doi.org/10.4018/978-1-7998-5792-1.ch009

Poulaki, P., Kritikos, A., Vasilakis, N., & Valeri, M. (2022). The Contribution of Female Creativity to the Development of Gastronomic Tourism in Greece: The Case of the Island of Naxos in the South Aegean Region. In M. Valeri (Ed.), *New Governance and Management in Touristic Destinations* (pp. 246–258). IGI Global. https://doi.org/10.4018/978-1-6684-3889-3.ch015

Radosavljevic, M., & Andjelkovic, A. (2017). Multi-Criteria Decision Making Approach for Choosing Business Process for the Improvement: Upgrading of the Six Sigma Methodology. In J. Stanković, P. Delias, S. Marinković, & S. Rochhia (Eds.), *Tools and Techniques for Economic Decision Analysis* (pp. 225–247). Hershey, PA: IGI Global. doi:10.4018/978-1-5225-0959-2.ch011

Radovic, V. M. (2017). Corporate Sustainability and Responsibility and Disaster Risk Reduction: A Serbian Overview. In M. Camilleri (Ed.), *CSR 2.0 and the New Era of Corporate Citizenship* (pp. 147–164). Hershey, PA: IGI Global. doi:10.4018/978-1-5225-1842-6.ch008

Raghunath, K. M., Devi, S. L., & Patro, C. S. (2018). Impact of Risk Assessment Models on Risk Factors: A Holistic Outlook. In K. Strang, M. Korstanje, & N. Vajjhala (Eds.), *Research, Practices, and Innovations in Global Risk and Contingency Management* (pp. 134–153). Hershey, PA: IGI Global. doi:10.4018/978-1-5225-4754-9.ch008

Raman, A., & Goyal, D. P. (2017). Extending IMPLEMENT Framework for Enterprise Information Systems Implementation to Information System Innovation. In M. Tavana (Ed.), *Enterprise Information Systems and the Digitalization of Business Functions* (pp. 137–177). Hershey, PA: IGI Global. doi:10.4018/978-1-5225-2382-6.ch007

Rao, Y., & Zhang, Y. (2017). The Construction and Development of Academic Library Digital Special Subject Databases. In L. Ruan, Q. Zhu, & Y. Ye (Eds.), *Academic Library Development and Administration in China* (pp. 163–183). Hershey, PA: IGI Global. doi:10.4018/978-1-5225-0550-1.ch010

Ravasan, A. Z., Mohammadi, M. M., & Hamidi, H. (2018). An Investigation Into the Critical Success Factors of Implementing Information Technology Service Management Frameworks. In K. Jakobs (Ed.), *Corporate and Global Standardization Initiatives in Contemporary Society* (pp. 200–218). Hershey, PA: IGI Global. doi:10.4018/978-1-5225-5320-5.ch009

Rezaie, S., Mirabedini, S. J., & Abtahi, A. (2018). Designing a Model for Implementation of Business Intelligence in the Banking Industry. *International Journal of Enterprise Information Systems*, *14*(1), 77–103. doi:10.4018/IJEIS.2018010105

Richards, V., Matthews, N., Williams, O. J., & Khan, Z. (2021). The Challenges of Accessible Tourism Information Systems for Tourists With Vision Impairment: Sensory Communications Beyond the Screen. In C. Eusébio, L. Teixeira, & M. Carneiro (Eds.), *ICT Tools and Applications for Accessible Tourism* (pp. 26–54). IGI Global. https://doi.org/10.4018/978-1-7998-6428-8.ch002

Rodrigues de Souza Neto, V., & Marques, O. (2021). Rural Tourism Fostering Welfare Through Sustainable Development: A Conceptual Approach. In A. Perinotto, V. Mayer, & J. Soares (Eds.), *Rebuilding and Restructuring the Tourism Industry: Infusion of Happiness and Quality of Life* (pp. 38–57). IGI Global. https://doi.org/10.4018/978-1-7998-7239-9.ch003

Romano, L., Grimaldi, R., & Colasuonno, F. S. (2017). Demand Management as a Success Factor in Project Portfolio Management. In L. Romano (Ed.), *Project Portfolio Management Strategies for Effective Organizational Operations* (pp. 202–219). Hershey, PA: IGI Global. doi:10.4018/978-1-5225-2151-8.ch008

Rubio-Escuderos, L., & García-Andreu, H. (2021). Competitiveness Factors of Accessible Tourism E-Travel Agencies. In C. Eusébio, L. Teixeira, & M. Carneiro (Eds.), *ICT Tools and Applications for Accessible Tourism* (pp. 196–217). IGI Global. https://doi.org/10.4018/978-1-7998-6428-8.ch009

Rucci, A. C., Porto, N., Darcy, S., & Becka, L. (2021). Smart and Accessible Cities?: Not Always – The Case for Accessible Tourism Initiatives in Buenos Aries and Sydney. In C. Eusébio, L. Teixeira, & M. Carneiro (Eds.), *ICT Tools and Applications for Accessible Tourism* (pp. 115–145). IGI Global. https://doi.org/10.4018/978-1-7998-6428-8.ch006

Ruhi, U. (2018). Towards an Interdisciplinary Socio-Technical Definition of Virtual Communities. In M. Khosrow-Pour, D.B.A. (Ed.), Encyclopedia of Information Science and Technology, Fourth Edition (pp. 4278-4295). Hershey, PA: IGI Global. doi:10.4018/978-1-5225-2255-3.ch371

Ryan, L., Catena, M., Ros, P., & Stephens, S. (2021). Designing Entrepreneurial Ecosystems to Support Resource Management in the Tourism Industry. In V. Costa, A. Moura, & M. Mira (Eds.), *Handbook of Research on Human Capital and People Management in the Tourism Industry* (pp. 265–281). IGI Global. https://doi.org/10.4018/978-1-7998-4318-4.ch013

Sabuncu, I. (2021). Understanding Tourist Perceptions and Expectations During Pandemic Through Social Media Big Data. In M. Demir, A. Dalgıç, & F. Ergen (Eds.), *Handbook of Research on the Impacts and Implications of COVID-19 on the Tourism Industry* (pp. 330–350). IGI Global. https://doi.org/10.4018/978-1-7998-8231-2.ch016

Safari, M. R., & Jiang, Q. (2018). The Theory and Practice of IT Governance Maturity and Strategies Alignment: Evidence From Banking Industry. *Journal of Global Information Management, 26*(2), 127–146. doi:10.4018/JGIM.2018040106

Sahoo, J., Pati, B., & Mohanty, B. (2017). Knowledge Management as an Academic Discipline: An Assessment. In B. Gunjal (Ed.), *Managing Knowledge and Scholarly Assets in Academic Libraries* (pp. 99–126). Hershey, PA: IGI Global. doi:10.4018/978-1-5225-1741-2.ch005

Saini, D. (2017). Relevance of Teaching Values and Ethics in Management Education. In N. Baporikar (Ed.), *Management Education for Global Leadership* (pp. 90–111). Hershey, PA: IGI Global. doi:10.4018/978-1-5225-1013-0.ch005

Sambhanthan, A. (2017). Assessing and Benchmarking Sustainability in Organisations: An Integrated Conceptual Model. *International Journal of Systems and Service-Oriented Engineering*, *7*(4), 22–43. doi:10.4018/IJSSOE.2017100102

Sambhanthan, A., & Potdar, V. (2017). A Study of the Parameters Impacting Sustainability in Information Technology Organizations. *International Journal of Knowledge-Based Organizations*, *7*(3), 27–39. doi:10.4018/IJKBO.2017070103

Sánchez-Fernández, M. D., & Manríquez, M. R. (2018). The Entrepreneurial Spirit Based on Social Values: The Digital Generation. In P. Isaias & L. Carvalho (Eds.), *User Innovation and the Entrepreneurship Phenomenon in the Digital Economy* (pp. 173–193). Hershey, PA: IGI Global. doi:10.4018/978-1-5225-2826-5.ch009

Sanchez-Ruiz, L., & Blanco, B. (2017). Process Management for SMEs: Barriers, Enablers, and Benefits. In M. Vemić (Ed.), *Optimal Management Strategies in Small and Medium Enterprises* (pp. 293–319). Hershey, PA: IGI Global. doi:10.4018/978-1-5225-1949-2.ch014

Sanz, L. F., Gómez-Pérez, J., & Castillo-Martinez, A. (2018). Analysis of the European ICT Competence Frameworks. In V. Ahuja & S. Rathore (Eds.), *Multidisciplinary Perspectives on Human Capital and Information Technology Professionals* (pp. 225–245). Hershey, PA: IGI Global. doi:10.4018/978-1-5225-5297-0.ch012

Sarvepalli, A., & Godin, J. (2017). Business Process Management in the Classroom. *Journal of Cases on Information Technology*, *19*(2), 17–28. doi:10.4018/JCIT.2017040102

Saxena, G. G., & Saxena, A. (2021). Host Community Role in Medical Tourism Development. In M. Singh & S. Kumaran (Eds.), *Growth of the Medical Tourism Industry and Its Impact on Society: Emerging Research and Opportunities* (pp. 105–127). IGI Global. https://doi.org/10.4018/978-1-7998-3427-4.ch006

Saygili, E. E., Ozturkoglu, Y., & Kocakulah, M. C. (2017). End Users' Perceptions of Critical Success Factors in ERP Applications. *International Journal of Enterprise Information Systems*, *13*(4), 58–75. doi:10.4018/IJEIS.2017100104

Saygili, E. E., & Saygili, A. T. (2017). Contemporary Issues in Enterprise Information Systems: A Critical Review of CSFs in ERP Implementations. In M. Tavana (Ed.), *Enterprise Information Systems and the Digitalization of Business Functions* (pp. 120–136). Hershey, PA: IGI Global. doi:10.4018/978-1-5225-2382-6.ch006

Schwaiger, K. M., & Zehrer, A. (2021). The COVID-19 Pandemic and Organizational Resilience in Hospitality Family Firms: A Qualitative Approach. In A. Zehrer, G. Glowka, K. Schwaiger, & V. Ranacher-Lackner (Eds.), *Resiliency Models and Addressing Future Risks for Family Firms in the Tourism Industry* (pp. 32–49). IGI Global. https://doi.org/10.4018/978-1-7998-7352-5.ch002

Scott, N., & Campos, A. C. (2022). Cognitive Science of Tourism Experiences. In R. Augusto Costa, F. Brandão, Z. Breda, & C. Costa (Eds.), Planning and Managing the Experience Economy in Tourism (pp. 1-21). IGI Global. https://doi.org/ doi:10.4018/978-1-7998-8775-1.ch001

Seidenstricker, S., & Antonino, A. (2018). Business Model Innovation-Oriented Technology Management for Emergent Technologies. In M. Khosrow-Pour, D.B.A. (Ed.), Encyclopedia of Information Science and Technology, Fourth Edition (pp. 4560-4569). Hershey, PA: IGI Global. doi:10.4018/978-1-5225-2255-3.ch396

Selvi, M. S. (2021). Changes in Tourism Sales and Marketing Post COVID-19. In M. Demir, A. Dalgıç, & F. Ergen (Eds.), *Handbook of Research on the Impacts and Implications of COVID-19 on the Tourism Industry* (pp. 437–460). IGI Global. doi:10.4018/978-1-7998-8231-2.ch021

Senaratne, S., & Gunarathne, A. D. (2017). Excellence Perspective for Management Education from a Global Accountants' Hub in Asia. In N. Baporikar (Ed.), *Management Education for Global Leadership* (pp. 158–180). Hershey, PA: IGI Global. doi:10.4018/978-1-5225-1013-0.ch008

Sensuse, D. I., & Cahyaningsih, E. (2018). Knowledge Management Models: A Summative Review. *International Journal of Information Systems in the Service Sector, 10*(1), 71–100. doi:10.4018/IJISSS.2018010105

Seth, M., Goyal, D., & Kiran, R. (2017). Diminution of Impediments in Implementation of Supply Chain Management Information System for Enhancing its Effectiveness in Indian Automobile Industry. *Journal of Global Information Management, 25*(3), 1–20. doi:10.4018/JGIM.2017070101

Seyal, A. H., & Rahman, M. N. (2017). Investigating Impact of Inter-Organizational Factors in Measuring ERP Systems Success: Bruneian Perspectives. In M. Tavana (Ed.), *Enterprise Information Systems and the Digitalization of Business Functions* (pp. 178–204). Hershey, PA: IGI Global. doi:10.4018/978-1-5225-2382-6.ch008

Shaqrah, A. A. (2018). Analyzing Business Intelligence Systems Based on 7s Model of McKinsey. *International Journal of Business Intelligence Research, 9*(1), 53–63. doi:10.4018/IJBIR.2018010104

Sharma, A. J. (2017). Enhancing Sustainability through Experiential Learning in Management Education. In N. Baporikar (Ed.), *Management Education for Global Leadership* (pp. 256–274). Hershey, PA: IGI Global. doi:10.4018/978-1-5225-1013-0.ch013

Shetty, K. P. (2017). Responsible Global Leadership: Ethical Challenges in Management Education. In N. Baporikar (Ed.), *Innovation and Shifting Perspectives in Management Education* (pp. 194–223). Hershey, PA: IGI Global. doi:10.4018/978-1-5225-1019-2.ch009

Sinthupundaja, J., & Kohda, Y. (2017). Effects of Corporate Social Responsibility and Creating Shared Value on Sustainability. *International Journal of Sustainable Entrepreneurship and Corporate Social Responsibility*, *2*(1), 27–38. doi:10.4018/IJSECSR.2017010103

Škarica, I., & Hrgović, A. V. (2018). Implementation of Total Quality Management Principles in Public Health Institutes in the Republic of Croatia. *International Journal of Productivity Management and Assessment Technologies*, *6*(1), 1–16. doi:10.4018/IJPMAT.2018010101

Skokic, V. (2021). How Small Hotel Owners Practice Resilience: Longitudinal Study Among Small Family Hotels in Croatia. In A. Zehrer, G. Glowka, K. Schwaiger, & V. Ranacher-Lackner (Eds.), *Resiliency Models and Addressing Future Risks for Family Firms in the Tourism Industry* (pp. 50–73). IGI Global. doi:10.4018/978-1-7998-7352-5.ch003

Smuts, H., Kotzé, P., Van der Merwe, A., & Loock, M. (2017). Framework for Managing Shared Knowledge in an Information Systems Outsourcing Context. *International Journal of Knowledge Management*, *13*(4), 1–30. doi:10.4018/IJKM.2017100101

Sousa, M. J., Cruz, R., Dias, I., & Caracol, C. (2017). Information Management Systems in the Supply Chain. In G. Jamil, A. Soares, & C. Pessoa (Eds.), *Handbook of Research on Information Management for Effective Logistics and Supply Chains* (pp. 469–485). Hershey, PA: IGI Global. doi:10.4018/978-1-5225-0973-8.ch025

Spremic, M., Turulja, L., & Bajgoric, N. (2018). Two Approaches in Assessing Business Continuity Management Attitudes in the Organizational Context. In N. Bajgoric (Ed.), *Always-On Enterprise Information Systems for Modern Organizations* (pp. 159–183). Hershey, PA: IGI Global. doi:10.4018/978-1-5225-3704-5.ch008

Steenkamp, A. L. (2018). Some Insights in Computer Science and Information Technology. In *Examining the Changing Role of Supervision in Doctoral Research Projects: Emerging Research and Opportunities* (pp. 113–133). Hershey, PA: IGI Global. doi:10.4018/978-1-5225-2610-0.ch005

Stipanović, C., Rudan, E., & Zubović, V. (2022). Reaching the New Tourist Through Creativity: Sustainable Development Challenges in Croatian Coastal Towns. In M. Valeri (Ed.), *New Governance and Management in Touristic Destinations* (pp. 231–245). IGI Global. https://doi.org/10.4018/978-1-6684-3889-3.ch014

Tabach, A., & Croteau, A. (2017). Configurations of Information Technology Governance Practices and Business Unit Performance. *International Journal of IT/Business Alignment and Governance*, *8*(2), 1–27. doi:10.4018/IJITBAG.2017070101

Talaue, G. M., & Iqbal, T. (2017). Assessment of e-Business Mode of Selected Private Universities in the Philippines and Pakistan. *International Journal of Online Marketing*, *7*(4), 63–77. doi:10.4018/IJOM.2017100105

Tam, G. C. (2017). Project Manager Sustainability Competence. In *Managerial Strategies and Green Solutions for Project Sustainability* (pp. 178–207). Hershey, PA: IGI Global. doi:10.4018/978-1-5225-2371-0.ch008

Tambo, T. (2018). Fashion Retail Innovation: About Context, Antecedents, and Outcome in Technological Change Projects. In I. Management Association (Ed.), Fashion and Textiles: Breakthroughs in Research and Practice (pp. 233-260). Hershey, PA: IGI Global. https://doi.org/ doi:10.4018/978-1-5225-3432-7.ch010

Tantau, A. D., & Frăţilă, L. C. (2018). Information and Management System for Renewable Energy Business. In *Entrepreneurship and Business Development in the Renewable Energy Sector* (pp. 200–244). Hershey, PA: IGI Global. doi:10.4018/978-1-5225-3625-3.ch006

Teixeira, N., Pardal, P. N., & Rafael, B. G. (2018). Internationalization, Financial Performance, and Organizational Challenges: A Success Case in Portugal. In L. Carvalho (Ed.), *Handbook of Research on Entrepreneurial Ecosystems and Social Dynamics in a Globalized World* (pp. 379–423). Hershey, PA: IGI Global. doi:10.4018/978-1-5225-3525-6.ch017

Teixeira, P., Teixeira, L., Eusébio, C., Silva, S., & Teixeira, A. (2021). The Impact of ICTs on Accessible Tourism: Evidence Based on a Systematic Literature Review. In C. Eusébio, L. Teixeira, & M. Carneiro (Eds.), *ICT Tools and Applications for Accessible Tourism* (pp. 1–25). IGI Global. doi:10.4018/978-1-7998-6428-8.ch001

Trad, A., & Kalpić, D. (2018). The Business Transformation Framework, Agile Project and Change Management. In M. Khosrow-Pour, D.B.A. (Ed.), Encyclopedia of Information Science and Technology, Fourth Edition (pp. 620-635). Hershey, PA: IGI Global. https://doi.org/ doi:10.4018/978-1-5225-2255-3.ch054

Trad, A., & Kalpić, D. (2018). The Business Transformation and Enterprise Architecture Framework: The Financial Engineering E-Risk Management and E-Law Integration. In B. Sergi, F. Fidanoski, M. Ziolo, & V. Naumovski (Eds.), *Regaining Global Stability After the Financial Crisis* (pp. 46–65). Hershey, PA: IGI Global. doi:10.4018/978-1-5225-4026-7.ch003

Trengereid, V. (2022). Conditions of Network Engagement: The Quest for a Common Good. In R. Augusto Costa, F. Brandão, Z. Breda, & C. Costa (Eds.), *Planning and Managing the Experience Economy in Tourism* (pp. 69-84). IGI Global. https://doi.org/10.4018/978-1-7998-8775-1.ch004

Turulja, L., & Bajgoric, N. (2018). Business Continuity and Information Systems: A Systematic Literature Review. In N. Bajgoric (Ed.), *Always-On Enterprise Information Systems for Modern Organizations* (pp. 60–87). Hershey, PA: IGI Global. doi:10.4018/978-1-5225-3704-5.ch004

Vargas-Hernández, J. G. (2017). Professional Integrity in Business Management Education. In N. Baporikar (Ed.), *Management Education for Global Leadership* (pp. 70–89). Hershey, PA: IGI Global. doi:10.4018/978-1-5225-1013-0.ch004

Varnacı Uzun, F. (2021). The Destination Preferences of Foreign Tourists During the COVID-19 Pandemic and Attitudes Towards: Marmaris, Turkey. In M. Demir, A. Dalgıç, & F. Ergen (Eds.), *Handbook of Research on the Impacts and Implications of COVID-19 on the Tourism Industry* (pp. 285–306). IGI Global. https://doi.org/10.4018/978-1-7998-8231-2.ch014

Vasista, T. G., & AlAbdullatif, A. M. (2017). Role of Electronic Customer Relationship Management in Demand Chain Management: A Predictive Analytic Approach. *International Journal of Information Systems and Supply Chain Management, 10*(1), 53–67. doi:10.4018/IJISSCM.2017010104

Vieru, D., & Bourdeau, S. (2017). Survival in the Digital Era: A Digital Competence-Based Multi-Case Study in the Canadian SME Clothing Industry. *International Journal of Social and Organizational Dynamics in IT, 6*(1), 17–34. doi:10.4018/IJSODIT.2017010102

Vijayan, G., & Kamarulzaman, N. H. (2017). An Introduction to Sustainable Supply Chain Management and Business Implications. In M. Khan, M. Hussain, & M. Ajmal (Eds.), *Green Supply Chain Management for Sustainable Business Practice* (pp. 27–50). Hershey, PA: IGI Global. doi:10.4018/978-1-5225-0635-5.ch002

Vlachvei, A., & Notta, O. (2017). Firm Competitiveness: Theories, Evidence, and Measurement. In A. Vlachvei, O. Notta, K. Karantininis, & N. Tsounis (Eds.), *Factors Affecting Firm Competitiveness and Performance in the Modern Business World* (pp. 1–42). Hershey, PA: IGI Global. doi:10.4018/978-1-5225-0843-4.ch001

Wang, C., Schofield, M., Li, X., & Ou, X. (2017). Do Chinese Students in Public and Private Higher Education Institutes Perform at Different Level in One of the Leadership Skills: Critical Thinking?: An Exploratory Comparison. In V. Wang (Ed.), *Encyclopedia of Strategic Leadership and Management* (pp. 160–181). Hershey, PA: IGI Global. doi:10.4018/978-1-5225-1049-9.ch013

Wang, J. (2017). Multi-Agent based Production Management Decision System Modelling for the Textile Enterprise. *Journal of Global Information Management, 25*(4), 1–15. doi:10.4018/JGIM.2017100101

Wiedemann, A., & Gewald, H. (2017). Examining Cross-Domain Alignment: The Correlation of Business Strategy, IT Management, and IT Business Value. *International Journal of IT/Business Alignment and Governance, 8*(1), 17–31. doi:10.4018/IJITBAG.2017010102

Wolf, R., & Thiel, M. (2018). Advancing Global Business Ethics in China: Reducing Poverty Through Human and Social Welfare. In S. Hipsher (Ed.), *Examining the Private Sector's Role in Wealth Creation and Poverty Reduction* (pp. 67–84). Hershey, PA: IGI Global. doi:10.4018/978-1-5225-3117-3.ch004

Yablonsky, S. (2018). Innovation Platforms: Data and Analytics Platforms. In *Multi-Sided Platforms (MSPs) and Sharing Strategies in the Digital Economy: Emerging Research and Opportunities* (pp. 72–95). Hershey, PA: IGI Global. doi:10.4018/978-1-5225-5457-8.ch003

Yaşar, B. (2021). The Impact of COVID-19 on Volatility of Tourism Stocks: Evidence From BIST Tourism Index. In M. Demir, A. Dalgıç, & F. Ergen (Eds.), *Handbook of Research on the Impacts and Implications of COVID-19 on the Tourism Industry* (pp. 23–44). IGI Global. https://doi.org/10.4018/978-1-7998-8231-2.ch002

Yusoff, A., Ahmad, N. H., & Halim, H. A. (2017). Agropreneurship among Gen Y in Malaysia: The Role of Academic Institutions. In N. Ahmad, T. Ramayah, H. Halim, & S. Rahman (Eds.), *Handbook of Research on Small and Medium Enterprises in Developing Countries* (pp. 23–47). Hershey, PA: IGI Global. doi:10.4018/978-1-5225-2165-5.ch002

Zacher, D., & Pechlaner, H. (2021). Resilience as an Opportunity Approach: Challenges and Perspectives for Private Sector Participation on a Community Level. In A. Zehrer, G. Glowka, K. Schwaiger, & V. Ranacher-Lackner (Eds.), *Resiliency Models and Addressing Future Risks for Family Firms in the Tourism Industry* (pp. 75–102). IGI Global. https://doi.org/10.4018/978-1-7998-7352-5.ch004

Zanin, F., Comuzzi, E., & Costantini, A. (2018). The Effect of Business Strategy and Stock Market Listing on the Use of Risk Assessment Tools. In *Management Control Systems in Complex Settings: Emerging Research and Opportunities* (pp. 145–168). Hershey, PA: IGI Global. doi:10.4018/978-1-5225-3987-2.ch007

Zgheib, P. W. (2017). Corporate Innovation and Intrapreneurship in the Middle East. In P. Zgheib (Ed.), *Entrepreneurship and Business Innovation in the Middle East* (pp. 37–56). Hershey, PA: IGI Global. doi:10.4018/978-1-5225-2066-5.ch003

About the Contributors

Kesavan Dhanapal is currently an Assistant Professor of Finance at SRM Institute of Science & Technology, Vadapalani, Chennai. Prior to his academic career, he worked for 4 years as a Scale I officer at City Union Bank, where he gained expertise in Credit and Startups and was instrumental in introducing Cash Deposit Machines (CDMs) throughout the country. He also worked for 4 years as a Business Analyst at Client Digital Ltd, Chennai, where he was responsible for Fund Raising and New Projects Handling. With 4 years of teaching and research experience, Dr. Dhanapal's research interests include Service Marketing, Financial Management, Renewable Energy, and Sustainable Development. He has published 47 articles in various journals and authored 3 books. Notably, he has also served as an advisor to the Telangana Government for the Direct Beneficiary Transfer scheme in Agriculture Development.

Mari Anand N. has a rich experience of 10 year in the field of teaching and expertise in the field of Marketing and Human Resource Management. Currently he is working as Faculty Member, Department of Business Studies, University of Technology & Applied Sciences, Salalah, Sultanate of Oman. He is also a Member in Research Advisory Committee at VELS Institute of Science, Technology & Advanced Studies, Chennai. To his credit he has published 27 articles in Scopus and UGC Listed Journals. He has guided 63 UG and 22 PG projects. He served as Member of Board of Studies for Business Administration and Member for University Examination Board of SRM Institute of Science & Technology. The author is an Editorial Board Member for International Journal of Advance Research in Commerce Management and Finance (IJARCMF). The author has organized various International Conferences and International Conclave during his tenure. The author was an ISO Convener and served as IQAC coordinator & Exam Cell convener. He is also an External Academic Auditor and Chief Examiner for various institutions. The author was resource persons for different Faculty Development Program (FDP) organised by various colleges. He is an active Member in Federation of Indian Chamber of Commerce and Industries (FICCI) & Madras Management Association (MMA).

***

Elaiyaraja A. is working as Assistant Professor in the Department of Commerce at St. Thomas College of Arts and Science, Chennai. He has more than 15 years of teaching experience and is actively involved in research of fintech products. He has published more than 15 articles in various reputed journals.

Sayantani Banerjee is a certified Accounting Technician from The Institute of Chartered Accountants of India and holds a Ph.D. in International Finance. Having completed her formal education in commerce, her expertise lies in the broader areas of accounting, taxation and finance. She is also associated with ASSOCHAM as part of core-team member of CSR and Sustainability Committee, Southern region. Dr. Banerjee is actively involved in research in allied areas of international finance, decentralised financing and taxation. She is also associated with Jesuit Worldwide Learning, a global organisation providing higher education at the margins, as a subject-matter expert where she is involved as content developer and online facilitator for disadvantaged and displaced students all across the world. She has a total experience of 16 years in teaching undergraduate and post-graduate students.

Suresh Esakki is serving as a faculty member in the College of Economics and Business Administration, University of Technology and Applied Sciences, Salalah, Sultanate of Oman. He is a very dynamic teacher and actively participating in research and extension activities in the past few years. He has gained teaching and research experience from international dais such as Ethiopia and Oman. He has published a good number of research articles in national and international level journals and frequently delivering special lectures in international level forums.

J. Fathima Farzana is working as Assistant Professor of Commerce in St.Joseph's University Bangalore. She is an expert in Finance and Accounting, her area of specialization ranges from Taxation, GST, IFRS and FInancial Services. She has published more than 15 articles in various reputed journals. She has taken up research in the area of Fintech and other financial technologies. At present she is persuing a research on Sand Box and innovative Fintech technologies in Indian Perspective.

Arifenur Güngör is an Asistant Professor of Economics at Istanbul Topkapı University, Turkey. She holds a BA degree in economics and an MA degree in money, capital, and financial institutions from Istanbul University, Turkey, and a Ph.D. degree in economics from Yildiz Technical University, Turkey. Dr. Güngör's research interests focus on international finance and financial econometrics.

Mahmut Sami Güngör is an Assistant Professor of Economics at Marmara University, Turkey. He has received both an MA and a Ph.D. degree in economics from Istanbul Technical University, Turkey. He holds a BA degree in economics and a BA degree in econometrics from Istanbul University, Turkey. His research interests focus on empirical macroeconomics, financial economics, the economics of education, and poverty.

Nur Aqilah Adilah Hj Abd Rahman is working as Assistant Professor Technology Management at School of Business, Universiti Teknologi Brunei. He has published several articles in Scopus Listed Journals.

Ramya J. obtained a doctoral degree from the College of Engineering (CEG) Guindy, Anna University. She holds a master's degree in business administration from College of Engineering (CEG) Guindy, Anna University, and a bachelor's degree in computer science engineering from Avinashilingam Deemed University. Dr.J.Ramya works at SRM Institute of science and technology as an Assistant Professor and has several years of work experience in the areas of teaching, research, and administration. She has authored international publications on varied management subjects. She also presented various academic as well as research-based papers at several national and international conferences. Her current research interests include enhancing the customer experience for organized retailing customers and dynamic pricing strategies.

Sadeesh J. is currently working as Assistant Professor in Department of Commerce at SRM Institute of Science & Technology, Vadapalani, Chennai. He obtained a doctoral degree from University of Madras. He has published more than 10 articles in various reputed journals. He has authored a book chapter in The Handbook of Management Thoughts. His current research interests include Negative Advertising and its Impact, Consumer Behaviour, Brand Celebrities.

Bharathi Ravi is working as Assistant Professor of Management at St. Joseph College of Engineering, Chennai. Her area of Research includes Game Theory, Innovative HR practices, Learner Management System development and Crypto Currencies. She has been researching in the field of Crypto for the past 6 years and an active investor across 85 various tokens. She is conducting active research in the field of Crypto currencies relating to multiple payment and peer to peer interaction process. She has published more than 15 articles across various reputed journals.

Sathish Kumar S. is currently working as Assistant Professor in Department of Commerce at SRM Institute of Science & Technology, Vadapalani, Chennai. He obtained a doctoral degree from University of Madras. He has published more than 5 articles in various reputed journals. His current research interests include Digital Banking and e-Marketing.

Sivaprakkash S. has done all his degrees from Loyola College, Chennai. He is a Gold Medalist in M.Com. and M.Phil. Currently working as Assistant Professor in the Department of Commerce at Central University of Tamil Nadu. To his credit he has published 15 articles in listed journals. He is a recipient of Rajiv Gandhi National Fellowship for Persons with Disabilities for the year 2016-17. His areas of interest include Investment Management: Mutual Funds & Stock Market, Business and Company Law, Marketing: Global Perspective of Marketing, Human Resource Management, Statistics Analysis and Research Methodology.

Subashree S. is working as Assistant Professor in Department of Business Administration at SRM Institute of Science & Technology, Vadapalani, Chennai. She is currently pursuing her Ph.D. in Management at Manonmaniam Sundaranar University. She holds a master's degree in business administration from College of Engineering (CEG) Guindy, Anna University and a bachelor's degree in commerce from University of Madras. She has 11 years of teaching experience and has published more than 10 articles in various reputed journals. Her areas of interest are Financial Derivatives, Securities Market and Commodity Market.

Thowseaf S. is working as Assistant Professor, Centre for Distance and Online Education (CDOE) in B. S. Abdur Rahman Crescent Institute of Science and Technology, Chennai, India. His area of research includes Agriculture, Agro Economics, Innovative financial products. He has published more than 20 Articles in various journals.

Vevek S. is a Gold Medalist in M.Phil. Currently working as Assistant Professor in the Department of Commerce in SRM Institute of Science & Technology, Chennai. To his credit he has published 10 articles in listed journals. His areas of interest are Financial Derivatives, Security Market Operations, Statistics Analysis, Research Methodology, International Business and Accounting.

Srimathi Thilakar is working as Assistant Professor of Finance at SRM Institute of Science & Technology, Vadapalani, Chennai. Her area of lecturing includes Financial Management, Financial Accounting, Derivatives, Security analysis and Portfolio management. She has published more than 10 articles in various reputed journals. She has authored a Book chapter on Dividend policy and implications. Her present research is focussed towards Lintner model of Dividend application and its association with policy making. She is also an expert in innovative financial Instruments.

Mohammed Umair working as Assistant Professor of Commerce in St. Joseph's University Bangalore. He has published more than 10 articles in various reputed journals. He has taken up research in the area of financial technologies.

Raja V. is currently heading the Department of Computer Science Application & Data Science at SRM Institute of Science & Technology, Vadapalani, Chennai. He as vast experience of more than 15 years in teaching field. He has obtained his Ph.D. in Computer Science from Bharathiar University and holds bachelor's and master's degree in Computer Science from University of Madras. He has presented various research papers at several national and international conferences. His area of interest is Network Security and it's Applications.

Naveenraj X. is working as Assistant Professor at SRM Institute of Science and Technology. He has obtained his Ph.D. in Organizational Behavior from Vellore Institute of Technology. He also holds M.B.A. (HR & Marketing) from Panimalar Engineering College and Bachelor's Degree in Physics from St. Joseph's College. His areas of interest are Organizational Psychology, Stress Management and Organizational Development. He has published more than 10 articles in various reputed journals.

Index

F

G

H

I

L

M

N

P

R

S

T

V

W

www.ingramcontent.com/pod-product-compliance
Lightning Source LLC
LaVergne TN
LVHW061536290926
849162LV00004B/817

* 9 7 8 1 6 6 8 4 5 6 9 1 0 *